TV Format Mogul

For Noela
With warm gratitude for her great love and support

First published in the UK in 2013 by
Intellect, The Mill, Parnall Road, Fishponds, Bristol, BS16 3JG, UK

First published in the USA in 2013 by
Intellect, The University of Chicago Press, 1427 E. 60th Street,
Chicago, IL 60637, USA

Copyright © 2013 Intellect Ltd

All rights reserved. No part of this publication may be reproduced, stored in a retrieval system, or transmitted, in any form or by any means, electronic, mechanical, photocopying, recording, or otherwise, without written permission.

A catalogue record for this book is available from the British Library.

Cover designer: Ellen Thomas
Production manager: Tim Mitchell
Copy-editor: MPS Technologies
Typesetting: Planman Technologies

Print ISBN: 978-1-8415-0623-4
ePUB ISBN: 978-1-78320-078-8
ePDF ISBN: 978-1-78320-077-1

TV Format Mogul
Reg Grundy's Transnational Career

Albert Moran

intellect Bristol, UK / Chicago, USA

Contents

Foreword *by Toby Miller* — ix

Preface — xi

Acknowledgements — xv

Abbreviations — xvii

Chapter 1: The TV Format Mogul — 1

Chapter 2: Early Years: 1923–47 — 9

Chapter 3: Apprenticeship I: Learning About Broadcasting, 1947–53 — 25

Chapter 4: Apprenticeship II: Quiz-show Schooling, 1953–59 — 39

Chapter 5: Apprenticeship III: Mastering Television Formats, 1959–64 — 55

Chapter 6: Domestic Consolidation, 1964–70 — 77

Chapter 7: Transnational Ambitions I: First Moves, 1969–74 — 99

Chapter 8: Transnational Ambitions II: Retooling for Domestic and Offshore, 1974–79 — 119

Chapter 9: Transnational Ambitions III: Australia, the United States and South-East Asia, 1979–85 — 139

Chapter 10: Transnational Ambitions IV: Australia, the United Kingdom and the United States, 1985–89 — 159

Chapter 11: Transnational Ambitions V: Worldwide, 1989–95   175

Chapter 12: Buyout and Beyond: Since 1995   197

Chapter 13: A TV Format Mogul Among TV Format Moguls   211

Appendix: Grundy's Television and Film Output   227

References   239

Index   253

Foreword

Reg Grundy went from being a man behind a microphone to being the man behind the men and women behind the microphones. He built a national and international company, for all the world like some Joseph Schumpeter fantasy figure. He did not want bricks and mortar to mark his stature, preferring transitory forms and spaces as the market dictated. He seems to have been as much an entrepreneur as a mogul, and his media successes were not part of a wider play for power over everyday life. He made money from entertainment; he sailed then sold his yacht; he snapped pictures of animals and shared them (Reg Grundy Wildlife website). Bermuda International Airport has a permanent exhibit of Dr Grundy's work. May we all see it some day.

In Albert Moran, Reg Grundy has the best imaginable chronicler and analyst. Long Australia's foremost ethnographer and historian of television, Albert has wanted to write this book since before I met him a quarter of a century ago, when he taught me what little I know as we lectured together.

When I visited Grundy's official web page, I was enchanted to see that 'About Reg Grundy' was essentially empty, devoid of information. It was a blank, dark slate, as if awaiting the picture that Albert has painted of this game show host and owner. But eventually it loaded, revealing the great man in a safari jacket, his face obscured by his camera, and describing him as 'one of the media's most respected statesmen'.

That description made me wonder about the idea of the media statesman, so hard to disinter from its gendered privilege and so rarely associated with media owners. The term barely exists in online usage. Can it be applied to Beaverbrook? Sulzberger? Newhouse? Black? Hearst? Lebedev? Maxwell/Ludwig Hoch? To Grundy's fellow nationals, the thankfully now pitiful Murdoch and his simple male progeny? Tycoons or moguls, perhaps, albeit often with interests in public policy: how to evade it, how to shape it, how to denounce it, how to applaud it. But are they statesmen?

Many things set Grundy apart from these personalities, not least that he focused principally on one genre: the game show – humble, apolitical, uncontroversial, fleeting, popular, entertaining, fun. Not at all like news and current affairs. So what is he talking about when presenting himself as a media statesman? Let's be a little inventive.

I think a statesman transcends his or her time, providing a flexible vision rather than being captive to the present. Statesmen have the capacity to look beyond immediate interests to see what can and should be of lasting significance.

In many ways, Reg Grundy's staple of the game show is very partial indeed. It is popular television's exemplar of a minor literature, very minor. But think again, please. Deleuze and Guattari (1983: 16) define the concept of a minor literature as follows:

> A minor literature is not the literature of a minor language but the literature a minority makes in a major language. But the primary characteristic of a minor literature involves all the ways in which the language is affected by a strong coefficient of deterritorialization.

Australian television had a talent for remaking and remodelling genres from elsewhere, as numerous critics of Albert Moran's generation pointed out in their recuperation of the national screen from charges of banal mimesis.

In Grundy's case, this process went a step further. He both domesticated foreign material and repurposed it for export elsewhere, and in the process transcended his beloved game shows to make drama as well.

Grundy deterritorialized television as he shifted genres, languages, executives, nations and formats. He took an evolving international trade in television and made it his own.

Today, as Albert Moran has shown in countless books and articles, format sales and co-productions are the name of the game. Grundy understood that in business terms before virtually anyone else, and Albert understood it in academic terms before virtually anyone else. As Albert explains in his preface, it took them decades to come together, but here they are, and we are all the better for it. Bravo! Statesmanlike indeed.

Toby Miller
October 2011

Preface

This book has been a long time in the making, and it is worth recording its development. One might say that Reg Grundy and I were good television friends in the very early 1960s, although situated on different sides of the television screen. In apparently marathon Saturday-afternoon programme sessions on Sydney's Channel 9, wedged in between Nock and Kirby's *Joe the Gadget Man* and a serious-looking bespectacled Brian Henderson among rock 'n' rolling teenagers on *Bandstand*, Reg was there greeting contestants on *Wheel of Fortune*, asking the quiz questions and spinning the wheel. I played my part in the pact, sitting in my lounge room, alone or with family, watching the comings and goings on a black and white, seventeen-inch Admiral television set, bought on hire purchase and still being paid off.

This timing was entirely coincidental. Our family, newly arrived from Dublin, had settled in Sydney in 1959 and bought the television set just as *Wheel of Fortune* was making its transition from radio to television. Reg disappeared off our television screens about two years later, although I was glad to hear that he was a producer and not out of a job. Still, it was a bit disappointing to notice that the very familiar neatly moustached 'Face That Helped Launch 1000 Spins of the Wheel of Fortune' had retreated into the shadowlands of programme production. At a time when almost everyone else wanted to get their face on television, Reg Grundy had disconcertingly taken his off the screen.

Fast-forward nearly fifteen years to the end of 1974: I had almost completed an apprenticeship for an academic career in media studies. I was planning a brief return to Sydney when a La Trobe University colleague in Melbourne, Mick Counihan, suggested I conduct an interview with Reg Grundy. What a great idea! A telephone call to Grundy Enterprises evoked no response. In any case, I realized that I knew little about the Australian television business, and that I first needed to work up a background to avoid asking dumb questions of the quiz-show supremo. The result was much time spent poring over programme notes in back issues of *TV Times*, a lot of interviews and conversations with television professionals in Brisbane, Sydney and Melbourne, and several books on the subject of Australian television production. All the same, there had not been an interview with Reg Grundy. Indeed, the latter had become a kind of Howard Hughes of Australian television. He was rarely encountered even by his own employees in Grundy House on Sydney's North

Shore, never reported in newspaper gossip columns and had become a name but no longer a face for the public at large.

Fast-forward again: in 1992, I was fortunate enough to visit Grundy House with Professor Stuart Cunningham and Dr Marie Delofsky. Stuart and Marie were there to interview Ian Holmes, Grundy Worldwide's president, as part of the research that would result in the magisterial book *Australian Television and International Mediascapes* (1996), written by Stuart Cunningham and Elizabeth Jacka. I had previously interviewed Ian Holmes as part of the work on Australian television, but had failed to keep up with the company's international developments, first in the area of programme distribution and later in the area of format adaptation and remaking. Like others, I was conscious of the process of programme copycatting, whereby television programme ideas from elsewhere metamorphosed into Australian productions and vice versa. Reg Grundy had long been the butt of jokes in the Australian media about this practice. Nevertheless, I was surprised to learn in the interview with Ian Holmes that this kind of content exchange took place under regular business arrangements rather than by some kind of mysterious osmosis.

This realization rekindled the Grundy project. I resolved that if the company could transnationalize itself by going offshore, then it behooved me as researcher in an era of increasing globalization to pick up the trail of this development. I began to visit Grundy's and other format companies' offices in London, Amsterdam, Cologne, Paris and elsewhere, asking questions and gathering whatever printed and VHS material I could. The result of this protracted investigation has been a series of further books, essays and chapters, beginning with *Copycat TV* in 1998, that have dealt with the detail and meaning of television programme formats.

The old ambition of a career-related biographical interview was also stirred. Reg Grundy sold his international organization in 1995. Living in Bermuda at the time, he collapsed his Sydney offices into a modest operation with the enigmatic label of RG Capital. Shortly after the sale, I managed an interview of sorts by dint of having some questions faxed to the principal in Bermuda. An attempt to arrange a face-to-face meeting was, however, turned down by a local employee. The project went back on hold until, more recently, I decided that I must either publish a Grundy business profile or allow the whole project to perish.

As luck would have it, Grundy's own autobiography appeared in 2010. It is probably the closest to an interview that one would ever achieve. Elsewhere, I have published a review essay concerning the memoir (Moran 2010), which has all the pluses and minuses of an interview with valuable information that allows one to cross the 't's and dot the 'i's alongside more homely domestic information. The publication had the very useful effect of helping me to see the wood for the trees so far as the principal's business development was concerned. Significantly, Grundy's autobiography was aimed at Australian readers who could recall at least some of the many Grundy programs over the previous 40 years.

By contrast, this study is published by Intellect, an international publisher with one foot in the United Kingdom and the other in the US marketplace. It follows in the wake of other monographs and edited collections of mine dealing with the phenomenon and meaning of the worldwide system of television format exchange. The study is addressed to an international readership interested in the evolution of programme franchising from the point of view of one particular company, and especially the producer who established that company. Reg Grundy did not originate the practice of programme adaptation and remaking, although he was certainly one of its pioneers. This anatomy of his career is offered in the hope of filling in gaps in an international history, and encouraging others to investigate comparable national developments elsewhere. In that way, the project will have been worth all the time that it has taken.

Albert Moran
Brisbane

Acknowledgements

Two Australian institutions supported and nourished the research and writing that have gone into this book, and I gratefully acknowledge their support. First, the project was funded under Australian Research Council Discovery Award DP0667066, held between 2006 and 2009. In addition, Brisbane's Griffith University has been my alma mater for over 30 years, and has continued to provide a stimulating and congenial environment in which my research finds meaning and support.

Various research assistants have worked at different times on parts of this undertaking: I am deeply indebted to the labour, ideas, tenacity and encouragement of Margaret Cook (Pullar), John Davies, Chris Keating, Cory Messenger and Rea Turner. Closer to home, my son James and daughter Kate have also contributed in a marvellous variety of ways, and I am very appreciative of their efforts.

Professor Bridget Griffen-Foley at Macquarie University has generously provided newspaper articles and other references concerning Sydney commercial radio in the 1940s and early 1950s while my colleague, Dr Tony van Fossen, has been most helpful in sharing his knowledge and insight about celebrity tax havens. I am very obliged to both these scholars. Furthermore, Reg Grundy was kind enough to answer a series of faxed questions in 1995, and I acknowledge this assistance.

Over the years, various television industry professionals and others have made time available to speak to me, whether in person or on the telephone. I would like to thank the following for these interviews: Lionel Baart, Don Battye, Brian Bury, Ron Casey, Bob Crystal, John Culliton, Tony Culliton, Jason Daniel, Max Drummond, John Franco, Bill Grantham, Jack Grimsley, Roy Hampson, Brian Henderson, Ian Holmes, Richard Lane, Len Mauger, Lyle McCabe, George Morotoff, Gary O'Callaghan, John O'Grady, Peter Pinne, Ted Simmons, Tony Skinner, Reg Watson, Barry Weston and Warren Whitfield. Deep appreciation for extraordinary help, ongoing assistance and support must go to librarians and archivists at the Australian War Memorial (Canberra), Coles Myer Ltd's Archives Department, David Jones Archives (Sydney), Griffith University's Interlibrary Loans section, the Mortlock Library (Adelaide), John Martin's Archive Collection and Mr R. W. Fisher, former School Archivist, St Peter's College, Adelaide.

Finally, I greatly value the copy editing work of Sue Jarvis in Brisbane and the input of Tim Mitchell and Holly Rose at Intellect. Long may our relationships continue.

Abbreviations

AAI	All-American International
ABC	American Broadcasting Company
ABC	Australian Broadcasting Corporation
ABCB	Australian Broadcasting Control Board
ABT	Australian Broadcasting Tribunal
ATO	Australian Taxation Office
AWA	Amalgamated Wireless Australasia
BBC	British Broadcasting Corporation
BHP	Broken Hill Proprietary Company
B&T	*Broadcasting and Television* (Australian trade journal)
CBC	Columbia Broadcasting Corporation
CBD	Central business district
CBS	Columbia Broadcasting System
CEO	Chief executive officer
CLR	Compagnie Luxembourgeoise de Radiodiffusion
CTL	Compagnie Luxembourgeoise de Televisione
CVA	Coventure agreement
FRAPA	Format Recognition and Protection Association
IRS	Inland Revenue Service
ITV	Independent Television (Network)
MCA	Music Corporation of America
NBC	National Broadcasting Company
OB	Outside broadcast
OBE	Order of the British Empire
RCA	Radio Corporation of America
RAI	Radiotelevisione Italia
RPA	*Radio Pictorial of Australia* (trade journal)
RTL	Radio Television Luxembourg
SMH	*Sydney Morning Herald*
TBI	Television Business International

Chapter 1

The TV Format Mogul

Introduction

The aim of this study is to investigate the career in Australia, the United States, the United Kingdom and elsewhere of television producer Reg Grundy. That historical trajectory is analysed systematically in the next thirteen chapters, which trace Grundy's commercial path from his beginnings to his life as a businessman to his retirement in 1995. This passage was a remarkable one for a broadcaster who spent most of his working life in Australia before extending his television production empire into other places. Even so, Grundy's rise depended on particular business and cultural circumstances that were already in play. It also followed a pattern in media industries that is repeated elsewhere, to a greater or lesser extent. The study's title highlights this continuity by addressing Grundy as a particular kind of media magnate. For, unlike some other tycoons of publishing and broadcasting such as William Hearst, Rupert Murdoch and, in Australia, Kerry Packer, Grundy did not benefit from a media inheritance from a communications magnate father; rather, he started from scratch. All the same, the would-be entrepreneur was intelligent enough to recognize the crucial importance of television programme remaking as a means of high-volume, fast-turnover content output. Long before the term 'format' was used to describe this practice, Grundy had embarked on a television business career that would see him become one of a small group of international TV format moguls, and certainly the first (and to date the only) TV format mogul to originate in Australia. In this chapter, I establish the analytical framework for the history that follows. I explain the terms 'format' and 'television format', and discuss the implications of the label 'mogul'. What is a TV format mogul, and why is the name applied to Reg Grundy? There are solid historical and sociological reasons for labelling the rise of this Australian television producer in such a way. I offer a preliminary answer by briefly explaining who Grundy is and why he warrants investigation as a TV format mogul.

The television programme format

What, then, is a television format, the entity on which Grundy built a media production empire? I suggest that the term relates to the identification of a body of practical knowledge associated with a programme, formula or structure that facilitates its remaking in another place and time. This view is echoed by other recent writers on the subject. According to Chalaby (2009: 40–41):

> Formats or shows sold under license for local adaptation are inherently transnational ... since a licence cannot be bought twice in the same territory (for the same period of time), a programme becomes a format only once it is adapted outside its country of origin.

For Bourdin (2011: 166–70), the term designates that which is a 'standard, replicable, internationally marketable, and potentially successful formula'.

Somewhat disconcertingly, the term 'format' is relatively widely used. It had its origins in the early printing industry, where it was used to refer to a book of a specific size. From there, the term passed into wider use in the twentieth century in particular areas of knowledge, including business, computer science, and the radio and film industries. Even so, 'format' has gained a specific meaning, alongside its more general deployment, in the international television industry over the past quarter century to designate the adaptability of television programs for different audiences in different television settings (Moran 1998: 7–11). Of course, the remaking of programmes in television (and before that, in radio) is an old practice with even more ancient roots in such industries as the book trade, newspaper publishing and the advertising industry. Even so, past practices of programme adaptation and remaking tended to be ad hoc and occasional, so that an agreed-upon term to designate the practice was hardly necessary. When mention was needed, the labels used were frequently those of 'idea' or 'expression'. More recently, as the practice of programme adaptation and remaking has become increasingly systematic and widespread, the term 'format' has been preferred as a way of designating the practice (Bourdin 2011: 16–37; Moran 2009).

Moguls and media

In turn, I have used the term 'mogul' in my title to suggest the range and power associated with a business empire. I might have used other terms such as 'magnate', 'tycoon', 'emperor' or even 'godfather', so why is the label 'mogul' preferred? I take the term from pioneer British media researcher Jeremy Tunstall, who first outlined characteristics of the figure as early as 1970 and more recently has returned to further sociological analysis of the type (see Tunstall 1970: 13–15; Tunstall 2001: 17; Tunstall & Palmer 1991: 17, 105–13; Tunstall & Palmer 2001: 17, 65–70). He suggests the existence of a hierarchy of occupational and professional types in media organizations, based on levels of power and control. At the top of his typology is the media mogul, the self-made owner and operator of one or more media companies. Next comes the media baron, who is a top executive who works for the media mogul. Further down the organizational ladder is the media star, a category requiring little explanation.

Tunstall's explanation of the media mogul is clear and succinct: 'A "media mogul" we define as a person who owns and operates major media companies, who takes entrepreneurial risks, and who conducts these media businesses in a personal or eccentric style' (2001: 2). Further qualities are added to this profile. The media mogul, for instance, has mostly developed a media empire from scratch, building it up through entrepreneurial effort, but also through mergers with and the acquisition of other companies. The figure largely operates in one or several parts of media industries, such as newspaper publishing, but may also own some non-media businesses. Additionally, the media business operated by the mogul can confer a good deal of attention and celebrityhood on others, yet the mogul may have 'a highly distinctive personal publicity stance' (2001: 4). Tunstall suggests that the latter frequently can involve a low-publicity profile, where the media proprietor downgrades publicity, rarely agrees to open-ended interviews and is shy of photographs (2001: 5). Such a bashfulness also has a business dimension: given that the media mogul is mostly self-made and seeks to control public exposure, it is often not surprising to discover that the mogul dabbles in other private companies and pursues business interests in other fields. Additionally, as someone who owns and operates a company, the media mogul takes risks and tends to follow a personal set of hunches.

Two other elements can be added to round out Tunstall's profile. He notes that the figure has an all-consuming interest and involvement in business, which spills over into private domestic life to the point where there is little distinction between the two. Finally, there is the fact that media power also sometimes overflows into the political sphere, where this kind of tycoon often has strong interests and commitments. Tunstall notes that the mogul's political inclinations are likely to be right wing and conservative.

Typical examples of this type of media mogul are not hard to find. Tunstall identifies such captains of media industries as William Randolph Hearst in the United States, Rupert Murdoch internationally and Silvio Berlusconi in Italy as classic instances (Tunstall & Palmer 2001: 65–68). He further identifies a kind of lower rung of media moguls, who are less well known outside specific national settings: they include Axel Springer and the head of the Bertelsmann family in Germany, Robert Hersant in France and Emilia Azcarraga in Mexico (Tunstall 2001: 17). Equally, I would suggest that there are other moguls associated with particular areas of media industries who also warrant attention, even if their power, wealth and influence are no match for the grand moguls listed by Tunstall. Accordingly, this book advances the claims of a particular type of media czar, namely the TV format mogul. In the next twelve chapters, I flesh out this figure through a consideration of the business career of Australian television producer Reg Grundy. The last chapter places this case study of the TV format mogul in the context of the career of several other such tycoons, past and present, to make the case for a general type, as well as further highlighting the particular significance of Grundy for the development of the field of television format adaptation.

Before suggesting the high degree of correspondence between Grundy's industry situation and the features of the mogul as outlined by Tunstall, it is useful to sketch the broad contours of Grundy's broadcasting career as a prelude to the intensive account that follows.

Reg Grundy: a brief outline

Born in Sydney, Australia in 1923, Reg Grundy joined commercial radio as a sports commentator and time salesman (Moran 2004a). He developed a radio game show, *Wheel of Fortune*, which he took to the Sydney television station TCN9 in 1959. He teamed up with Channel 9 not as a station employee but as an independent producer who would 'package' the quiz-show for the station. Following a trend in Hollywood and US network television, Grundy incorporated himself as a company, Reg Grundy Enterprises, thereby achieving considerable tax savings. The 36-year-old worked as both master of ceremonies and producer on the television version of *Wheel of Fortune* as he had done with the radio version. The show itself was Grundy's own invention. The new 'packager' soon discovered that he did not have the time or capacity to develop new quiz programmes; instead, realizing that US network television could serve as a ready source of new quiz-show ideas, Grundy began visiting the United States to spot attractive formats for adapting and remaking back in Australia.

During the 1960s, Reg Grundy twice suffered the simultaneous cancellation of all his shows, but by 1970 he had rebounded. His Australian television production empire grew apace. To safeguard itself against programme cancellations, it stepped up its quiz-show output and brought in independent producers to make drama series, telemovies and children's fiction. It also added a very successful drama serial division, with hit series that included *The Young Doctors*, *The Restless Years*, *Prisoner*, *Sons and Daughters* and *Neighbours*.

As early as 1972, Reg Grundy planned to expand his production operation to the United States. Beginning in 1980, the company began to move offshore using the cash flow from its Australian operation to bankroll this move. Television systems internationally were undergoing multiplication, commercialization and, in the case of public-service systems, privatization. A US Grundy production office was set up in 1979 and Grundy sold several game shows to US networks for their daytime line-ups. One of the most successful of these was *Sale of the Century*, a quiz show that originated in the United States, but that that Grundy had copied as early as 1970; Grundy would later purchase *Sale of the Century* outright and remake it in over a dozen different territories. The Grundy US operation also found itself devising other quiz and game shows, some of which became US network programmes; other versions of the shows were remade in various territories. Although Grundy personally was committed to triumph in the US television market, as if to show that the master's apprentice had come of age, the daytime network market closed up as the growing popularity of talk shows squeezed opportunities to sell quiz shows. Moreover, a spin-off of one of his successful Australian soap operas, *Prisoner*, which he financed, did poorly in the US syndication market.

The company now known as Grundy Worldwide outside Australia (where it continued to trade as the Grundy Organisation) fared much better in the United Kingdom, Western Europe, South America and parts of Asia. Altogether, it produced quiz shows and dramas in more than twenty countries, so it became very wealthy indeed. In 1995, Reg Grundy sold the company to the UK-based Pearson Television group for US$279 million (A$380 million). It was one of twenty company acquisitions by the group, which eventually was bought by the German Bertelsmann Group, adopting the name FremantleMedia. The Australian branch of the conglomerate was known as Grundy Television from 1995 to 2005, but finally came under the name of the parent company. Why did Grundy sell? There was no heir to carry on the business and the mogul himself was 72 years old at the time. Grundy probably smarted from the US disappointment, and in any case realized that he did not have the war chest to turn his company into a megaconglomerate through merger and acquisition, as did others. Instead, by selling when the company was at the height of its success, he achieved an excellent price with himself still at the helm.

Grundy as a format mogul

Reg Grundy is a media mogul who has operated in the field of television formats. A career review according to Tunstall's yardsticks supports this claim. First, there is the fact that there was no media inheritance with which to get started and no particular background advantage when it came to a broadcasting career. Instead, Grundy started from scratch and built a television empire, largely through his own efforts. He owned and operated what became a major media company in the area of television programme production, especially involving the remaking of formats adapted from elsewhere. In addition, while not a gambler, the Australian-born television entrepreneur frequently was prepared to venture into unknown waters so far as business was concerned, taking triumph and disaster in his stride. Further conforming to Tunstall's model of the media mogul, Grundy mostly operated in the area of television programme production, although he strayed into other business ventures on occasion including briefly contemplating the purchase of an Australian commercial television network in 1992 (Shoebridge 1991).

Likewise, Reg Grundy developed a personal style in business that was characteristic of the media-mogul figure, exemplified by his very low public profile. Family life took a back seat to his business career, often with no suggestion of where one ended and the other began. Several of these qualities also found expression in the fact that all three of the companies that Grundy operated were his own private businesses. By capitalizing all his ventures from accumulated revenues, the TV format mogul ensured that he never had to disclose the financial details of his company operations to either shareholders or lending institutions. That all of these qualities entitle Reg Grundy to the name of TV format mogul will be seen concretely in the pages that follow. Here, though, it is worth adding some remarks about Reg Grundy's politics. This is noted because it is part of Tunstall's paradigm of the media mogul, and because it does not directly arise in the pages that follow.

Structure of the book

Having summarized the case for Grundy to be viewed as a TV format mogul, it remains to outline the chapters that follow. This chapter has spelt out the reasons for a study that is historical and sociological rather than personal and domestic. Nevertheless, Chapter 2 affords space to the early life, offering a prologue to the business career, and covering background, childhood, school, war service and breakthrough into commercial radio broadcasting. A long period of practical learning was required to provide Grundy with the necessary background to build a business empire. He came to know about the details and context of a trade in which he would spend the next five decades of his working life.

I have split this period of broadcasting apprenticeship into three chapters that cover Grundy's time in commercial radio and his early years in commercial television. The newcomer mastered three different cultural and commercial sets of skills: first, those related to broadcasting in general; then those specific to quiz and audience-participation programmes; and finally, the skills needed to embark on programme adaptation and remaking. Independent television programme production was always a risky matter for television entrepreneurs, but business expansion was the only form of insurance possible in the world of television programme packaging, where the independent operator invariably was dependent on the more powerful office of the broadcaster.

Chapter 6 marks a halfway point in the story of his career. The period 1964–69 saw Grundy and his company recover from a major cancellation by a broadcaster. Significant domestic consolidation was also achieved, despite one last business hiccup. The stage was set for further expansion, first into another area of television programme production drama and then, building on this foundation, into markets in other parts of the world. The next five chapters follow the course of this development. The Grundy company became a major corporate transnational entity with a large number of branches scattered around the world, and Grundy himself becoming a TV format mogul.

As Chapter 11 explains, the early 1990s were an especially propitious time for international television programme producers with a worldwide multiplication in the number of television broadcasting channels on the air. The Grundy company went from strength to strength, with its output continuing to expand across the planet. Suddenly, this movement stopped: Reg Grundy offered his company for sale and a buyer was found; his years as a TV format mogul were at an end. Two chapters round out the account of Grundy's career. Chapter 12 brings the story up to date at the time of writing by outlining the subsequent history of Grundy without his company and the company without Grundy. The last chapter steps back from the detail of Grundy's business life to reflect further on the figure of the TV format mogul. Reg Grundy's significance is further highlighted by locating him in the company of several other TV format moguls, past and present. Such comparisons enable us to more fully understand the figure of the TV format mogul in general, and Grundy in particular.

Chapter 2

Early Years: 1923-47

Introduction

This chapter offers some background on the early years of Reg Grundy's life between 1923, when he was born, and 1947, when he managed to obtain a full-time job in commercial radio in the largest advertising and listening market in Australia.

Once he secured a foothold in broadcasting, Grundy brought a genius to bear on the institution that helped launch the business career that is the object of this study.

Like the period after 1995 briefly discussed in Chapter 12, these first years are not crucial to the business career that followed. Nevertheless, they are offered here in summary form for three reasons. First, they highlight the fact that Grundy did not have any kind of exceptional background, on the one hand, or particular handicaps, on the other, but could look back to happy circumstances associated with being the only child of lower-middle-class parents. The self-made man would look back to neither advantages nor disadvantages.

Second, it also highlights the degree to which his early life was affected by two great world events, the Great Depression and World War II. Young Grundy was not immediately affected by either of these events, but they did have a powerful impact on a world in which he struggled to answer the question 'What shall I do?' The third reason for this preliminary chapter is to detail how Grundy groped towards an answer to this question from 1939 to 1947.

Frustration was, finally, followed by triumph, so mid-1947 saw him embarking on a career in commercial radio broadcasting in the largest broadcasting market in Australia. My chapter is split into two parts: the first dealing with his childhood in Sydney and Adelaide, and the second following the youth from the outbreak of the war to his landing of his first full-time job with a Sydney commercial radio station.

Infancy, Depression, re-establishment

Reginald Roy Grundy was born on 4 August 1923 in Sydney. His parents were Roy Harold Grundy and Lillian Josephine Grundy (née Lees). Their marriage took place at the New South Wales (NSW) Registrar General's Office on 31 July 1923. The baby boy was to be the couple's only child, although both his father and mother had several brothers and sisters as well as extended families. Like most of the population of the island continent in 1923,

Grundy's parents belonged to families whose Australian roots stretched back several generations, even if much of their earlier ancestry had its origins in one of the four kingdoms of the British Isles. The newborn baby had two family lines through the Grundys and the Lees, both of which had their origins in England. The Grundy surname is a family name, chiefly derived from the county of Lancashire.

The Grundy branch of the family had been somewhat itinerant over the previous half century. Reg Grundy's paternal grandfather, John Grundy, was born in 1864 in Koroit on the western shores of Victoria next to the port of Warrnambool (O'Farrell 1987: 33–41). By 1898, when Reg Grundy's father, Roy Harold Grundy, was born, the family was living closer to Sydney. Grundy notes in his memoirs that his grandfather was a sewing-machine salesman in Albury on the NSW–Victoria border (Grundy 2010: 11–13). Grundy's father was the second child in his family to live beyond youth, joining an older brother known as Jack. Later, in Grundy's father's death notice, his existing brothers and sisters were named as John (Jack), Clive, Jean, Hazel and Irene (Dot). Lillian Josephine Lees, Reg Grundy's mother, came from a large extended family that had lived on the Central Coast about 50 miles north of Sydney for four generations (Whitfield 2005). The family could trace its lineage back to at least as early as the mid-seventeenth century in England. Two descendants who were brothers were transported to NSW in 1790. Settling on the coast, their families and they farmed, hunted and fished.

By contrast, Grundy's parents appeared to see themselves as Sydneysiders. Certainly Grundy senior was born when his parents were living in Sydney. Over the next eight years, Roy, Lillian and young Reg 'lived somewhere near or in the inner city' (Grundy to author 1995; Grundy 2010: 10–11). His mother had, undoubtedly, ceased outside employment when the baby came, devoting herself to family and home. There was no lack of contact among relatives in these early years. The parents seem to have been personable, friendly and outgoing, and there was probably much social interaction with their extended family in the form of visits and get-togethers in inner Sydney and on holidays on the Central Coast.

While the life of the young family was probably ordinary, this could not be said about the city that surrounded them (Spearritt 1978: 119). This was a boom time in Sydney. By 1923, the city's inhabitants numbered one million, with gold mining, pastoralism and agricultural industries in its hinterland and a manufacturing sector in its midst sustaining this population. Sydney's development was becoming increasingly enmeshed with national and international markets in import, export, investment and migration. A large, consuming public was forming with various kinds of outlets making available the goods and services that were part of this consumption economy. Grundy senior worked in confectionery and chocolate manufacturing, itself an early formation of a modern all-encompassing amusement and gratification industry that would later recruit his son (Kasson 1978; Bard 1983; Peiss 1986; Leach 1993; Matthews 2004).

Roy Grundy was manager of one of the outlets of the Ernest Hillier chocolate and confectionery company (Grundy to author 1995), which had come into existence in Sydney in 1912 as part of a trend that first began in England and the United States. Coincident with and dependent on the rise of such popular commercial entertainments as the skating rink, amusement park, Vaudeville theatre and dance hall, various food and drink venues sprang up. These commercial outlets offered such mouth-watering delicacies as aerated soda drinks, ice cream, chocolates and popcorn. Born in the United Kingdom, and learning the craft of chocolate-making in the United States, Ernest Hillier himself had opened the first soda fountain in Australia: Hillier Refreshment Services. This was located at the Imperial Skating Rink at Rushcutters Bay's White City on the Sydney Harbour foreshore. Shortly afterwards, the company was servicing two other established outlets in Sydney, and within two years had opened a downtown city outlet shop that pioneered the manufacture and retail of chocolate. Hitherto, this sweet delicacy had been imported from the United States and United Kingdom (Ernest Hillier website).

However, from 1926, Australian export commodities suffered a price decline on international markets (Selleck 1998). Increasingly, London-based financial institutions were reluctant to pursue further investment. In 1929, a new loan issue was rebuffed, US financial institutions suffered a dramatic collapse and Australian unemployment rose sharply, peaking at 30 per cent in 1932. Grundy senior was one of the lucky ones who managed to continue in his line of work – not too surprising, given the senior position he occupied at Ernest Hillier. Yet the Depression did affect the business climate in general, with the market for luxury food items seriously undermined. Indeed, the company's owner decided in 1933 to relocate the business to Melbourne. By then, father, mother and young child had uprooted themselves from friends, family and familiar surroundings to move to South Australia.

Another city, schooldays, radio delights

The city to which the Grundy family came in 1930 differed significantly from Sydney (Whitelock 1977; Colwell & Naylor 1977; Brownhill 1978; Prest 1998). Founded on schemes of land speculation and the promotion of rural industries in its hinterland, the colony (later state) of South Australia had begun a process of industrialization from the 1890s onwards. Mining was an important engine of this development, with Adelaide interests establishing mining operations at Broken Hill in the far west of NSW and a smelting industry at Port Pirie to the north of the South Australian capital (BHP Billiton website).

Taking up a senior company position as catering manager with the most important retail department store in the city, Reg Grundy's father was in a secure financial position to ride out the Depression. The job demanded that the family live close to the city in suitable middle-class surroundings (Colville & Naylor 1977: 95–104). Accordingly, the family rented a succession of houses in garden suburbs to the south.

Grundy senior did not belong to the landed gentry of South Australia; instead, he was part of the retinue of servants who helped cater to its needs and wants, and also enjoyed some of the material advantages associated with this function.

Roy Grundy joined the department store as catering and restaurant manager. Founded in 1866 as a small general store, the company was the largest retail department store in Adelaide, proclaiming itself 'the Big Store' (Anon. 1946: 144). At a time when Australia's department store retailing was state-based, John Martin was one of the joint owners of the Intercontinental Buying Group, designed to facilitate its purchase of supplies from overseas mostly from the United Kingdom.

In mid-1936, Roy Grundy oversaw the official opening of a new John Martin Restaurant. This arrangement was necessary not only for the comfort of diners but also because the hall served as a location for social entertainment in Adelaide society. An orchestra regularly played there for the pleasure of patrons. There was also a busy round of important social functions spread across the year, including dances, dinners, luncheons and bridge parties.

While Reg's father was busy at his workplace and his mother concentrated on running the home, Reg Grundy was very active at school. Over the nine years spent in South Australia, the boy undertook his primary education at a succession of state primary schools in inner suburbs. He seems to have been an excellent pupil as far as schoolwork was concerned, being awarded 624 marks out of 700 at his primary school graduation, an overall average of 89 per cent across all subjects.

Initially, as the 1937 school year began in Adelaide in early February, the youngster very briefly took his place in Class 1A at Adelaide High School, the only non-fee-based state school offering classes to university matriculation level.

Shortly, his parents were offered a place for their son at the most prestigious secondary school in Adelaide, St Peter's College. His father had been told by his employer that St Peter's College would be a more desirable school for his son's education (Grundy 2010: 14).

The Collegiate School of St Peter was the oldest and most pre-eminent secondary school in the state (Price 1947; Peake-Jones 1978). It was founded in 1847 to educate the sons of Adelaide's upper and middle classes for the professions, the church, officer life in the military or life on the land.

During the Depression, the school increased its scholarships for day students (St Peter's School Archives). Boys were prepared for an Intermediate Certificate and a Leaving Certificate. The young Grundy spent two years at the school, achieved good grades in English, Geography, Latin and German and discovered a capacity for drawing, wood cuts and design. On his departure, the headmaster supplied him with a handsome testimonial. He wrote:

> He is a thoroughly intelligent and able boy, intelligent well above the common average. I have always found him a most willing person, full of initiative. He has made quite a mark in our community which looks to him as our No. 1 School Artist and stage scene painter. This boy has ideas and is able to execute them. I have considerable confidence in his reliability.

Young Grundy had discovered a talent and a passion that briefly threatened his school work. The claim that Grundy was the school's 'No. 1 artist' was no empty boast. In both 1937 and

1938, the school magazine, which was published three times a year, featured a succession of linocuts and drawings by Grundy. These images, the only visual competition for which was the usual humdrum group photos of prefects, sporting teams and the like, had pride of place in the magazine's pages, suggesting that the editor and the school were appreciative of the visual skills and imagination of the young boy. The headmaster's comments also noted his involvement in school drama, which seemed to not only include behind-the-scenes stage work but also a willingness to undertake acting roles, with him being cast in the role of a servant in *She Stoops to Conquer*, which St Peter's Dramatic Society planned to stage in 1939.

If retail work at John Martin and Company and schooling at St Peter's College were important pillars in the life of the small Grundy family, another pastime for the Grundys, like many other families in Adelaide and elsewhere, was listening to the radio. Broadcasting, which had been a fledgling notion in Sydney in 1923 when Reg was born, was well on its way to becoming an indispensable part of everyday domestic life in Australia.

Adelaide listeners had a total of six radio-broadcasting stations to choose from. Two of these were provided by the relatively newly formed Australian Broadcasting Commission (ABC) (Inglis 1983: 115), while the other four were independent commercial stations. All stations were involved in audience-participation programmes of one kind or another, including talent quests, community singing and vox populi interviews (Mittell 2004). Such programmes made sense from a broadcaster's point of view: they followed straightforward patterns of production, cost very little to put together and were quick and easy to produce. They offered the public the opportunity to be part of a live production and participate in proceedings, with the added excitement of being spontaneous and immediately on the air. Young Reg Grundy and his mother attended some of these shows in Adelaide. A profile written some 25 years or so later would recall:

> [He] sought a childhood dream in radio. 'Heaven knows how but I never had the confidence to appear on radio. I used to go every Saturday night to a children's show in Adelaide. I'd sit there with my mother, gaping in awe at the compère, but I couldn't get up from that seat to go on the air.'
>
> (*TV Week* 1962: 21)

A false start

Shortly, however, the family's life was again disrupted. Early in 1939, Roy Grundy received an offer of a highly suitable management position at a leading Sydney department store. He accepted the job. Reg was now a youth of 15 years of age who had completed his intermediate education. So what would Reg do? How would he earn his livelihood? The remainder of this chapter explores his attempt to settle on a career, and the frustrations and obstacles he encountered in this search.

Sydney was still suffering the after-effects of the Great Depression, so employment may have been difficult to find. Nevertheless, young Reg had three factors working in his favour. First, he had completed his education at a highly prestigious college, the second-oldest secondary boys' school in the country, and he had good school reports and a glowing testimonial from his headmaster. His father, Roy Grundy, had had extensive commercial retail experience and would have had good connections in both Sydney and Adelaide department stores

There was also the possibility that the young boy may have had some casual Christmas employment with John Martin. The upshot was that, shortly before he turned 16, Reg Grundy secured his first job at a major Sydney department store, David Jones (Grundy 2010: 15–16). He was following in Roy's footsteps, even if this meant putting on hold the talent and enthusiasm for drawing and woodcut graphics that had become evident while he was a schoolboy. However, this job was to be the first of a series of career disappointments and frustrations that would continue over the next eight years.

Of all the big department stores in Sydney in the 1930s, David Jones could claim to be the oldest and one of the best traders in the Central Business District (CBD) (Wolfers 1980; Thompson 1980). In what was a typical pattern for the establishment of the great Australian department stores of the second half of the nineteenth and first half of the twentieth century, the company was originally co-founded by a merchant hailing from Britain. It began trading in Sydney as early as 1835 (Thompson 1980: 14). By around 1840, the Welshman David Jones had a store in Sydney's George Street, close to the General Post Office. The store was rebuilt in 1887 and was still operating in 1939 when Reg Grundy began work as a trainee. The early start gave the company a twenty-year break on potential retail competitors who only established their city stores in the period of 1906–10 (Wolfers 1980: 18–20). By 1939, the David Jones company had capitalized on its excellent mid-city location to add two additional stores a short distance away. In 1927, the company opened a large store in Elizabeth Street, opposite Hyde Park, which would specialize in women's wear, while two years before young Reg Grundy joined, a nearby Market Street store began operation, with menswear being its specialty (Wolfers 1980: 19; Thompson 1980: 5).

With a staff of approximately 2000 women and men, David Jones targeted white-collar workers and high-income earners, with a particular focus on customers from the city's more affluent Eastern Suburbs. The Grundy family's address in Double Bay would have helped young Reg land this first job. The development of the city underground railway, including the opening of the nearby St James railway station, had considerably increased custom, and had induced the company to add further outlets to its array of city stores. David Jones also benefited from the redistribution of Sydney city shopping associated with the opening of the Harbour Bridge, the expansion of the city railway system and the coming of motor buses, which had helped concentrate big store trade between Park and Hunter Streets along George, Pitt and Castlereagh Streets (Spearritt 1978: 44; Wolfers 1980: 23).

Reg Grundy spent two-and-a-half years at David Jones before he left to join the Australian Army Reserve. The young man deliberately seems to have been rotated through different sections of the store, undertaking a variety of duties as part of a loose scheme of on-the-job training (Thompson 1980: 10–30; Grundy 2010: 15–18). Under the company's Junior Executive Program, Grundy's first posting was to the Women's Wear department, where he worked in accounts as a trainee clerk with the princely wage of £22 6s a month. Later, he would sometimes refer to this position as 'not much more than a glorified office boy' (Grundy 2010: 18). A later posting saw him working as assistant buyer in Women's Sportswear. At another time, he seems to have been selling men's socks. Garry O'Callaghan, who later worked with him as an assistant at the radio station 2SM in the early 1950s, mentioned how generally useful this kind of shop-floor selling at David Jones would be for Grundy during his career:

> He used to say once you knew how to sell something, selling air time or autographed photos was no different. He had a happy knack of turning someone who really didn't want to know him into someone who wanted to be his friend.
>
> (O'Callaghan 1995)

Another false start

The possibility of a rather different career briefly opened up during this time even while working at the department store. This was due to the skill and enthusiasm for drawing and graphic art the young Grundy had displayed while at St Peter's College. He mentions in his memoirs that he was summoned to meet the managing director of David Jones, who announced that the company was prepared to pay his tuition fees to attend art college as a part-time student in the evening while continuing to work in the store in the daytime (2010: 15 17). This was not necessarily a benevolent gesture by the company; rather, it hoped to profit if Grundy acquired practical skills and knowledge in the area of design and decoration.

In 1939, he was enrolled as a part-time student at the Julian Ashton Art School in George Street near the Central Business District (McCullough 1955: 2002; Julian Ashton website). The original Julian Ashton had been born in England in the mid-nineteenth century and moved to the colonies, settling in Sydney in 1892 and establishing the Sydney Art School, which later changed its name to the Julian Ashton Art School. By 1939, the school was well established as a teaching centre for all aspiring Australian painters and artists, but it also taught practical art that might have application in such areas as visual display, decoration, advertising and publicity. Many Sydney men and women undertook part-time studies there while working in applied arts jobs in advertising, commercial design and graphic display.

Reg Grundy took classes in the Antique Drawing course at the school (Grundy 2010: 18). The emphasis was on practice, creating charcoal sketches of plaster-cast heads that needed to be accurate in proportion and line. He attended for one term on Tuesday nights, taking classes at the end of the working day. By late 1939, however, this initiative seemed to stall and his enthusiasm for art evaporated (Grundy 2010: 18). There was a postscript to this second, more specialized would-be career, however. In March 1940, Grundy was promoted to become a junior assistant at David Jones. Ironically, his last position with the company before he left to join the military tapped into some of the training and skills in visual composition and presentation that he had unearthed while at school and further refined in his one term at art school (Grundy 2010: 18). The position saw him deployed in the display section of the company, working on the planning of a new floor for David Jones' Elizabeth Street store. However, World War II intervened and the career in art and design went on hold. In late 1941, Japanese forces attacked the US navel fleet at Pearl Harbor. World War II ceased to be half a world away from Australia, but was suddenly much closer. Grundy joined the Army Reserve and in late January 1942 was ordered to report for duty. He formally took leave from David Jones, although like others who were volunteering, he was promised that his position would be kept for him. This probably meant little to the 18-year-old. Instead, he could hope that military duty might offer a way out from the career dead ends he had encountered.

A third cul-de-sac

The Japanese attack on Hawaii signalled the beginning of World War II in the Pacific Ocean for the United States. For Australia, a big island in the southern Pacific with a very large, mostly undefended, coastline and a sparse population spread across the continent, the attack reawakened a nightmare scenario whose roots lay in the nineteenth century – the fear of invasion from multitudes of Asian peoples to the north. As the Australian alarm mounted, the 18-year-old Reg Grundy enlisted in the Citizen Military Forces (CMF) two days before Christmas Day and two weeks after the Pearl Harbor attack. He had some rudimentary defence training, joining the school cadets while at St Peter's in Adelaide. The CMF was a part-time, voluntary service, equivalent to the peacetime Army Reserve. Young Grundy was posted to the 1st Cavalry Division Signals at Allendale in the Hunter Valley, just north of Sydney. He was not required immediately, so there was time to enjoy Christmas and the summer with family and friends.

In mid-January, he formally left David Jones for military service. His feelings must have been mixed. After over two-and-a-half years at the big department store, his work life was routine and predictable, whereas wartime military service held the promise of adventure, excitement and danger. This was not to be, however. After all, for every fighting soldier, a large number of military personnel must be deployed in the capacity of backup. The army decided that Grundy was medically unfit and would not be allocated to combat duties (Grundy 2010: 19–20). Instead, he had valuable administrative skills as a result of working at David Jones. Hence in March 1942, after almost two months of basic training, the young Reg Grundy qualified as a clerk. He was posted to a personnel unit that specialized in administrative duties.

For Australia, 1942 was the grimmest year of the war so far. Singapore fell, as did Manila; Darwin was bombed; and several Japanese submarines attacked Sydney Harbour. Responding to this threat, Reg Grundy enlisted for unrestricted full-time service, which went under the name of Universal Service. As a private, he was posted to the District Accounts Office, Sydney, part of the Royal Australian Army Pay Corps, in September. He continued to serve as a clerk. A little more than a year later, in November 1943, he was promoted to corporal, rising the following year to the rank of sergeant. The former David Jones trainee's service was probably satisfactory, but in any case this kind of promotion was useful from an administrative point of view, because it ensured that pay staff had seniority over many of the personnel whose wages they were administering.

Grundy probably first grew his moustache at this time. As an element of male grooming, the moustache was at the height of its popularity in the 1930s and 1940s. For men, it indicated the growth of facial hair, a kind of confirmation of manhood. Clark Gable at MGM and Errol Flynn at Warner Bros sported moustaches, as did several other minor Hollywood male stars and actors. Australian commercial radio, the closest show-business institution the island state had to Hollywood, also saw a vogue for the moustache, which was sported by such broadcasting celebrities as Bob Dyer, John Dease, Howard Craven and Nigel Lovell. Not surprisingly, the moustache was acceptable and common in the armed forces.

By this time, the danger to Australia had passed as the Allied Forces pushed the Japanese military northwards across the Pacific. Reg Grundy's war had turned out to have none of the adventure, excitement and danger that he might have imagined (Grundy 2010: 19–21). Instead, life in the Pay Corps was likely to have been as routine and even as boring as clerical duties in David Jones had proved to be. Nor had there been any travel. Ironically, as Grundy explains in his memoirs, he had ended up working for the last two years of the war at the Hordern Pavilion in the Sydney Showground, a short distance from where he had been living with his parents since the family had returned from Adelaide (2010: 22). Like many, the young Grundy would have looked forward to the end of the war and his return to civilian life. However, a resolve not to resume clerking must have been strong. Fortunately, the showground itself would soon offer him a way out of his career stalemate. Consequently, something needs to be said about this venue and its most important annual event.

The Sydney showground and the Royal Easter Show

The Sydney Showground is a tract of 72 acres set among more extensive parklands on the city's south-east edge. The land was leased permanently to the Royal Agricultural Society (RAS) of NSW at this time. The location contained various show rings, large halls and a host of ancillary buildings that served two main functions. The showground was the headquarters of the RAS and also functioned as the setting for the annual Royal Easter Show

(Mant 1972: 1–55). This was an annual hallmark agricultural event lasting for ten days, where agricultural products of all kinds were bought, sold and exhibited; where practices, skills and products associated with life on the land competed; where exhibitions of all things related to agriculture were mounted; and where a galaxy of sideshow amusements furnished other forms of entertainment.

The 1940 Easter Show had been the last for several years. In May 1941, the showground facility was acquired by the Commonwealth under wartime National Facilities Regulations (Mant 1972: 66). The site was, in effect, transformed into a self-contained army town. As Mant notes, the venue became an important recruit reception depot, with many units being formed there in the early days of the war (1972: 76). It also functioned as a general details and staging depot, with facilities for general staff, commanding officers, the pay office, accounts office, adjutant and quartermaster, as well as hospitals, post office, banks, canteens, entertainment halls and other facilities. A constant procession of troops passed through, and many units were formed there in the early days of the war (RAS 1944–45: 1–19). Despite the suspension of the Royal Easter Show between 1941 and 1946, some activities of the RAS were maintained. Various cattle and dog shows were held in smaller venues, and the Society continued to undertake other activities (Mant 1972: 55).

In fact, after August 1945, two separate trains of events were happening side by side at the showground. Reg Grundy was involved in one of these and an onlooker at the other. The first involved the demobilization of military personnel as the showground became the main centre for discharging personnel in Sydney. The other event involved preparations for the Royal Agricultural Society's resumption of its main annual event, the Royal Easter Show. Demobilization was to continue at the showground into the second half of 1946, so that the first post-war Royal Easter Show could not be scheduled before 1947. Over twenty months, the showground slowly transformed from an army city full of demobilizing personnel back to a massive agricultural facility. As a young, unmarried man, Reg Grundy was among the last of the wartime military personnel to be demobilized. During his continuing duties in the Pay Corps at the showground, he would have had a first-hand view of preparations in progress for the 1947 Royal Easter Show.

The Sydney Royal Easter Show was a major event in the social calendar of both the city and the state, and the city's big stores were intimately involved in many events at the venue (Wolfers 1980: 25–28). Several had permanent pavilions there for trade and allied purposes. The showground also played host to numerous exhibitions and demonstrations by most of the great Sydney department stores, mounted inside its buildings and along its roadways. The city retail companies, including Grace Bros and David Jones, also sought favourable publicity and goodwill with country and city visitors by donating prizes for the competitive ring events during the ten days of the show. Cumulatively, these connections of army, venue, big store links and upcoming show were probably sufficient to push chance the way of a smart, eager young man, unwilling to re-enter the dull routines of his former mode of employment.

The first break

An agricultural show is a multifarious event, and one of its many parts involves the buying and selling of farm livestock such as cattle, sheep, pigs and chickens. Daily information about these livestock sales and prices at the Sydney Royal Easter Show was of considerable interest to farmers, both those who managed to come to Sydney for the event, and those who had to remain on the land in regional and rural parts of NSW. During the Royal Easter Show, different animals were allocated to different pavilions and stockyards at the showground, with their own particular sales times, so a good geographical knowledge of the setting and the clerical skills of accuracy of price tabulation, sales volumes and so on were necessary for reliable livestock sales reporting.

Newspapers traditionally had covered livestock price news at the show since its inception in 1877, but radio had the advantage of offering more up-to-date coverage and wider dispersal. One particular NSW regional radio station, 2GZ, was in a unique position to broadcast such information on a daily basis for the ten days of the Easter Show. The station was headquartered in the city of Orange in Central Western NSW, but maintained a basement studio in the Sydney CBD in Hoskins Place, near the offices of the Postmaster General's Department in Martin Place. The station was owned by two brothers, one of whom had a major involvement with Sydney commercial station 2UE. The regional station used transmission lines in its basement studio to send a broadcast signal to Orange, having boosted the power of their output with the approval of the Postmaster General's Department Wireless Branch in 1936 (Jones 1995: 38). This technical boost had been part of a deliberate plan by the Wireless Branch to upgrade a number of country stations across Australia to greater transmission power (1995: 39). 2GZ now had 2 kilowatts, which allowed station coverage to extend north and south to neighbouring states, and even spill over their borders, whereas other country radio stations in the area had far more limited transmission power. These arrangements of landline and transmission power enabled 2GZ to provide up-to-date broadcasts of livestock prices to the station's rural constituency from the 1947 Royal Easter Show.

At some point, Grundy learned that 2GZ wanted someone to undertake this livestock reporting for the ten days of the show. Seizing this opportunity, the 23-year-old managed to secure an interview with the 2GZ Sydney manager and landed the job (Grundy 2010: 201). Grundy's duties involved visiting the different livestock pavilions housing cattle and pigs on a daily basis, compiling information about sales volume and prices into a summary report, and undertaking these for the period of the show. The 2GZ Sydney manager then read these bulletins into the microphone for transmission via landline to rural NSW.

In his memoir, Grundy reports suggesting that the programme manager also conduct interviews with livestock buyers and sellers. The enterprising young man would supply questions and arrange the guest interviewees. The programme manager in turn suggested that Reg conduct these interviews himself (2010: 22–23). He grabbed the chance to do so. He also took the opportunity to have a recording of one of these interviews preserved in the form of an acetate recording. Impressed with his work, 2GZ offered him a job as an announcer at the station's main studios in Orange, but Grundy preferred to take his chances closer to home, looking for a broadcasting job with one of the commercial radio stations in Sydney. Although still a novice, Grundy now had a calling card in the form of the acetate recording.

A full-time job in radio

By this time in early 1947, Reg Grundy had been demobilized and was living back with his parents at Double Bay. Rather than returning to David Jones and his old position, the would-be broadcaster had set aside his accumulated CMF savings to draw upon as he searched for another job. Grundy's memoir documents his interest in show business. He had already served an apprenticeship of sorts albeit mostly as a fan to the world of entertainment, mass amusement and popular culture. He mentions listening to the Hollywood Reporter on radio as a youngster in Adelaide, and later being inspired by visiting US entertainers such as crooner Bing Crosby and clarinetist and big band leader Artie Shaw. Grundy had worked out front before an audience as a would-be crooner at the Grace Auditorium and behind the scenes operating the stage lights; he also put on a show each Wednesday at the Sydney Showground while stationed at the District Finance Office (Grundy 2010: 93–100). Radio broadcasting seems to have been especially attractive to Grundy: 'How glamorous and exciting it was, working in radio,' he would later remark when he had the opportunity to get close to visiting Field Marshall Douglas Montgomery in Sydney in 1947 (2010: 29).

Getting the 2GZ stint had been a fortunate break, even if he had had to wait almost eight years for it to happen. But the prospects of securing a full-time, permanent job in radio did not seem bright. Grundy was both too old and too young for the commercial radio industry. At 23 years of age, the young hopeful was too old to enter radio as a junior assistant, with the average age of entrants about 16. Instead, because he was in his twenties, Grundy might have been expected to have had some broadcasting-related experience but, of course, he lacked such a background. As a later profile once put it: 'No station wanted a man of his age without training' (*TV Week* 1962: 21).

A second stroke of fortune occurred when Grundy gained an introduction to Sydney radio announcer John Harper (Griffen-Foley 2009: 60–70). As part of commercial radio's move in the direction of turning its on-air announcers into celebrities, Harper was regarded as 2KY's leading announcer and was known in newspaper reports and elsewhere as 'The Playboy of the Air' (RPA 1 August 1937: 9; 1 November 1939: 16–17; 1 May 1944: 16–17, 34; 1 February 1949: 12–13). Following the US motion picture company MGM's self-proclamation of Clark Gable as the 'King of Hollywood', Harper was also crowned by station publicity as the 'King of Sydney radio'. The 2KY celebrity announcer was a gruff, somewhat older man, who had begun his announcing career with commercial

Sydney radio station 2GB before switching to another Sydney station, 2KY, owned by the Australian Labor Party (ALP). It occupied a middle level of popularity among Sydney's six commercial radio stations.

The older man now took the time to have Grundy visit 2KY, where he questioned him about his broadcasting aspirations and listened to his 2GZ acetate recording (Grundy 2010: 23–24). Harper had some influence at 2SM, another Sydney commercial radio station. The two stations had an overlapping listenership, which was working class, inclined to vote for the ALP and often belonged to the Catholic Church. Harper may also have been aware that 2SM was looking for a sports announcer (Simmons 1995). There was already an incumbent in the position but he seems to have wanted to transfer to other duties while the station management wanted a different voice behind its sports broadcasts.

Briefly taking on a mentoring role towards the young man, Harper arranged for Reg Grundy to have an audition with 2SM's general manager (Grundy 2010: 24–25). The audition was not successful, but two weeks later 2SM contacted him and asked him to audition by describing part of a boxing match at the Sydney Stadium. He reported into a ringside microphone that transmitted back to the radio station in the heart of the CBD. This second audition was more positive, and the young hopeful secured a job with 2SM. At the beginning of July in 1947, Reg Grundy's broadcasting career began. Early the next month, the novice broadcaster would turn 24.

Afterword

Grundy was lucky to break into commercial radio in Sydney at this time. After eight years of frustration and waiting, he had got a start in a career that seemed glamorous, exciting and well rewarded. Australian commercial radio had boomed in wartime and, by 1947, it was clear that this prosperity was following it into the post-war period. Nevertheless, for the young Grundy just starting out in the broadcasting industry, there was to be a very long way ahead before he became captain of a major organization in the business of broadcasting. In fact, Grundy was just beginning his life work, and would spend the best part of another two decades learning the distinctive tricks of the broadcasting trade, first in commercial radio and then in television. The next three chapters are devoted to this long apprenticeship.

Chapter 3

Apprenticeship I: Learning About Broadcasting, 1947-53

Introduction

In 1947, Reg Grundy started a full-time permanent job with a Sydney commercial radio station. A career in broadcasting had begun, one that would see him occupied in different parts of the business for almost the next 50 years. The novice had much to learn and the next seventeen years were spent refining his craft and defining his ambition. He would, eventually, focus on a highly profitable component of the industry that was well known but not widely understood. First, though, the young man had to learn the ins and outs of his craft before he was in position to spot opportunity where others saw none. The next three chapters of this study are devoted to successive stages of this apprenticeship. Reg Grundy's first career was in radio broadcasting in general and sports broadcasting in particular. Lacking any background in sport, Grundy had to learn how sport worked (or might work) in radio. In the process, he was to discover much more about himself including his capacity to take significant initiatives, to tackle new challenges, to prepare for contingencies, to delegate tasks to others when this was possible, to work hard, to learn from mistakes and to grasp whatever opportunities came his way. This chapter is concerned with Reg Grundy's first six years in radio with Sydney commercial station 2SM, where he developed skill and shrewdness as a radio presenter, producer and time salesman, specializing in sports broadcasting.

Time and place

In 1947, Australia, like the other Allies who had fought against the Axis powers, looked forwards as well as backwards. The exigencies of wartime had overcome the dire circumstances of the Great Depression but the question was whether there would be a resumption of those conditions following the cessation of hostilities (Moran 1991: 30–35). Despite the fact that wartime rationing and restrictions had continued into peacetime, there were grounds for believing that economic and social conditions would continue to improve. Apart from the military skirmishes mentioned in the previous chapter, Australia had suffered none of the physical damage of war seen in the United Kingdom, Europe and parts of Asia. Its primary industry products continued to be in strong demand internally as well as externally while its nascent manufacturing sector, which included branch plants of British and US companies, had received an enormous boost from the war (Scurfield 1998: 410–11). The federal government was determined to continue this wave of industrialization and embarked on an ambitious migration drive with newcomers in demand as industrial workers, consumers and inhabitants helping to swell an underpopulated continent (Davison et al. 1998: 520–22).

The broadcasting sector that Grundy joined was still consolidating after wartime and continuing to enjoy a boom that had begun in 1940. Although the first radio transmission of content in Australia had begun as early as 1923, radio broadcasting as a viable financial and social institution had only come into existence in Australia in the late 1930s (Mackay 1956; Potts 1988; Jones 1995). Until 1932, the federal government had persisted in a succession of schemes whereby national radio broadcasting would be undertaken as a service provided by the state with content provided by different consortiums of commercial providers whose base lay in such arenas as music, theatre, newspapers and the retail trade (MacKay 1956: 1–20). The year 1932 saw the establishment of a national programme provider, the Australian Broadcasting Commission (ABC), modelled after the example of the British Broadcasting Corporation (BBC) (Inglis 1982). A large group of lower-power transmitting licensees, the B-class stations, the forerunners of the commercial radio sector, continued to mark time through much of the rest of the 1930s, held back in their search for a viable revenue base under the general impact of the Great Depression and the claims of the newspaper sector that radio lacked a demonstrable, quantifiable listening public (Mackay 1956: 1–4). Commercial radio networking after the example of US broadcasting only began in 1938 with the establishment of the Macquarie Network. This organization was the first formal networking arrangement to be set up in commercial radio and sat alongside a looser association of stations headed by 3DB in Melbourne, flagship of the Herald and Sun publishing group, which called itself the Major Network (MacKay 1956; Moran & Keating 2003: 271–72).

As Miller has noted, radio networking set itself the task of addressing a national audience whether as a polity or a commercial market (2004: 157–59). And yet, unlike their counterparts in the United States in the form of the National Broadcasting Company (NBC) and the Columbia Broadcasting System (CBS), networks were not the most powerful entities in Australian commercial radio. This title was reserved for advertising agencies, most especially the Big Two of the J. Walter Thompson Advertising Agency and the George Patterson Advertising Agency, the first a Sydney branch of the US parent, which had been formed soon after the American Civil War, and the second a home-grown organization with US and UK associations (Potts 1988: 33–39; Moran & Keating 2003: 16–17). What the agencies had in common was their long-term affiliation with Australian branch plants of US manufacturing giants such as Colgate-Palmolive, Lever Brothers and Kelloggs.

One sign of the might the agencies wielded on behalf of these powerful clients was the establishment in 1938 of the Colgate-Palmolive radio unit as a separate division of the George Patterson agency (Patterson 1956: 64–81; Potts 1988: 59–77; Moran & Keating 2003: 96–97). The war triggered a big leap forward in its output after a first variety show called *Vanity Fair* had been heard in 1938 (Lane 1994: 252). Under government wartime price-fixing regulation, advertising expenditure was pegged to sales, and increased sales boosted production budgets considerably (Potts 1988). The Colgate-Palmolive Unit employed the most famous Australian radio stars, a 40-piece orchestra and, from 1942, broadcast from the new Macquarie Auditorium at 2GB in Sydney (MacKay 1956: 7–19). Its roll-call comprised three hours of headline programmes each week, including *Rise and Shine* (an army quiz), *The Youth Show, Star Parade* (later *Calling the Stars*), *Quiz Kids* and *First Light Frazer*). The unit moved to 2UE in 1946 and continued to package this kind of premium output until the early 1950s (Jones 1995: 45).

World War II had turned out to be a massive boon for Australian commercial broadcasting in general. The war had two major effects so far as helping to create a thriving radio industry was concerned (Moran & Keating 2003: 82–84). Overseas currency became scarce, and networks and stations were forced to turn to the local production of radio programming content. Additionally, paper for newsprint was in short supply, and Australian advertisers were forced to seek other outlets besides newspapers and magazines to promote their goods and services. The upshot was that commercial radio stations increasingly had the revenues to support the production of a very large, local programming output. In effect, World War II brought about an 'Australianization' of the local commercial radio sector even if the sector continued to remain wedded to ways of thinking first derived from US network broadcasting. Nor did this boom end with the coming of the peace. Rather, the sector continued to thrive until the mid-1950s when the inception of regular television broadcasting forced Australian commercial radio to begin to change what it did and how it did it.

The lure of commercial radio

Despite these general developments in the institution of commercial radio, the question of Grundy's career choice still needs to be raised. Just why was the young man drawn to the industry? The answer was that commercial broadcasting seemed to be immensely more attractive, alluring, exhilarating and lucrative than just about any other line of work available in 1947. Here was what had been singularly unavailable to Reg Grundy while he was at David Jones and during the war. In the United States, Hollywood already had this same kind of allure for almost 40 years for young men and women across the country. Many hopefuls went to Los Angeles with the expectation of getting work in front of or behind the camera in 'the dream factory', as the film studios were collectively known. Australia had no 'Hollywood' in the form of a highly successful movie production, distribution and exhibition industry. Neither did it have a popular recording music industry of any consequence that would act as magnet for young hopefuls. What Australia did have, though, was a kind of displaced version of Hollywood. This was the Australian radio broadcasting industry, especially its commercial sector, concentrated in Sydney and, to a lesser extent, in Melbourne, in the period between 1940 and 1956.

Australian radio had not always held out this promise of riches, glamour and excitement. In the 1920s, radio had been dominated by amateur enthusiasts interested in its technical challenges (Jones 1995: 1–33). By the 1930s, large commercial interests had bought into the sector, but mainly to protect their other outside commercial operations. Most of a company's advertising budget in the economy at large still went to newspapers, ensuring that commercial radio broadcasting struggled for profitability. Indeed, in the early to mid-1930s, several stations in regional Australia had had to sell out. By the late 1930s, as I have already noted in Chapter 2, things were improving so far as the financial returns of commercial station operations were concerned with a surge in sales of half a million receiving sets recorded between 1934 and 1938. All the same, it was the advent of World War II that triggered real profitability and the glamorization in Australian commercial radio (Potts 1988). Wartime import restrictions on US programme transcriptions had the effect of considerably boosting opportunities for local writers, actors, announcers, producers, sound technicians and others in the radio programme production sector (Lane 1994: 39–44; Jones 1995: 45).

The exotic glamour that Australian radio acquired was a rather different matter to this profitability even if the two went hand-in-hand. The advent of talking pictures in the United States by around 1930, as the adoption of sound-on-film was called, brought three major American entertainment industries closer together (Hilmes 1990; 2004a). The sectors in question were the Hollywood film industry, the US radio network industry and the American popular recorded music industry. These sectors did not merge. Instead, there was a series of coalescences of different commercial and cultural interests in such matters as ownership, technology, station operation, recorded music, market strategy, publicity, promotion and gossip (Hilmes 1990; 2004). The US radio networks derived many benefits from setting up additional broadcasting studios in Los Angeles in the mid-1930s, thereby recasting a good deal of their output in terms of entertainment and show-business values. Hollywood could teach radio a lot because it already had almost two decades of experience in promoting itself and its products by means of ballyhoo and imagery that emphasized stars, celebrity, glamour, the exotic, the erotic and the utopian (Buxton & Owen 1972: 49–88). The US radio networks progressively absorbed this outlook, most especially in the 1930s.

Such a change was not lost on Australian commercial radio, which looked to the United States for principles and practice. By 1940, Australian commercial radio had become heavily 'Hollywoodized' in terms of the excitement, luxury and reward that it seemed to entail (Potts 1988: 66–87; Moran & Keating 2003: 96–97). There appeared to be no other line of work other than commercial radio broadcasting for a young man of talent and energy, eager to find challenge and reward after almost eight years of frustration as a trainee and clerk.

Radio station 2SM

In 1947, Sydney was served by six commercial broadcasters as well as two stations provided by the ABC. As might have been expected, the airwaves were principally dominated by stations with strong network affiliations. 2UE was linked to Melbourne's 3DB as members of the Major Network while 2GB was the flagship of the Macquarie Network (Jones 1995). These broadcasters, together with 2UW, were the leading Sydney radio stations so far as budgets, programmes, personalities and listeners were concerned. Next came the Labor Party's 2KY, which tended to attract a slightly smaller listening audience. Sharing a bottom rung so far as popularity was concerned were 2SM and 2CH. No doubt part of their narrower appeal was due to the fact that the licences for the two stations were held by religious groups. This affected programming in various ways, including restricting what might be broadcast by one or other station and setting significant amounts of time aside for programming of religious worship.

2SM was located on the seventh and eight floors of the Australia House building in Carrington Street near Wynyard Railway Station close to Sydney's CBD (Simmons 1995). It was a small station occupying two floors of the Australia House building. There was a small office on the seventh floor of the building from which salesmen worked but all other station activities happened on the eight floor. 2SM had various features in common with 2CH, most especially the fact that both stations technical operations and equipment was provided by Amalgamated Wireless Australasia (AWA) which was housed nearby in York Street. A Sydney Catholic priest, Monsigneur James Meany, was managing director of 2SM, having taken out the original licence on behalf of the Sydney diocese of the Catholic Church in 1932 (Walker 1973: 15). The priest had adopted a radio call signal acronym based on the name of the parish church that he ran in a nearby suburb. Working in an office at the station each day, Meany saw 2SM as a Catholic radio station whose prime function was to provide a service of devotion and instruction to Catholic listeners across the metropolitan area (Griffen-Foley 2009: 85).

This still left many broadcasting hours when ordinary listeners could tune in for a more secular service of information and entertainment. The upshot was that, for the most part, 2SM sounded like the other Sydney commercial stations, although lacking their glamour, affluence and grandeur. With his parish duties continuing, Meany left the actual running of the station to a general manager. The upshot was that 2SM promoted itself not so much as a Catholic station but rather as a 'family station', an orientation that could be heard in its programming, which attempted to appeal to housewives and mothers, to men, to younger members of the family and to children (Simmons 1995). The idea of the family as audience helped to organize the broadcasting day with some programmes arranged for the general listener and other time zones set aside for particular listeners such as the housewife and the child.

As it turned out, 2SM was an excellent station to join for an ambitious young man who was belatedly beginning his broadcasting career. Sitting on the bottom rung of Sydney commercial radio stations so far as the industry, the public and its programming was concerned, the station would provide opportunities for the taking. 2SM did not boast any big programmes such as *Calling the Stars* or *The Lux Radio Theatre*, nor top-line radio stars such as Jack Davey or Bob Dyer. There were no jealous rivals who might want to cut a newcomer down to size. Instead, there was plenty of opportunity for a young man with ambition, energy and imagination. Although Grundy was hired as sports director and initially employed to commentate on boxing, he was soon involved in other broadcasting activities at a station where announcers were also expected to be all-rounders. Seeking sales and sponsors became a prominent, ongoing activity but so, too, were such duties as preparing news copy, reading the news and putting together other shows including attracting sponsorship and recruiting artists (Grundy 2010: 26–42). Other opportunities would soon offer themselves to a young man anxious to make up for aimless years as a retail store trainee and clerk. First, though, Grundy needed to establish himself as 2SM's sports director, in the process mastering the art of sports broadcasting.

Radio sport and Sydney boxing

As noted in Chapter 2, Reg Grundy seems not to have had any particular interest or aptitude for sport while at St Peter's College in Adelaide. Hence, in entrusting him with the job of sports director, 2SM was assuming that he would quickly learn how sport functioned in radio. Sport was and is a form of actuality broadcasting with the public perceiving the sporting event as being unscripted, spontaneous and (unless otherwise indicated) transmitted live-to-air (Battema 2004: 1320–23; Goldberg 1998: 29–37; Gorman, Kirk & Rozin 1994: 1–22). In this respect, the sporting broadcast has much in common with other forms of actuality broadcasting such as documentary, public events coverage and outside news broadcasts. Yet this actuality was never regarded as completely sacrosanct so far as the broadcast of sporting events was concerned. Mediation of one kind or another was (and is) seen as frequently necessary to enhance the broadcastability of the sporting event. Besides, because of the competitive nature of sporting events, radio sport was also understood as a form of broadcast entertainment with the element of struggle or battle linking it to audience-participation programmes and quiz shows. In fact, intervention of one kind or another on the part of the broadcaster was often necessary. Broadcast equipment could be faulty or the live sporting event might be unpredictable and unmanageable in part because it was controlled by outside interests and could be affected by unexpected circumstances. In short, 'liveness' and 'actuality' were effects to be striven for by the radio professional even if it was necessary, on occasions, to revert to 'phantom' broadcasts and other events staged for the microphone (Griffen-Foley 2009: 298).

Boxing had been one of the major early attractions of radio broadcasting (Buxton & Owen 1972: 14–22). In the United States in the 1920s and 1930s, live descriptions of major boxing matches featuring such heavyweight champions as Jack Dempsey and Joe Louis attracted very large numbers of listeners, helped in the sale of radio receivers, further popularized the pugilistic arts, and increased the attraction of sports broadcasting on radio (Battema 2004). Australian professional boxing was at its height of popularity during and immediately after World War II. In Sydney and Melbourne, the most attractive venues were those owned and operated by Stadiums Limited, an interest controlled by legendary sporting entrepreneur and gambler John Wren (Griffen 2004: 144–49; Casey 1995). In 1947, boxing happened at the Sydney Stadium on Monday nights while wrestling occurred on Thursday. Tickets were at a premium, and many Sydney notables – including 2KY celebrity announcer John Harper and Consolidated Press media mogul Frank Packer – were regular attendees at the boxing matches.

The Monday-night event was reported to the public at large by a retinue of newspaper sports writers as well as a host of radio broadcasters. In fact, the radio broadcasts only covered the main bout of the evening preceded by a summary of earlier fights (Grundy 2010:

26–35; Casey 1995). Grundy had been hired by 2SM because of his vocal chords rather than any sporting background. After all, urbanity and clear diction were the keys to progress in radio announcing. Regulations promulgated by the Postmaster General's Department stated: 'Every announcer shall be of good education, style and personality, and possessed of clear enunciation, as far as possible free from any characteristic dialect' (Jones 1995: 43). Or as a colleague who had joined 2SM a year earlier put it, comparing Grundy with a 2SM predecessor John Sherwood: '[Sherwood] wasn't a very good sporting commentator, and we all knew this so we looked for somebody who would have the type of voice … Reg's voice on the tape didn't get too excited as they do these days; you could hear everything he said' (Simmons 1995).

Vocal range and quality were a good start but Grundy also needed to master the art of boxing commentary. He would later explain: 'I'd seen two fights in my life. I got every Joe Palooka comic book I could and a couple of books on wrestling and boxing. I threw in all the color I could to save me calling punches and hands' (*TV Week* 1962). In his memoir, he adds that he also sought out one of the press corps for feedback and suggestions about his boxing descriptions (2010: 33–34). Clearly, he soon mastered the art of the boxing commentary and his Monday-night fight descriptions were to continue on Sydney radio for more than ten years.

Unlike the more popular Sydney radio stations, 2SM did not broadcast racing. And while Monday-night boxing was the most important weekly event on the station's sporting calendar, nevertheless, there were other sporting opportunities awaiting the 2SM sportscaster that will be discussed below (Griffen-Foley 2009: 283–96). There were, for example, the NSW tennis titles and the McWilliams Wines golf tournament (Grundy 2010: 38). These were, however, one-off contests and the young sportscaster looked around for more regular sporting events to cover during the 2SM broadcasting week.

Rugby League, a world bout and a sporting farce

The involvements in question illustrate the three other sporting involvements that helped to consolidate Grundy's legendary if minor status as a sportscaster among the public at large, his colleagues and even in his own subsequent store of anecdotes. This range of Grundy's activities as 2SM sports director had to do with the pioneering of football broadcasting, the airing of an international overseas boxing match, and a well-publicized incident at the Sydney Stadium that turned a sporting event into a farce. The football code in question was Rugby League. Broadcast of the popular winter game was not new to Sydney commercial radio. However, racing broadcasting was king so Rugby League fans had to be content with snatches of the Match of the Day heard between the calling of races on a Saturday afternoon. Grundy recognized an obvious fit between 2SM's listeners and the very popular Sydney football code. He arranged to call games in their entirety over the last part of the 1949 season. Having only played Australian Rules football at school, he undertook a rapid study of the rules of Rugby League, had his backup systems in place, met the players and memorized their faces (Grundy 2010: 37–40). His commentary was delivered from the sidelines with Grundy also relying on a former player to help him identify referee decisions, players' identity, and on-field moves. A six-game trial set of broadcast commentaries took place in 1949 and led to 2SM becoming a permanent radio broadcaster of the game, with Grundy immediately securing sponsors for the following season (Grundy 2010: 39–40). Over the next three and a half years, the 2SM sports director was to call all competition games as well as Test Matches with England, France and New Zealand (Grundy 2010: 40).

The second initiative had to do with Grundy's coverage of the world bantamweight championship boxing match between Australian Jimmy Carruthers and South African Vic Toweel, held in late 1952 (Casey 1995). The bout was to occur in Johannesburg. Australia would only learn of the encounter by means of the international wire service because no newspaper or radio station could afford to send a reporter or commentator to cover the bout. By booking the only radio-telephone links between Johannesburg and Sydney, Johannesburg and London, and London and Sydney, Grundy ensured that he would have an exclusive scoop of the event as well as technical insurance if one set of cables was to prove mechanically faulty.

How, though, was he to get to the contest in South Africa? Qantas, Australia's international airline, had opened a 'Kangaroo Route' between Sydney and Johannesburg a short time before (Qantas history website). Grundy secured a ticket in a contra deal that would involve frequent promotions of the airline during the broadcast. 2SM approved the arrangement, and Grundy flew off for his first trip overseas, itself a kind of down payment on the many international flights that he would make later in his career.

The fight itself was sensational, with Carruthers knocking out the South African just two minutes and nineteen seconds into the first round. Then followed two problems that highlighted the unpredictability of sporting contests and the need for sports broadcasters to be ever artful and inventive. First, there was the fact that the bout had not run for sufficient time to allow the inclusion of a string of Qantas promotions in the broadcast. Luckily, Grundy had recorded a large number of vox populi interviews beforehand that would help overcome this problem. A larger difficulty lay in the fact that the first minute of Grundy's description of the boxing contest had been lost by a sound engineer loaned to him by the South African Broadcasting Corporation. This called for a 're-recording' along the lines pioneered by early radio descriptions of baseball in the United States and Test cricket in Australia where, unknown to the listener, commentary and sound effects could be used to simulate the live broadcast of an unfolding contest (Jones 1995: 16–20). In fact, on this occasion, sound engineers used a recorded disc of a US baseball crowd to provide backing for Grundy when he simulated his commentary of the missing first minute of the boxing match. Grundy had had a practical introduction to the art of the 'phantom' broadcast.

The last incident further highlighted Grundy's awareness that sports broadcasting could also have obvious elements of show business and entertainment, even descending into obvious comedy and farce. Just as other genres of radio could involve the stunt, so sport on radio could also give rise to what might be called the sporting-stunt broadcast. One Thursday night, Reg Grundy was calling a wrestling match at the Sydney Stadium. The great majority of the Stadium wrestling troupe were American. Even by then, wrestling had ceased to be a sport and had crossed over into the domain of theatre and performance, where wrestlers improvised holds and moves with an arranged outcome in mind (Casey 1995). Grundy was calling a contest from a crow's nest position on one of the corners of the ring where he could be seen from every corner of the stadium. Suddenly, one of the contestants, Big Chief Littlewolf, seemed to grow angry at Grundy's commentary and gave voice to his feelings. The wrestler began to climb the pole to attack the commentator. Grundy, in turn, helped continue the joke by climbing higher and higher, beating off the apparently enraged wrestler with his microphone. As befits that kind of event, the incident entertained the crowd, captured headlines for Thursday-night wrestling, and won some useful publicity for the 2SM sports director.

Seizing opportunities

The period at 2SM was a productive time for a young man with drive and ambition. Besides the sports broadcasting work mentioned above, there were other occasions and openings for Reg Grundy to advance his reputation and, sometimes, gain additional remuneration. Several examples of this extra curricular enterprise can be mentioned by way of rounding out this discussion of the first stage of Reg Grundy's broadcasting career. A minor illustration involved a small mail-order business in autographed photographs of champion boxers appearing at the stadium that Grundy conducted from home, which was mentioned by one of his 2SM colleagues (O'Callaghan 1995).

Another initiative occurred when a 2SM assistant was undertaking National Service. Seizing the chance, the young sports director arranged for a series of boxing matches at Holsworthy Army Camp to raise money for Legacy, a well-known charity. The camp's commanding officer approved the idea and Grundy arranged for a series of boxers and wrestlers who performed at the Sydney Stadium to take part. He then commentated the bouts as part of his regular 2SM broadcasts (O'Callaghan 1995). The Holsworthy venture was good public relations, as was a third venture: a charity auction that Grundy organized in connection with the death of a Sydney Aboriginal boxer, Dave Sands. Sands held boxing titles at middleweight and heavyweight levels and boxed at the Sydney Stadium and at another city venue, Leichardt Stadium (Casey 1995; Gillespie-Jones 1995). In late 1952, the boxer was killed in a truck accident, whereupon the sportscaster persuaded the owner of a Sydney nightclub to allow him to run a charity auction for Sand's wife and family with show-business and sporting-world folk donating time and money for the occasion.

Two other examples of Reg Grundy's enterprise involved profitable sidelines put his way by another announcer at 2SM. I have already noted that when Grundy joined the station in 1947, he was unaware of the fact that the station already had an announcer who called the boxing and wrestling. This was film, theatre and radio actor Patrick Tuohill, whose stage name was John Sherwood (Simmons 1995). Sherwood had appeared in the major Australian war-features *Forty Thousand Horsemen* and *The Rats of Tobruk* and was the station's principal announcer. He would later move to the United Kingdom to appear in such features as *The Hasty Heart* (1953). Possibly anticipating this departure, he introduced Grundy to two profitable voice-based sidelines. One involved recording the anonymous voice-overs for advertising slides that played in cinemas between the support and main feature film, while the other involved becoming one of the off-screen commentators for Cinesound Newsreels when Sydney boxing stories were included in the weekly offering (Grundy 2010: 35–38). This second assignment was approved by Cinesound's manager in the person of Ken Hall. Hall himself was a veteran of the Australian film industry (such as it was), serving successively as Union Theatres' publicity manager, assistant to the general manager, producer and director of a dozen feature films and, finally, overseeing the occasional documentary and the weekly *Cinesound Review* (Moran & Vieth 2005: 97–98). As we shall see in Chapter 5, making Hall's acquaintance would later prove useful for Grundy's career.

2SM resignation

A little over six months after the Carruthers victory in South Africa and his own professional triumph in completing this first overseas broadcasting engagement, Grundy suddenly found himself leaving the station. He was not alone. Instead, there were six individual decisions to resign from 2SM in mid-1953 consisting of those of the general manager, Grundy as sports director, one of the news journalists as well as three women secretaries. This dramatic coup was sufficiently unexpected to warrant a moment of general publicity for events at the station (Griffen-Foley 2009: 185–86).

The event came about for political, religious and professional reasons. The Cold War was intensifying with politics and religion frequently becoming intricably intermixed while, from an industry perspective, Griffen-Foley has described the background to these resignations as a struggle between professionalism and sectarianism (2009: 182–88). The unexpected death of Monsignor Meany, the station's managing director, triggered the crisis. For the most part, as has already been noted, the latter had not behaved like a chief executive, preferring instead to leave most administrative and programming decisions to the station's general manager, although this relationship between the two had recently deteriorated.

Meany had kept the 2SM board of directors in the dark for a long time about station activities, including the state of its finances. By 1953, the Sydney Catholic hierarchy had been planning to centralize control of all Catholic broadcasting in another church body and the sudden death helped precipitate these discussions. There were other matters that were also canvassed by a hastily convened board meeting that was led by a newly installed managing director, appointed by the Sydney bishop. Administrative problems enumerated included the lack of new programming for several years, the station's low ratings, concerns about station profitability and the imminent threat posed by the inauguration of television. Sectarian tensions were also in the air, and there were anxieties over the fact that several males on staff at 2SM were not Catholic. Reg Grundy was one of them. Within days, matters became inquisitorial. Another employee at the time, Ted Simmons, has described the situation as follows:

> There was an internal power struggle between one faction of management who wanted to impose a set of rules and conditions on all members of staff and those who didn't agree with those rules. I was called in to the office. I was pre-warned by someone else on the staff and when I was questioned I knew not to give a direct answer, and so they were not prepared to sack me and I stayed on the staff. Quite a lot of my close work mates went in the purge. Religion was part of it and the faction wanted all employees to be Catholic. It didn't work out that way and it wound up being mixed staff as far as religion was concerned. The efficiency of the staff was considered more important. It was a management decision and when the hierarchy of the Church found out they were horrified.
>
> (Simmons 1995)

Given the fact that he was leaving the station, it was ironic that one of the few positives to be outlined to the board had been Grundy's performance as sports director (Griffen-Foley 2009: 186). For over six years, the young sportscaster had been successfully selling radio advertising time to would-be sponsors. In resigning from 2SM, he was gambling that he could sell himself as an employee to another one of Sydney's commercial radio stations. Broadcaster 2CH was an obvious first port of call. Overlaps between the two stations have already been mentioned. 2CH and 2SM had a good deal in common: both broadcasting licences were held by religious bodies; they both looked to AWA for technical services; both received their station news from the evening newspaper *The Sun*; listeners could find the two stations next to each other at the bottom of the radio receiver dial; their managements sometimes cooperated – as occurred when 2CH used 2SM's broadcasting facilities after a fire at the NSW Council of Churches' station; and 2SM and 2CH staff sometimes socialized for friendly games of cricket. Shortly, Grundy was hired by 2CH although this hardly represented an upward move for the 30-year-old radio broadcaster. 2SM, meanwhile, retained its association with sport for a long time after Grundy's departure. His assistant took over the Rugby League descriptions for the rest of the 1953 season. The station then appointed former player and prominent Catholic Frank Hyde not only to continue to call the football but also to cover the Monday-night boxing (Grundy 2010: 51).

Family business: romance

One other element of Reg Grundy's six years at station 2SM should be noted. This had to do with a courtship in progress when he resigned from the station. 2SM dubbed itself 'the family station', and this domestic warmth spilled over into the social and working relations of the staff. Because most of those employed at the station were Catholic, social interaction among the staff was encouraged. There were, for example, many friendly cricket matches both among the staff and with rival radio stations that became excuses for office picnics with other female and male staff in attendance. Other incidental activities included going to Sydney horse racing together on Saturday afternoon with the station's general manager Bernie Stapleton, himself the keen owner of a racehorse. Romance and marriage also happened among those who worked at 2SM.

Thus, it was not surprising that in 1952 Reg Grundy had met a young woman at the station whom he would marry some two years later. Her name was Lola Powell. Like all the women on staff at Radio Station 2SM, she was Catholic and single. Lola was twelve years younger than Reg Grundy, having been born in 1935 in the same Double Bay/Rose Bay area where the Grundy family had lived since moving back to Sydney in 1939. Lola Powell had attended Holy Cross College in Woolahra for both her primary and secondary education and had been hired as secretary to the station sales manager. Soon, she and Grundy were romantically involved.

After the death of Meany and the sudden staff resignations, the two decided that it would be wise for Lola to resign from the station (Gillespie-Jones 1995). Her religion made her safe from the purge that was then taking place but her attachment to one of the dissidents might have made her vulnerable to pressure. Lola Powell resigned from 2SM, moving first to another radio station, 2UW, and shortly afterwards to a job as secretary to the advertising manager for a sewing-machine franchise, secured through Grundy's uncle, Harry Lees. The two continued their courtship and decided to marry in late 1954.

Afterword

Reg Grundy had made remarkable progress in his broadcasting career in the span of six years. After a late start in radio because of World War II, he had mastered much to do with broadcasting. Selling was the main pathway to success. The 2SM sports director realized that hard work, thorough preparation, accepting advice from old hands and learning from mistakes needed to be matched by entrepreneurship and initiative. Opportunity was there for the taking provided it could be recognized and harnessed. His motto might have been to think ahead, prepare, adapt and take advantage of unexpected openings. Boldness was also a feature of his makeup, as was confirmed in his decision to resign from 2SM.

Indeed, it was a mark of how confident Reg Grundy had become that the young man who only got his toe in the door of commercial radio in 1947 should now resoundingly slam a career door behind him when he left his first radio employer in mid-1953. This chapter has chartered this rising optimism on Grundy's part over this period by investigating his successes in different areas of broadcasting. The 30-year-old had mastered many of the skills and secrets of sports broadcasting. Changing stations meant changing routines and opportunities, however. Further practical schooling beckoned. Reg Grundy soon found himself in a new career situation where new skills and capacities would have to be learned. A second phase of his apprenticeship was at hand.

Chapter 4

Apprenticeship II: Quiz-show Schooling, 1953-59

Introduction

The second stage of Reg Grundy's practical learning in the more specialized areas of broadcasting now began. He believed he had moved to a station similar in terms of both geography and industry outlook to 2SM. Yet Grundy soon discovered that this was not quite the case. 2CH had little interest in sport, so the former sports director at 2SM gradually had to reinvent himself and what he did. This change took place over the next half-dozen years. Grundy began to concentrate on audience-participation and quiz programmes. He cobbled together a succession of shows that depended on surrounding circumstances, on the example of other radio hosts and producers, and on whatever his own memory and imagination could conjure up.

By learning on the job, Reg Grundy was in fact serving an apprenticeship to a genre of popular entertainment in broadcasting that would serve him well for the rest of his working life. Meanwhile, Australian television finally became a reality in 1956, with a slow but irresistible effect on radio broadcasting. It soon became obvious to Grundy that further change was necessary if his career was to thrive. This chapter follows Grundy's personal and professional life in the latter half of the 1950s. The former saw marriage, death and birth, while the latter witnessed another six years in commercial radio. Reg Grundy appeared to mark time in his business career. Crucially, though, he changed from being a sporting personality to becoming a quiz-show host and producer. This second phase in radio provided him with an invaluable apprenticeship for the upcoming mode of mass broadcasting of image as well as sound that was taking on its own institutional forms in Sydney in this period.

The general setting

Australia in the years 1953–59 saw a high degree of economic prosperity, political hegemony and social orthodoxy (Moran 1991: 55–68). The 'long boom' that many Western nations enjoyed after the end of World War II was underway, generating full employment in primary industries as well as in secondary industries, where rapid industrialization was occurring behind a strong wall of domestic protection. Labour was in short supply, and very high levels of employment attracted hundreds of thousands of migrants, leading to high rates of home ownership, house building and the rapid spread of suburbs in the major metropolitan centres. The Cold War had a local impact, with a split in the Australian Labor Party in 1956 that had the effect of further enshrining the existing political hegemony. However, if politics ceased to be an area of social variation, social habits and routines could become an area of difference. This was certainly the case for migrants from Europe and elsewhere, who were formally required to 'assimilate' to a supposed Australian way of life, even while that practice was itself changing due to successive waves of consumerism and popular culture, much of it coming from the United States.

Radio broadcasting seemed not to register these changes, continuing in a form set in place over two decades earlier. No new radio stations came on the air in Sydney, and broadcasting continued to operate on the AM (Alternate Modulation) frequency band. Six commercial radio broadcasters continued on air, with the two most popular and successful, 2GB and 2UE, functioning as dominant stations in the Macquarie and Major radio networks. One of the few events to ruffle this durability was the occasional movement of radio personalities from one radio station to another. Grundy's resignation from 2SM and his employment by 2CH were briefly worth a media mention, as was 2GB's signing of John Hudson as breakfast announcer in 1954 and 2CH's consequential recruitment of Brian Henderson from New Zealand radio in 1955 (Henderson 1995). For the most part, though, there were no deep-seated changes afoot and it was business as usual in Sydney commercial radio broadcasting.

US radio know-how goes Down Under

Australian commercial radio was undergoing change at other levels, however. One of these related to the dominance by the early 1950s of the quiz-show genre in the commercial radio programming schedule (Mackay 1959: 14–19). The stocks of this genre had been rising steadily through the previous decade, and by elevating this genre to a pre-eminent place in station programming, Australian commercial radio was following a US programming trend towards audience-participation and quiz shows (Mittell 2004). From 1934 onwards, Australian radio executives had contact with their counterparts across the Pacific, leading to a steady stream of radio industry ideas and know-how, radio programme transcriptions, personnel and other elements taking root in Australian commercial radio (Potts 1988: 26–29; Lane 1994: 26–28, 55–59).

The advent of *Professor Quiz* and the rapid development of the US radio quiz show after 1936 soon made their presence felt in Australia. By 1942, for example, 2GV Macquarie could boast of a clutch of quiz shows in its evening line-up, including *Rise and Shine*, *Ask the Army* and *The Quiz Kids*. Whether the first two of these were original is unclear, but the latter was an adaptation and remake of a US original that had made its first appearance in 1938 on one of NBC's radio networks. It was an overwhelming temptation to tap into US know-how in different radio genres, with or without the permission of copyright owners. In fact, when US radio programme formats were overtly imitated, sometimes without the permission of their copyright owners, it was not uncommon for threats of legal action to ensue.

This could be the case with quiz shows, but it especially came into play when more valuable intellectual property violations were seen to be involved. For instance, in 1950 Ron Beck Productions had remade its own radio version of the popular US comic-strip series *Blondie*, starring local actor Willie Fennell in the principal role of Dagwood Bumstead. *Blondie* was an extremely valuable franchise, having given rise to comic books, a US radio network version and two Hollywood feature films. The Australian clone came to the attention of the US copyright owners and legal threats were made. This local version of *Blondie* was dropped in 1953 in favour of a kind of local sibling, *Life with Dexter*, which starred the same actor in the same kind of role as a bumbling husband and father (Griffen-Foley 2009: 23–34).

Other arrangements were also possible. One of these was highlighted by Bob Dyer, a highly popular quiz host and producer on Australian commercial radio in the 1940s and 1950s. Dyer grew up in the United States and first came to Australia to perform in Vaudeville as a ukulele-playing Southern hillbilly. He stayed on to become a radio variety star, and by 1944 had begun to package his own radio shows, such as the stunt-based quiz show *Can You Take It?*, which began in 1946, and a big giveaway question-and-answer programme, *Pick-a-Box*, which debuted on 2GV Macquarie in 1948. There followed a string of other quiz shows that made Dyer one of the kings of Australian commercial radio (Moran & Keating 2003: 148–49). Not surprisingly for someone with extensive US show-business contacts, many of Dyer's audience-participation and quiz shows had originated in the United States. In fact, under an arrangement with leading US radio host and producer Art Linkletter, who had originated the stunt-based audience-participation success *People are Funny* in 1942 (Mittell 2002: 326–41), Dyer had access to Linkletter's catalogue of audience-participation and quiz shows for remaking in Australia (Grimes 2010: 33).

Commercial and cultural charms of radio quiz shows

As I have already suggested, if variety had been the dominant 'headline' form of Australian commercial radio in the early 1940s, the late 1940s and early 1950s saw the genre displaced by audience-participation programmes and quiz shows. The reasons were not hard to find. On the negative side, the rising costs of variety were unsustainable, especially in an economic recession that briefly occurred in the very early 1950s. On the positive side, the quiz shows were a highly profitable format: they required little money for 'talent' (only hosts and announcers), only necessitated small writing staffs and could be produced quickly without many rehearsals. Although prizes were often lavish, producers usually persuaded companies to contribute products to the prize packages in exchange for on-air mentions (Mittell 2004: 1150).

After a study trip to the United States, a Macquarie executive reporting on the increasing popularity of the radio quiz show drew attention to a CBS report that found 'quiz shows gave listeners a shot at something for nothing, a feeling of superiority when contestants could not answer easy questions', and a chance to satisfy the 'curiosity that all people have about other human beings' (Griffen-Foley 2009: 228–29). Locally produced quiz shows, whether original or adapted from overseas predecessors, had the added advantage of generating production-related employment, thereby winning the support of local guilds and other industry unions.

The upshot of this development was that Australian commercial radio was awash in radio quiz shows in the decade from the late 1940s to the late 1950s. Many of these were 'headline' night-time shows hosted by Dyer or Davey on 2GV Macquarie. The two were equally adroit in handling the different subtypes of the genre. Thus Dyer presided over the knowledge-based *Pick-a-Box*, the comedy-gag variant *It Pays to Be Funny*, the stunt-based adaptation *Can You Take It?* and the 'giveaway' show *Cop the Lot* among other quiz-show outings. Davey was just as busy, and his offerings included the factual knowledge quiz shows *Give It a Go* and *The Dulux Show*, a novelty variation *Auction Quiz* and the panel comedy quiz show *The Pressure Pack Show*.

Nor was the quiz show restricted to night-time, top-rating stations and personality hosts. Quiz shows could also feature at less popular times of the day or evening, and come from stations that did not figure so prominently in audience ratings. The music quiz show was a type that was particularly easy to mount, with a station only needing a turntable, a collection of musical recordings and a telephone to call up listeners, as witnessed in 2UE's *UE Calling* and 2CH's *Colda Music Quiz* (*B&T*, 24 May 1954: 15).

Making way for television

Despite the general popularity of commercial radio, and the dominance of the quiz show, broadcasters increasingly were haunted by the spectre of television during this period. Television had been discussed as early as the 1920s, so radio broadcasters had long believed that it was something that would happen a long time into the future. Between 1953 and 1959, however, the elephant finally got loose in the room. A succession of events brought the speculation into being (Moran & Keating 2003: 30–34). In 1954, engineers conducted a series of closed-circuit television broadcasts to hospitals as part of the coverage of the Royal visit of the newly crowned Queen Elizabeth II. In 1954–55, a Royal Commission on Television conducted lengthy hearings across the country in preparation for regular service. Early in 1956, test transmissions began, and in late 1956, regular television broadcasting started in Sydney and Melbourne.

There was no immediate panic on the part of radio broadcasters, but there was concern. After all, US commercial radio had learned to live with network television, so Australian radio executives were optimistic that a rapprochement favourable to their interests could be achieved. Some also believed that commercial radio had much to offer television in the area of experienced personnel, programme ideas, showmanship, news reporting and so on. Sometimes, however, the radio background counted for very little. This turned out to be the case when ATN7, one of the two new commercial television stations in Sydney, simulcast eight audience-participation programmes and quiz shows being broadcast by 2GB and the Macquarie Network (Pitts 2004; Felsenthal 2004). Several of these shows had been immensely popular on radio, with some showing themselves as perennial favourites. Some of their titles have been mentioned above. They included *The Dulux Show, Give It a Go, It Pays to Be Funny, The Pantomime Show, Pick-a-Box, The Pressure Pak Show* and *The Quiz Kids* (Moran & Keating 2003: 338–39). In the event, only one of these shows, Bob Dyer's *Pick-a-Box*, was to make a successful transition to the new medium. Television would not afford much respect for reputations built in radio. However, Grundy was probably too busy in his work at his new radio station to take too much notice of this mostly unsuccessful remaking of radio quiz shows for television. Having glimpsed the shadow of television, let us return to the 30-year-old as he began the second phase of his broadcasting career at another Sydney commercial broadcaster.

Radio Station 2CH

In his memoir, Reg Grundy entitles his move to his new radio station 2CH as 'A Stroll Across the Park' (2010: 534). Indeed, his new employer was situated a short diagonal distance from Carrington Street, through Wynyard Park, to the resplendent AWA building in York Street where 2CH was housed. From its completion in 1939 until 1958, the building was the tallest in Australia, with its modernist Art Deco style and a large metal spire fashioned after the Eiffel Tower. The AWA tower's height allowed it to relay broadcast radio signals from both 2CH and 2SM to all parts of the Sydney metropolitan area. Whether he was aware of it or not, Grundy was joining a station that was part of a large international family of radio, technological and broadcasting interests, founded by the Italian experimenter and inventor Guglielmo Marconi, that had come into existence almost fifty years earlier.

Following his development of radio communications technology and systems at the turn of the twentieth century, this son of an Italian father and an Anglo-Irish mother had set up the Marconi Company as a British corporation. The ambition of Marconi and his engineers was to establish an international monopoly over maritime ship-to-shore communication, and this necessitated establishing coastal radio stations in several parts of the world. Local subsidiaries of the British parent corporation were necessary to operate these radio stations. The advent of World War I nudged national governments into taking cognizance of this kind of international operations in their territories that had strategic implications. The US Marconi operation was 'Americanized' in the period of 1917–19 for political and commercial as well as military reasons. The Radio Corporation of America (RCA) was established as the corporate owner and operator of these resources, which included equipment, patents and human personnel (Finney 2004). In 1926, RCA established a broadcast network organization in the shape of the National Broadcasting Company (NBC) (Buxton & Owen 1972: 36–52). Meanwhile, in Australia, the local Marconi subsidiary had entered into a partnership with the state. A new company was established in 1922 under the name of AWA, with the Commonwealth as the largest shareholder (Moran & Keating 2003: 201).

As AWA's leading radio broadcasting station in Australia's premier market in terms of listening audience and the value of radio advertising, Grundy's new employer, 2CH, served as a primary link to AWA's older North American sibling, RCA, and its radio broadcasting arm, NBC. One of these had to do with radio broadcasting content. As part of an international service to its US listeners, NBC regularly aired very short overseas features, scattered through its programme schedule. These included 90-second shorts produced by 2CH that generally featured the station's production manager. More occasionally, there were opportunities for an ambitious and enterprising figure such as Grundy to be heard on the parent network. Thus, in late 1955, he recorded an on-air interview with Didi Pails, the former Davis Cup tennis star, regarding Australia's prospects of regaining the prized trophy. The interview was tape recorded and then flown to the United States, where it was heard nationally on NBC's *Monitor* programme. Under the headline '2CH Interview Aired in USA', *Broadcasting & Television* duly noted that '2CH sporting commentator Reg Grundy realized a long-term ambition to be heard by millions of listeners at once' (*B&T*, 11 October 1955: 6). A year later, Grundy was also featured in a daily 60-second report on NBC radio summarizing events at the Melbourne Olympic Games (Grundy 2010: 58).

Unfortunately, such opportunities for enterprise and initiative were less common at Grundy's new station than had been the case at 2SM. The tone of middle-of-the-road orthodoxy was set by the parent organization, AWA, which had been described in a 1956 industry profile as 'somewhat conservative and somewhat prim as a company' (*B&T*, 24 August 1956: 4). AWA operated the station on behalf of its licensee, the New South Wales Council of Churches, a body that had little interest in enhancing the station's general appeal. The licence owner only played a limited role in setting the ambience of the radio station, although it too favoured orthodoxy and conservatism. The Council of Churches was responsible for a ban on alcohol and cigarette advertising, and was against the broadcast of horse racing and Rugby League football. It allocated all of Sunday to the broadcast of religious services and devotion, and also set aside fifteen minutes each weekday morning for the discussion of ecclesiastical matters.

In other words, in moving to 2CH, Grundy was joining a Sydney radio station of only limited popular appeal; like 2SM, the station tended to come last in its share of the Sydney listening public. 2CH mostly steered a restrained pathway so far as its programming was concerned, with the emphasis placed on listener improvement and both moral and cultural upliftment (Hampson 1995). The main ingredient of its programming was familiar middle-of-the-road music with a combination of popular songs, including a smattering of light, classical music. 2CH projected itself as 'Sydney's music station' ('for which there was no substitute'). George Morotoff, who worked alongside Reg Grundy as a time salesman, programme host and announcer at the time, commented later: 'It was hard to work out our prime target audience. In those days the ratings were not sophisticated enough to give us breakdowns of demographics' (Morotoff 1995). So how was Grundy affected by this station culture?

From sportscaster to quizmaster

While he had undertaken various other duties at 2SM, including station announcements, news reading and time sales, Reg Grundy's title had been that of sports director, and his principal function had been to broadcast commentary on various live sporting events in which his audience was understood as being interested. Chief among these had been the sportscaster's Monday-night broadcast of the main boxing event at the Sydney Stadium, which had launched his career at 2SM. Several of Sydney's other commercial radio stations also broadcast boxing on a Monday night, and Grundy's new employer, 2CH, was agreeable to his continuing to cover this event. The station also seems to have been agreeable to him broadcasting the main Thursday-night wrestling bout at the stadium. Even so, the radio sporting event that Grundy was unable to take with him to 2CH was the weekly broadcast that he had created for 2SM, the Saturday-afternoon winter description of the main Rugby League match of the day. His former employer, 2SM, had seen an obvious fit between the station's Catholic listeners and Sydney's own code of football, with its strong working-class roots in Irish migrant communities. The previous chapter pointed out that 2SM had one of Grundy's assistants take over the commentaries, and then recruited Frank Hyde, a former champion player and prominent Catholic, as a permanent replacement in 1954. 2CH would have acquiesced this loss of Rugby League commentary because the game held little attraction for the station's management and for its more middle-class, Protestant listeners.

Despite this obstacle, Grundy continued to undertake sports broadcasts of one kind or another from outside locations for some time. Shortly after joining the radio station, he was describing baseball games from the Sydney Sports Ground and ice hockey from the Sydney Showground. There were also some notable one-off sporting events that were ideal for extended broadcast coverage, including the annual Davis Cup Tennis Challenge Rounds and various international golf matches. Reg Grundy also attended the 1956 Olympic Games in Melbourne and presented an evening roundup of sporting results from each day's events as well as a one-minute summary each day for NBC radio in the United States. The Games authority also had him call the final night of boxing, the Gold Medal events (*TV Week* 1959: 17).

2CH was always going to be more barren soil as far as sustaining a radio sporting career was concerned, however. In any case, Sydney did not host live sporting events on weekday evenings other than Monday and Thursday. This left several night-time slots for which Grundy, like other radio sporting specialists, had to devise various station-based programmes (Griffen-Foley 2009: 299–306). Initially, these programmes were heavily sports based, but soon Grundy's shows began to incorporate other generic elements. In fact, mixing programme types would soon lead Grundy in a new career direction. A string of generic crossover programmes over the next few years highlights this gradual disengagement from sports broadcasting. These included several combinations of talk and music into which Grundy had already strayed while at 2SM, and now included a Saturday-morning *Parramatta Hour*, which he both produced and hosted (Grundy 2010: 42).

The now-forgotten programme roll-call of late-evening sports-related shows that Reg Grundy put to air at 2CH during his six years there included *In the Groove with Grundy* and *Sportsmen in the Spotlight*, in which Grundy chatted on air to various sportsmen who had been persuaded to come on to the programme (*Sydney Morning Herald*, 9 February 1954: 43; *Sydney Morning Herald*, 24 May 1954: 27). Conversation between radio host and visitor could run dry, however, so there was a need to mix in other elements of radio to hold an audience and keep it entertained. Music was one perennial standby, hardly surprising given that 2CH labelled itself 'The Music Station'. Indeed, there is a possibility that Grundy may, on one occasion, have repeated a programme idea that he first probably used at 2SM. This involved assembling and playing, one after another, a series of different recordings of a popular early 1950s song 'Lucky Old Sun', a subtle reminder to the listener of how much the institution of broadcasting was (and is) founded on the notion of repetition (May 2010: 21–30). Certainly, in his memory of Grundy's time at 2CH, Roy Hampson remembered this musical novelty going to air (Hampson 1995). Another programme variant, *Sporting Scrapbook*, mixed sport and dramatization. This short-lived, once-a-week, night-time offering used a short play, hastily scripted by John O'Grady, a 2CH comedy writer, to highlight the essence of a particular sporting activity 'using the misadventures of a hapless fall guy' (O'Grady 1980; Grundy 2010: 55).

A more permanent solution to his programming problem lay in realizing that radio's strength lay in live broadcasting. Outside broadcasts of sports events had tapped into this power of spontaneity, but so too did audience-participation programmes. Radio had long been aware of the strength of shows that incorporated an audience, whether at home or in the studio, into its programmes. Grundy now had the idea of inviting his listeners to phone in and become part of proceedings in some of his shows. He was beginning to move in the direction of the audience-participation programme, a type whose most dominant form was the quiz show (Mittell 2004). Over the next half-dozen years at 2CH, Reg Grundy would metamorphose from sportscaster to quizmaster, his forte changing from athletic competition and sporting achievements to quiz contest and prize giveaways.

Producing quiz shows

Five shows that Reg Grundy produced and hosted while at 2CH highlight this move. Nor did he stick to one type of quiz show but rather tried his hand at various subtypes of the genre. This sampling would turn out to be a very useful tutoring for the long career in game shows that lay ahead of him. *Stump the Sportsman* was the first of these transitional programmes. It was a late-evening offering that appeared once a week in 1954. As its name suggests, *Stump the Sportsman* crossed the sports show genre with that of the quiz show. Listeners were invited to telephone in sporting questions for Grundy's guest sportsman in an effort to baffle the specialist (*B&T*, 20 November 1953: 4). In developing this variation of the quiz show, Grundy was probably unaware that the pattern of an expert sitting at the radio microphone and a listener phoning in the quiz question was in fact one of the earliest variations to appear in the evolving genre of the radio quiz show (Mittell 2004). In 1936, US radio network NBC had aired what was probably the first quiz show to appear on radio, *Professor Quiz*. Ordinary audience members were asked to answer questions devised by experts, which tested general knowledge and learning. Within a year, a variation occurred in the form of NBC's *Information Please*, where ordinary listeners phoned in questions designed to test the ability of experts who were part of the show. 2CH's *Stump the Sportsman* followed in the footsteps of *Information Please*, but also varied its pattern by crossing the quiz show with the sports programme.

Reg Grundy's next offering was also aimed at male listeners, although it was as much an audience-participation programme as a quiz show. In fact, *Deals on Wheels*, which first went to air in early 1955, was a significant transitional venture for Grundy because it had nothing to do with sport. The programme was a quasi-quiz show, with participants drawn from the listening public in competition with each other for a car being auctioned each week in the programme. Like *Jack Davey's Auction Quiz* on 2GB Macquarie some three years earlier, this programme replaced listeners competing against each other by correctly answering knowledge-based questions with listeners attempting to outdo each other with auction telephone bids (Griffen-Foley 2009: 227). *Deals on Wheels* was a crossover show in terms of being put to air in Grundy's night-time weekday sports zone, playing Thursday night at 9.00 p.m. and intended primarily for male listeners. The show consisted of an on-air auction of new-model cars, supplied by a car-auction sponsor. Listeners were able to phone in their bids, and Grundy acted as auctioneer while an employee of the sponsor helped out as announcer. *B&T* wrote of an opening bid of £1000 phoned in by an Adelaide listener for a 1955 Zephyr, although Grundy managed to up the winning phone bid to £1250 (*B&T*, 4 November 1955). Two new ingredients had been incorporated into the former sportscaster's quiz-show repetoire with this second foray into the genre of the audience-participation show. One of these was the element of direct rivalry or competition between listeners, while the second involved the promise of a valuable reward or prize for the most successful participant.

These two programmes had been transitional. Like *Sporting Scrapbook*, *Stump the Sportsman* and *Deals on Wheels* had their feet in two camps, making the shows hybrid and not easily promoted to a larger listening audience. Now, however, Grundy decided to highlight another quiz-show variation that had been familiar for some time in US network radio. This was the 'giveaway' show, which featured large, often spectacular, prizes. In US network radio, the 'giveaway' quiz show had first appeared in the late 1930s, and had resurfaced to great public attention and government ire with *Truth or Consequence* and *Stop the Music* in the 1940s (Mittell 2002: 330–33). In March 1956, 2CH announced a new sports-based quiz show entitled *Scoop the Pool*, which would be compèred and produced by Grundy (Grundy 2010: 56). Most importantly, the emerging quizmaster would also gather the prizes that were to be a dominant feature of the show, as heralded in its title. Once again, though, despite the increased attractiveness of the prizes over those in the first two outings, the programme remained aimed at a male listenership, going to air in Grundy's Thursday-night sports programming zone.

All the same, the quiz show constituted a breakthrough of sorts for the station, and for Grundy. *Scoop the Pool* was to run for 60 minutes each Thursday night, marking a significant vote of confidence by 2CH in the venture. Grundy had done a lot of homework for his new show, and it was appreciably bigger and better than its car-auction predecessor. Again he was host, and again the listening public contestants were contacted at the other end of the telephone line. Pacific Motor Auctions remained the sponsor and was joined by Dance Brothers from Sydney's western suburbs. These were responsible for the program's cash prizes. *Scoop the Pool* also offered other prizes raised by Grundy from commercial contacts, both old and new, including city theatre tickets, invitations to stadium boxing bouts and microgroove recordings (*B&T*, 23 March 1956: 22).

During this time, Grundy also became responsible as host and producer for another variant of the quiz show, suggesting that the station was aware of the direction in which his radio persona was moving and the skill that he was developing. *The Sorbent Show* was a daytime panel game show that featured a team of Sydney radio personalities and celebrities (Grundy 2010: 58–60). Once again, this variant of the quiz show was well known on US and Australian commercial radio. Two very popular evening versions *The Pantomime Show* and *The Pressure Pack Show* were running on 2GB at the time, both compèred by the Macquarie Network's top personality broadcaster, Jack Davey (Moran & Keating 2007: 127–28). The 2CH daytime adaptation was sponsored by Sorbent, and was broadcast live from the 2CH auditorium, with its seats usually filled by a lunchtime audience. The personality panelists competed by attempting to identify a phrase or object from a series of visual clues. Meanwhile, the audience listening at home was not forgotten, being invited to solve each puzzle from spoken clues (Grundy 2010: 58).

Wheel of Fortune

The last of Grundy's quiz shows at 2CH was his most successful. Its immediate predecessor, *Scoop the Pool*, had been sufficiently successful for its host-producer and station to launch an even more ambitious form of the quiz genre. The new programme was *Wheel of Fortune*, which completed Reg Grundy's transition from radio sportscaster to quizmaster. It was a daytime programme, squarely aimed at a housewife audience, and was to run each day in a two-hour timeslot from 2.00 p.m., a 2CH timeslot that previously had featured a comedy husband and wife in a live chat and humour show. After Grundy's generic variants on the quiz show, *Wheel of Fortune* represented a return to the original core of the type by being based around questions that tested the general knowledge and learning of contestants. But Grundy had also learned from other successful Australian radio quiz shows such as *Pick-a-Box* and *Scoop the Pool*. As its name implied, *Wheel of Fortune* was also a 'giveaway' programme, promising valuable and impressive prizes as well as more ordinary ones. Like many radio quiz shows, the new programme was phone-based rather than involving live contestants on station premises. The programme went to air from one of 2CH's smaller studios, with

Grundy on air randomly telephoning would-be contestants listed in the Sydney telephone directory. A telephone sat alongside the studio microphone. The station's copywriter provided the written quiz questions, while a small 'chocolate wheel' of the type universally found at fetes and carnivals balanced on the announcer's desk, ready to be spun to select a prize for successful contestants.

Wheel of Fortune reflected a great deal of faith and ambition on the part of Grundy and 2CH. For Grundy, the programme represented a final break with the area of radio sport, an arena to which he had devoted almost ten years of his broadcasting life. The quiz show was, in effect, the end of one career and the beginning of another. Two hours of on-air programming five days a week was a very demanding schedule, but excellent training for the work with television quiz shows that was to come. It required extensive behind-the-scenes effort. Armed only with a part-time secretary and his first de facto employee in the form of copywriter John O'Grady, who became the researcher and writer of the quiz questions, Grundy had to concentrate his attention elsewhere, including securing commercial goods and services as prizes from companies in return for on-air acknowledgement. Some of these prizes had to be significantly more valuable and attractive than city theatre tickets and LP records. However, Grundy, who had persuaded Qantas airlines to give him a return air ticket to Johannesburg in 1952, was up to the task. In October 1957, for example, advertising executive John Roy was reported as presenting 2CH *Wheel of Fortune*-winner Mrs McConnell with international return plane tickets to London, which Grundy had secured from Air India (*B&T*, 17 October 1957: 31).

Wheel of Fortune was a 'headline' programme for the station, and 2CH engaged in an extensive promotion and publicity campaign on its behalf. This included daily and trade press advertisements, window displays, broadcaster brochures and other station gimmicks. All of this had the desired effect, with 2CH's *Wheel of Fortune* debuting on air in highly dramatic circumstances. As industry news magazine *B&T* reported about the July 1957 launch:

> 2CH's biggest daytime quiz *Wheel of Fortune* 2–4 pm daily drew such phenomenal response on the first day that the volume of incoming calls completely disrupted Sydney telephone services, blowing every fuse in the York Exchange. The following day, the entire BX number series had the exchange put out of action making the situation so grave PMG officials were forced to complain to AWA's assistant general manager A. E. R. Fox requesting that the program's format be altered. Now instead of inviting listeners enthusiastic to participate in telephone quizzes, compère Reg Grundy is each day continuing questions to different suburbs. Apart from telephone calls listeners have come to the station with answers while over 200 are mailing their answers daily.
>
> (*B&T*, 28 June 1957: 5)

As a variant of the audience-participation show, the radio quiz programme relied heavily on the telephone to contact its audience contestants. This left a good deal to chance and to the good faith of all concerned. Under the existing *Broadcasting Act*, the telephone calls of contestants for a radio programme such as 2CH's *Wheel of Fortune* could not be put to air. Instead, Reg Grundy as compère had to repeat sufficient detail of such calls to help engage the attention of listeners. As the previous chapter has indicated, he already had learned that a degree of craftiness was useful and necessary in radio broadcasting to ensure that programmes ran well and entertained their listeners. Hence, with *Wheel of Fortune*, 2CH's copywriter John O'Grady, sat on the other side of the radio microphone to act not only as assistant but also to play the role of 'the judges'. Armed with a set of *Encyclopaedia Britannica*, he had the impossible task of somehow adjudicating in a matter of seconds on problematic answers to quiz questions (O'Grady 1980). However, phone-in contestants could sometimes be equally crafty in the privacy of their own homes. As Grundy later recounted:

> I remember asking one woman whether rayon burned or melted. She told me to hang on. She had a minute to answer. She came on the phone again in a few seconds and said: 'They melt.' I learned later that she had pulled off her stockings and shoved them into the fire to see what happened.
>
> (*TV Week* 1962: 20)

Leaving 2CH

By early 1959, Grundy must have felt himself under pressure at the station because of a decline in the fortunes of his quiz show. The initial popularity of *Wheel of Fortune* had proven to be short-lived. Regular television broadcasting had begun in Sydney in September 1956, and by early 1957, three stations were on the air (Hall 1976: 22–28). Weekday television broadcast hours initially were quite restricted at the time Grundy and 2CH were planning *Wheel of Fortune*. Even by the end of 1957, the Sydney television stations had made only limited time and programming incursions into afternoon scheduling. On weekdays, TCN Channel 9 began programme transmission at 1.00 p.m. and ABC Channel 2 started at 3.00 p.m. ATN Channel 7 did not open for broadcasting until 5.00 p.m.

Two years later, it was a rather different matter, however. Both of the commercial television stations began their broadcasts at 2.00 p.m. and the ABC started at 4.00 p.m. Television-set ownership was increasing rapidly among Sydney households, despite the high cost of a television receiver. Broadcast family radio was in crisis, and it was time for Grundy to take action. He seized the initiative and resigned from the station so that *Wheel of Fortune* finished on 2CH in February 1959.

The radio quizmaster seems to have been unemployed for the next three months. 'Reg left because he felt they were not responding to his ideas and memos about *Wheel of Fortune*, and he got out just before they fired him' (Morotoff 1995). Subsequently, Grundy also claimed that he had resigned from the station just ahead of being fired. Whether or not 2CH wanted to see him leave is a moot point. Grundy has added that he made numerous suggestions about improving *Wheel of Fortune*, but that the station failed to respond to these hints. Whether his departure was voluntary or forced, the fact was that a new arena of broadcasting, in the shape of television, was opening up and there was a significant opportunity now available that had not been there in 1953 when he had been forced to leave 2SM. It was time to investigate this new opening.

Family business: death, marriage, birth

Back in 1953 when he had joined 2CH, Grundy had had little time to settle down into his new job as sports and station announcer before family matters intruded. The small unit that was the Grundy family shortly recorded a departure, a union and an arrival. Within two months of joining 2CH, Reg Grundy suffered the death of his father, Roy Harold. As mentioned in Chapter 3, Roy had worked at Grace Bros department store on Sydney's Broadway since the family moved back to Sydney in 1939. Early 1954 saw extensive decorations underway at the Broadway store in preparation for the Royal visit of Queen Elizabeth II (Brasher 1985: 91–94). Roy Grundy could not take part in the preparations or the pageantry of the visit, however, because he was in poor health. In February, he retired from full-time duties as section manager, moving into part-time work in the Grace Bros Auditorium for several months before being admitted to Prince Henry Hospital in August and dying two weeks later. The cause of death was recorded as lung abscesses and periarteritis. A death notice in the *Sydney Morning Herald* (1 September 1954: 38) recorded Roy Harold Grundy as husband to Lillian and father to Reg. The notice went on to describe him as 'beloved son of John Grundy (Senior) and fond brother of Jack, Clive, Jean, Hazel and Irene (Dot)'. He was 56 years old (Grundy 2010: 82).

Plans for the marriage of Reg and Lola were already well in train, so the union went ahead. The two were wed in October 1954 in an Anglican Church in fashionable Vaucluse, close to where both Reg and Lola lived with their families. It was a small, quiet affair. They honeymooned by sailing to Adelaide and motoring back to Melbourne and on to Sydney. This allowed for several stops along the way, including visiting Albury where Roy Grundy's parents seemed to have originated (Grundy 2010: 14). Then it was back to work. The couple moved into a flat on New South Head Road at Double Bay, across the tramlines and near where Reg's widowed mother continued to live and close to where Lola's family also resided.

By the middle of 1955, Lola was pregnant. She recalled much later that the baby was planned (Gillespie-Jones 1995). The gender-neutral name of Kim was settled upon before the birth. When daughter Kim was born on 14 April 1956, the new parents also settled on a second name of Robin in memory of the child's recently deceased grandfather, Robin being an affectionate nickname that Lillian had bestowed on Roy (Grundy 2010: 82–86). Many years later, Lola believed that Kim might have had more siblings. Roy, Lillian and Lola herself had grown up in large families, even if Reg had been without brothers and sisters. However, the pressure of work, the subsequent break-up of the marriage and the later remarriages of both Reg and Lola to others meant that Kim would grow up alone. The couple had a second wedding ceremony in a Catholic Church in 1958 or 1959, and while it would not save the marriage in the longer term, it did ensure that Kim would attend the same Catholic schools in Sydney's Eastern suburbs as her mother.

Afterword

Reg Grundy probably made a significant mistake in moving from radio station 2SM to 2CH in 1953. In the longer term, however, the move triggered an important career change that otherwise might never have happened. He underwent a metamorphosis, transforming himself from a radio sports commentator into a quiz-show producer and host. As this chapter has suggested, the sportscaster turned quizmaster learned a great deal about the commercial and cultural tricks associated with audience-participation and quiz shows, mostly through a process of trial and error. In early 1959, Reg Grundy resigned for a second time from a Sydney commercial radio station. The move was part of a continuing change in the course of his business career. But he was at a crossroad of sorts because it was unlikely that he would find employment at a third radio station. In any case, television beckoned. After two and a half years on air, television stations in Sydney and Melbourne mostly had overcome their initial teething difficulties; more and more Sydney households had bought television sets; the sector was beginning to prove profitable for its operators. The 36-year-old radio broadcaster had long mastered the business of putting a programme together, recognizing the various elements needed and linking up the human resources – including himself as compère or host required to make such a combination work. Most importantly, Grundy had a successful programme package in the shape of *Wheel of Fortune*. In the television language of today, this was an effective programme format that had been produced successfully on radio. That amounted to a useful trialling and insurance that a Grundy-produced television adaptation of *Wheel of Fortune* would probably also be successful. It was time for Reg Grundy to complete his long apprenticeship both by mastering the new medium of image and sound, and learning how quiz-show devising could be fast-tracked with successful results.

Chapter 5

Apprenticeship III: Mastering Television Formats, 1959-64

Introduction

The years 1959 to 1964 marked the final stage of Reg Grundy's schooling in broadcasting. It had been a long training period, stretching back to 1947 when he first secured a short-term job for a country radio station. The apprenticeship had seen him master the possibilities of broadcasting and the craft of the radio quiz show. The last stage of his practical education was now beginning, with two further areas of activity to be mastered. The first was the business of commercial television itself, which was similar to but also unlike the operation of commercial radio. The quiz show had rapidly and successfully adapted to the new medium of television broadcasting. Mittell, for example, notes that:

> Unlike dramatic programs, quizzes did not have to create elaborate sets or visuals to appear on television. Cameras could easily capture the inexpensive live proceedings that studio audiences had been witnessing for years.
>
> (Mittell 2004: 11–52)

The second practice that Grundy would have to master was even more intriguing, and involved the television-programme format. With each of the audience-participation and quiz shows that he had produced and hosted in radio, Grundy had started from scratch in devising them. Stepping into the television industry, he discovered that Australian stations frequently had a faster way to develop new programmes: by adapting shows first devised by pioneer television industries in the United States and United Kingdom. Although it would be many years before the practice of adaptation and remaking was recognized under the 'format' label, Grundy immediately set about mastering the routine of television quiz-show format copying. This chapter deals with Reg Grundy's first five years in television. His long apprenticeship began paying off, with the independent producer showing a brilliance in developing quiz and game shows and a genius for television programme formatting. However, jealous forces would be set loose, and he would have to survive the most significant crisis of his business career.

Framework

Before looking in detail at Grundy's move into television production, it is useful to notice some broader features of the setting and situation in which he would find himself. The 1950s and early 1960s in Australia were characterized by economic stability and political consensus (Moran 1991: 55–65). Regular television broadcasting had begun in Sydney and Melbourne in late 1956. The year was an indicative one, for Australia belonged to a second tier of broadcasting systems that were dependent on the prior inauguration of television in countries that were wealthier, more densely populated and more technologically advanced than Australia. Television as an institution could not develop in the island continent from scratch, but had to be imported (Schatz 2004: 6968). Although this realization had been in place in the minds of some engineers, politicians and broadcasters since as early as 1942, even by the early 1950s, the federal government still wondered whether the national economy could afford the medium. Australia is the largest island continent in the world, with a population of less than ten million that, for the most part, is strung out along much of its very long coastline. As mentioned in Chapter 2, it had been unable to sustain a motion picture industry since the coming of sound, so some had strong reservations about the viability of a television industry. All the same, various sectors were enthusiastic about the new form of broadcasting. These included the newspaper and radio industries, the advertising sector and even sections of the defence industry (Attallah 1991: 58–98). Nonetheless, it was probably the moves by Canada, which had inaugurated services in 1951, and the United Kingdom to establish a commercial television sector in 1955 that finally precipitated the Australian move (Lucas 2004: 34–36).

By 1959, when Reg Grundy decided to attempt to take his quiz show *Wheel of Fortune* to television, the service was in full swing in the major state capital cities of Sydney and Melbourne and just beginning in the minor state capital cities of Brisbane and Adelaide (Moran 1993: 29). The new service was ambitious in both providing choice between one public-service station and two privately owned commercial stations, and in the rapid expansion of broadcast hours across all these cities. Imported programming from the United States and United Kingdom was very important in this setup, in the form of both finished, canned shows and programme samples or prototypes. The former helped offset station operating costs while the latter facilitated local, home-grown production by exemplifying what such shows might look like on air, and sometimes providing backup materials, including scripts and running sheets. This latter practice of importing programme know-how or formats for remaking had been the case with radio broadcasting since the 1930s. The legacy of quiz-show-format importing has already been described, but the practice was not confined to that genre. It was very widespread and even included borrowing in more expensive genres such as radio drama. Witness, for example, the inauguration of Australian versions of a 'headline' night-time drama series, *Lux Radio Theatre*, in 1939 and a series of daytime radio soap operas such as *Big Sister* and *Portia Faces Life* in 1942, all copied from US radio network predecessors (cf. Potts 1989: 53–54; Lane 1994: 67–68).

Television repeated this practice, particularly in Western Europe, South America and English-speaking countries, including Australia. The tendency was hardly surprising. After all, the United Kingdom and United States had been among the first territories in the world to begin regular television broadcasting, with the BBC establishing a regular service in 1937 (Blumler 2004: 330–37) and the US networks following suit in 1940 (Lucas 2004: 34–36). Later services repeatedly turned to these sources, not only for canned or finished programmes but also for programme formats. Take Western Europe, for instance (Bourdin 2011). Television started in the Netherlands in 1957. Shortly afterwards, viewers were watching *Alles of Nietss*, a domestic clone of the US quiz show *The $64,000 Question* while *Zo is Het Toevallig Ook Nog Eens Keer* was a Dutch reworking of the BBC's *That Was the Week That Was*. In nearby Belgium, where television had begun in 1953, the Flemish service was soon broadcasting *De Muziek Kampioen*, derived from the US quiz-show format *Name That Tune*. German public-service television was also to have a long history of imitating shows from elsewhere from 1955 onwards. So, for example, domestic viewers got to know the American *What's My Line?* in the form of its local remake, *Was Bin Ich*. Nor was adaptation only restricted to 'live' programmes in the areas of light entertainment and quiz shows. Fiction scripts could also be re-versioned elsewhere, as was the case when the BBC sitcom *Hancock* was remade in Finland as *Kaverukset* in 1960 (Schmitt, Bisson and Fey 2005).

Mostly, these format adaptations were being undertaken without the permission or even the knowledge of the original devisors or producers of such shows. The last chapter mentioned how an Australian radio producer was forced to change an adaptation of the sitcom series *Blondie* when the US copyright owner became aware of its unauthorized remake. To ward against the threat of legal action, fees were paid to US programme devisors as voluntary gestures of goodwill. This seems especially to have been the case on the part of public-service broadcasters. Witness the case of the BBC making such payment for the use of *What's My Line?* to Goodson-Todman and the German CBD to the CBS Network for *Tell the Truth* (Brunt 1985; Bourdin 2011).

The practice of programme adaptation and remaking already existed in Australia when Reg Grundy was planning to take his *Wheel of Fortune* radio format to television. The ABC looked to the BBC in the United Kingdom as both its model and parent, so that it not only imported a large amount of finished programming from British television but also adapted many programme formats to give its programming more Australian relevance and appeal. In 1961, for example, it inaugurated its own version of the BBC's weekly current affairs programme *Panorama* as *Four Corners*, while in 1967 it began a daily half-hour current affair programme titled *This Day Tonight* that was modelled on the United Kingdom's *Today Tonight* (Inglis 1982: 196, 311). The same tendency was also in evidence in Australian commercial television. Sydney station TCN9, where Grundy would take *Wheel of Fortune*, was no stranger to the practice, evidenced by such remakes as *Bandstand*, *Meet the Press* and *Name That Tune*, which had their origins in US television network programmes.

The Sydney television landscape

International traffic in television programme formats was important to Grundy's subsequent career, but not to his immediate situation in 1959 when he had just left radio station 2CH. For although there were three television stations operating in Sydney at the time, there was really only one possible market for a television adaptation of the *Wheel of Fortune* radio format. The public-service station, ABN2, was a closed shop so far as a fledgling independent television producer was concerned. Since its establishment in 1932, the ABC had produced all its local radio programming in-house, and was continuing with this policy in television. Meanwhile, Sydney's two commercial television stations differed markedly in their attitude towards involvement with a local would-be producer such as Reg Grundy.

ATN Channel 7 was quite nervous of such relationships, a fear that went back to a spectacular 'talent raid' (Hilmes 1990; Gomery 2007) on the Macquarie Radio Network in 1946, a foray that was dubbed the 'Colgate-Palmolive Affair' (Mackay 1959: 12; Patterson 1956: 110–12). In that year, through its advertising agency George Patterson, one of the Big Two of Australian radio advertising, Colgate-Palmolive sought to control which station members of the Macquarie Radio Network would be allowed to broadcast programmes supplied to it by the advertising agency on behalf of Colgate-Palmolive. This manoeuvre represented a direct challenge to the authority of the network, and Macquarie refused to allow such a move. The sponsor and its agency retaliated by taking all their programmes to a rival radio network. The 'Affair' almost destroyed the viability of the Macquarie Network, and it took several years for its fortunes to recover.

Even so, the 'Affair' left an indelible mark on the mind of management, including those who would run ATN7. Through the 1950s and 1960s, the station insisted on producing all its programmes in-house, not least as a means of preventing the recurrence of this kind of raid by its rivals. (The only notable exception was Bob Dyer who, as we have seen, had hosted and produced his own programme, *Pick-a-Box* for the 2GV Macquarie Network, and was allowed to continue this arrangement at ATN7.) Potential outside programme producers were not welcome at ATN7, and very few bothered calling (Moran 1993: 564–73).

Frank Packer, owner of the other commercial station TCN Channel 9, had not had a similar troubling experience in his commercial past, and in any case was in no doubt about who controlled and owned the television operation at his station (Moran 1993: 550–63). Grundy's choice of television client was, in effect, predetermined: TCN9 was both the logical and only viable market for a television remake of Grundy's radio quiz programme.

One other change to Australian commercial television happened in 1959. Grundy has suggested that he hesitated to move into television, believing that at 36 years of age he was too old to begin working in a new medium (2010: 66–68). The year and his age posed no problems, however. In fact, 1959 was a propitious year for a would-be producer to make such a move into the new form of broadcasting. Grundy probably would not have survived in television had he attempted the move in 1956, when only four commercial television stations existed in Australia. In 1959, the number doubled to eight, with commercial stations in Brisbane and Adelaide coming on the air (Hall 1976: 14–18). TCN9, like ATN7, now had three affiliate stations in the east coast state capital cities, whereas in 1956 it had just one affiliate (in Melbourne). The effect of this increase was to potentially further spread the costs of programme licensing from overseas or from a local would-be producer, such as Reg Grundy. But what of TCN9, the station to which several of Grundy's radio colleagues had gone to work both before and behind the cameras, and the station to which Grundy would pitch the idea of a television version of *Wheel of Fortune*?

TCN Channel 9

TCN9 was the television face of Consolidated Press, which was owned and operated by Sydney media mogul Frank Packer (Griffen-Foley 2000). Established in the very early 1930s, Consolidated Press had two mastheads in the shape of its two publications, the *Sydney Daily Telegraph* and the *Australian Women's Weekly*. The company had long been thwarted in its desire for a third outlet in the shape of a Sydney commercial radio station. Packer and the board of the company were determined that no such opportunity would be missed with the new medium of television, signalling its intention to apply for a television broadcast licence in evidence to the Royal Commission on Television in 1953 (Moran 1985: 22–26). A staunch supporter of the conservative federal Coalition government of the day, Packer was duly rewarded by the provision of a television broadcasting licence in 1955, so that TCN9 became the first television station to begin regular broadcasting the following year (Davidson 1968: 13).

Packer's station was as different from ATN7 as chalk and cheese. The Fairfax-Macquarie group was always more ready to spend money on the new operation than was the owner of Consolidated Press. ATN built a lavish headquarters at Epping on the northwest edge of the city while Packer was happy to settle TCN in a refurbished set of buildings in the suburb of Willoughby, just north of the Sydney Harbour Bridge and close to the Sydney television transmission tower at Gore Hill (Moran 2010: 343–56). ATN prided itself on presenting a service founded on notions of quality and a kind of cultural nationalism, whereas Packer wanted an unpretentious, no-frills television operation designed to be profitable sooner rather than later. Nor did the hard man of Australian media's ambitions stop with the developing success of TCN9. Instead, in 1960, when the Melbourne consortium that had secured the licence for GTV9 – hitherto an affiliate of ATN7 in Sydney – decided to sell the station, he immediately stepped in and bought it. The common ownership of Nine in Sydney and Nine in Melbourne would have a knock-on effect among interstate affiliates of TCN9 and ATN7 that would take several years to untangle, but nonetheless TCN9 and GTV9 immediately would begin to refer to themselves as part of the Nine Network. The buyout certainly brought Australian commercial television networking a step closer, despite whatever private misgivings the federal conservative government of the day may have had about the matter.

The common ownership did not cause any immediate change in management structures at either TCN9 or GTV9. In any case, in the period up to 1964, Reg Grundy only dealt with management at the Sydney station. These senior figures had occupied their television positions since 1955. Shortly after the commercial television licences had been granted to the parties already mentioned, Packer appointed Ken Hall, an old acquaintance and long-time head of Cinesound Newsreels, as the station's first manager (Moran & Keating 2003: 197–98). KG, as Hall was universally known, had been a good choice for the job of general manager of the television station. He was in his mid-fifties, with considerable experience in running the distribution arm of an Australian motion picture company for which he had also produced and directed almost a dozen feature films in the 1930s and 1940s. During his long screen career, he had never wavered from his firm commitment to Hollywood notions of entertainment and show business. Starting the last decade of his working life before retirement at the helm of TCN9, Hall represented for Packer a safe pair of hands to run the new venture in its formative years. Packer also put an heir apparent in place in the shape of a youthful Bruce Gyngell, who had been a cadet with ABC Radio, then worked briefly in television in New York and Hawaii under Packer's patronage before returning to help get TCN9 up and running (Jacka 2004: 1045–48). He was appointed as programme manager and inadvertently became the first face to appear on Australian television when he hosted TCN9's opening night of broadcast, including acting as last-minute compère of *Name That Tune*, a remake of a US quiz-show original that had premiered on the NBC network in 1953 and was devised by Harry Salter Productions (Schwartz, Ryan & Wosbrook 1987: 313–15).

The former 2CH radio producer of *Wheel of Fortune* was to be beholden to both these men. Hall was an old associate for, as we saw in Chapter 3, Grundy had moonlighted with Cinesound, providing voice-over boxing and other kinds of commentary for its weekly newsreels. Gyngell was in fact six years younger than Grundy, but the latter was happy to have the TCN9 programme manager become a mentor and friend who would, over the years, help provide useful industry knowledge and contacts in Australia, the United States and the United Kingdom.

The most immediate task, however, lay in the idea that Grundy might produce a television version of *Wheel of Fortune* for TCN9. The availability of Grundy suited the needs of the station. For while TCN9 had already produced in-house quiz shows such as the daytime *Balance Your Budget* and the night-time *Tell the Truth*, nevertheless no one at the station had any extended experience in the genre of quiz shows. Grundy had a valuable production background, most especially in the practice of securing consumer goods and services that could be given away as prizes to winning contestants. By late 1959, TCN9 (like ATN7) was planning to expand its hours of daytime weekday broadcasting. It needed low-cost, routine programming that would have a fast production turnaround. A daily quiz show undertaken by an outsider producer who would shoulder responsibility for budget, contestants, prizes and almost everything else was attractive to management, so TCN9 agreed to have Grundy produce a pilot for a television adaptation of *Wheel of Fortune* (Grundy 2010: 66–73). More hands were needed than had been the case with the radio version: TCN provided a television production crew and director while Grundy played host and producer and his wife, Lola, screened contestants and acted as hostess. Late in 1959, *Wheel of Fortune* began as a one-hour weekday show on TCN9 (Moran & Keating 2003: 384; Beilby 1981: 14–15; Murphy 1981: 60–89).

The quizmaster had been an employee at both 2SM and 2CH, receiving a wage as well as sales commissions. Now, however, Grundy was surprised to learn that he was not being appointed to the staff of TCN9. Instead, he was persuaded to head up his own private production company, Reg Grundy Enterprises (it later became Reg Grundy Services), which contracted with TCN9 to produce *Wheel of Fortune* for the station. Why this incorporation?

Reg Grundy Enterprises

The 'talent raids' that ATN7 feared after the 'Colgate-Palmolive Affair' had their origins in US commercial network radio (Becker 2004a: 1364–66; Gomery 2007: 153–67). In 1936, the Columbia Broadcasting System (CBS) had attempted to lure top radio stars and their shows away from NBC. The move was unsuccessful, but paved the way for a more determined and conquering set of raids in 1948. One of the key ingredients of the second onslaught was the package deal crafted by agent Lew Wasserman from the Music Corporation of America (MCA). Wasserman had realized that US taxation laws could be used as a means to lessen the tax that radio stars paid to the Inland Revenue Service (IRS). The move was currently working for Wasserman and his Hollywood clients, including stars, directors and others that he represented. There was no reason why the same strategy would not work in connection with the allied field of broadcasting. By forming their own company, which then sold their production services to the networks, stars rendered themselves liable for much lower rates of company tax than they were paying under personal taxation rates as direct employees of the radio networks.

The benefits of this system of television production services packaging were not lost on executives at the new Australian commercial television stations. The system of outsourcing production to an outside producer or programme packager had immediate benefits so far as reducing fixed labour and other costs at a television station (as it had already had at the Hollywood motion picture studios). Technical staff and others were no longer employed on a permanent, long-term basis but were instead contracted only for the run of a production. And while the salary rate for the latter might be higher than for long-term employees, nevertheless overall financial savings were achieved by dint of the fact that no remuneration was paid for down time.

By 1964–65, for instance, this system of independent production packaging or 'outsourcing' would be so visible that the Australian Broadcasting Control Board (ABCB) would note its ubiquity in its *Annual Report* (Moran 1985: 26). Even in the late 1950s, the outside independent production packaging system's financial and contractual advantages were sufficiently clear-cut for stations (perhaps with the exception of ATN7) to begin employing it in their dealing with service providers. Thus TCN9 executive Bruce Gyngell, who was already having difficulties explaining to Packer about the fixed costs and overheads involved in running the Channel 9 operation, would later claim credit for persuading Grundy to set up as the first independent television production packager in Australia (Jacka 2004: 1046). Reg Grundy would not become an employee of TCN9, although the station would make it increasingly clear that it regarded him as its very own outside producer, exclusively supplying only to Channel 9 (Grundy 2010: 87–92). Instead, a new private company, Reg Grundy Enterprises, was to be set up to contract with TCN to provide a specified number of programme episodes of a television version of *Wheel of Fortune* (Grundy 2010: 71–81).

Reg Grundy Enterprises had humble enough beginnings. The company initially employed three people: Grundy himself, his wife, Lola, and a former 2CH writer who researched and prepared quiz questions and later became involved in production managing. Lola Grundy acted as hostess on *Wheel of Fortune* and was also heavily involved in screening and preparing contestants before they appeared on camera. Grundy, who was the programme compère, had to find the prizes, liaise with the production crew at TCN9 and worry about everything else associated with *Wheel of Fortune* and the other quiz shows that TCN would begin to have him produce. Soon, the company's principal would be able to delegate the first of many tasks to others when a new employee became responsible for prize acquisition and on-air presentation.

For several years, Reg Grundy Enterprises operated from the Grundy family apartment in New South Head Road in Double Bay. Shortly after *Wheel of Fortune* began to air, the company spread into an adjacent vacant apartment. By 1962, things were becoming busier. More space and less travel time were necessary, whereupon Reg Grundy Enterprises left the Eastern Suburbs and moved into larger rented offices across the Sydney Harbour Bridge at Miller Street in North Sydney (Moran 2010: 343–56).

TCN9's quiz show format king

Grundy's first production task was to adapt and remake a pre-existing programme for television. He soon would begin doing this on a systematic basis, drawing from US network television, but this first remaking involved turning his own radio show into a television programme. A good deal of this kind of adaptation was happening in early television, which, in part at least, piggybacked on successful radio programmes (Fabe 1979; Graham 1988; Hoerschelmann 2004b: 1871–74; Felsenthal 2004: 2094–95). Nonetheless, making *Wheel of Fortune* as a television programme was by no means a straightforward or simple matter. As mentioned, ATN7 had already discovered this in 1957, when it telecast seven popular Macquarie Radio audience-participation programmes and had to cancel six of them by the end of the year. The crucial change with regard to the television version of *Wheel of Fortune* was that contestants would appear live on camera rather than being phoned at home (Mittel 2004: 336–37). The television quiz show was more immediately participatory so far as the audience was concerned than had been the case with its radio predecessor. In fact, there seemed to have been an early idea that *Wheel of Fortune* would offer prizes to the housewife home audience phoning in as well as for the onscreen contestants, but this idea was abandoned (*TV Week* 1959: 17).

Reg Grundy's voice was already familiar to the Sydney audience, so the daily half-hour television show now gave him a bodily presence. At 36, Grundy was approaching very early middle age, was clean-cut, of trim build and slight stature with dark hair and a short moustache, friendly but with the authority to move contestants through small talk and questions. *Wheel of Fortune* was extremely simple in its visual design, with Grundy standing beside a mounted wheel with a curtain in the background. Lola Grundy brought contestants on in pairs, and these had the choice of easier or more difficult questions, with correct answers resulting in a spin of the wheel, which carried up to 40 prizes. More lavish prizes had been assembled for contestants answering the most difficult questions, including a block of land and plane tickets to Singapore and London.

Grundy's timing in offering TCN9 a television version of *Wheel of Fortune* was fortuitous. The move of Sydney and Melbourne stations into daytime broadcasting was noted earlier. This move also coincided with the beginnings of a shift in audience preference away from imported shows in favour of locally produced programming (Moran 1985: 20–22). Overall, *Wheel of Fortune* would prove to be inexpensive and quick to produce, would follow a simple pattern of production and work with minimal set and props, would fill programming time and would be popular with the growing daytime television audience. Once broadcasts recording technology became available a short time later, there was also the possibility of airing the programme in other state capital cities with an increase in revenue for both the station and the producer (Odell 2004: 1263–64).

Joining TCN9 as an independent packager with his quiz show and the team of assistants that he now began to assemble, Reg Grundy must have seemed like an answer to a barely confessed programming prayer from the station so far as the production of quiz shows was concerned. The presence of Grundy and his company completed the third side of a triangle. After almost three years on air, TCN had technical experience and expertise in the form of directors, cameramen, sound recordists, booth announcers, lighting, wardrobe, carpentry and so on. Grundy formed the second side of the production triangle by providing the quiz-show content in the form of compères, hostesses, announcers, contestants, questions, prizes, slide presentations, attendant logistics and so on. US network television constituted the third side by regularly airing fresh crops of quiz and game shows that could provide the basis for lookalike programmes in Australia (Hoerschelmann 2004b: 1871–74). Like other television stations in Australia and elsewhere, TCN9 had no qualms about copying such programmes. The United States was not a signatory to the Berne Convention on copyright (Porter & Mun 2004: 593). Furthermore, Australia was a good distance from the United States, and in any case legal action would have had to be pursued in Australia, where the copyright breach would have to be alleged to have taken place (van Manen 1994: 2–7).

Packaging other quiz shows for TCN9

Up to this point in late 1959 when Grundy began packaging *Wheel of Fortune* for the station, TCN had produced only a handful of quiz shows. *Name That Tune* and *What's My Line?* were early adaptations of US network quiz shows that soon disappeared off the airwaves. Three years later, TCN9 – like ATN7 and even ABC2 – was intent on expanding its broadcast into weekday afternoons, and the genre of the quiz show would help this programming expansion. In February 1959, it began making *Concentration* as a weekly daytime half-hour quiz show produced in-house by the station (Moran & Keating 2003: 62). The programme was based on an NBC-produced and Goodson-Todman-originated format of the same name that had first appeared on US television in 1958 and would turn out to be one of the longest-running quiz shows on US network television (Schwartz, Ryan & Wosbrook 1987: 105–11). The concept of the show was based on a children's game and involved two contestants trying to match up prizes hidden between numbers on a giant board. *Concentration* briefly disappeared off TCN9 in 1960. When it returned mid-year, Reg Grundy Enterprises had taken over packaging the programme for the station.

Grundy would have welcomed the opportunity to have two daytime quiz shows on the air. Producing five hours of programming a week was a schedule with which he had become familiar while at 2CH. Such an output was also financially rewarding. And, in fact, as recording facilities came onstream, further opportunities began to open up. In 1962, for example, it was decided to syndicate the Sydney version of *Concentration* being produced by Reg Grundy Enterprises to Melbourne, where it replaced an in-house version produced and broadcast by TCN9's sister station, GTV9, on the basis that it was cheaper to purchase the syndicated version rather than continue to produce a Melbourne version (Grundy 2010: 79). Grundy had gone nationwide – or as near nationwide as was possible on the restricted airwaves of the early 1960s. In addition to the financial rewards, there was the matter of the security that multiple productions afforded an independent outside packager such as Reg Grundy Enterprises. Having two or more shows in production at any one time would help to overcome the business difficulties that would be created by the unexpected cancellation of any single programme.

Meanwhile, Grundy's lucky streak seemed to continue, as TCN9 now invited him to produce a third quiz show in the shape of *Tic Tac Dough* (Moran & Keating 2003: 124). In fact, almost immediately after getting *Wheel of Fortune* up and running, Grundy must have become aware of preparations afoot at the station for the launch of this 'big-ticket', once-a-week, one-hour night-time quiz show. *Tic Tac Dough* was also the offspring of a US quiz show original of the same name devised by producer and compère Jack Good (Schwartz, Ryan & Wosbrook 1987: 452–55). The programme had been one of the big-money US quiz shows of the mid- to late 1950s that had in part resulted in the banishment of the genre to daytime broadcasting when it was disclosed that programmes such as *The $64,000 Question* and *Twenty One* had been rigged (Hoerschelmann 2004b: 1874). The US *Tic Tac Dough* predecessor had begun as a daytime programme on NBC, running from 1956 to 1959,

Apprenticeship III

and also spawned a night-time version that ran from 1957 to 1959. Based on the nine-square game of Noughts and Crosses, the format pitted two contestants against one another with each square offering valuable cash prizes. As station publicity put it at the time: 'The contestants use an electronically operated board to play the quiz. The lucky contestant can win as much as £600 in a show. The scoreboard was built by TCN technicians' (*TV Week* 1959: 5). To help support this cost, the Australian version of the programme was sold to TCN9's affiliate stations and began early in 1960 as another quiz show being packaged by Reg Grundy Enterprises and seen interstate.

There were three other Grundy quiz shows in this period. The first was another night-time quiz show, although it made far less impact than *Tic Tac Dough*. This was *Surprise Package*, based on the parlour game of Twenty Questions, wherein two contestants had to reach an educated guess regarding a package's contents based on gaining twenty affirmative answers to their questions (Moran & Keating 2003: 120). It may have been developed in-house rather than being derived from a recent US predecessor. In any case, the only surprise associated with *Surprise Package* was the speed with which it came and went. This happened towards the end of 1961. The following year saw another casualty with the cancellation of *Wheel of Fortune*.

The loss of the latter would probably have come as a mixed blessing for Reg Grundy Enterprises. Grundy had become very busy as a quiz show producer at TCN9, so his continuing stint as host of *Wheel of Fortune* grew increasingly onerous. In fact, during the program's last eighteen months on air in 1962–63, he had employed two substitutes as host, a former Vaudevillian from 2CH followed by a TCN9 children's compère. Grundy's disappearance as the compère of *Wheel of Fortune* was unobtrusive and happened without fanfare. Yet it marked the beginnings of Reg Grundy's deliberate slide from public attention that would continue over the next dozen years, with interviews and photographs becoming increasingly rare. In his profiling of the media mogul, Tunstall (Tunstall & Palmer 1991) notes the characteristic preference for privacy and secrecy, and this was a path on which Grundy now embarked. The founder's name continued to appear under the company's banner of Reg Grundy Enterprises (the name Reg Grundy Services would also be used extensively) even while a long, slow process of 'de-Grundification' now got underway.

All this was in the future, however. In 1963, there was mostly the disappointment of having *Wheel of Fortune* cancelled. Reg Grundy Enterprises already had another daytime show on air five days a week: *Say When*, which commenced in early 1962 (Moran & Keating 2003: 114–15). Like *Concentration*, the adaptation was based on a Goodson-Todman game show format with the original debuting on NBC daytime a short time earlier, in 1961 (Schwartz, Ryan & Wosbrook 1987: 398–99). The game pitted two contestants against each other in attempting to build a predetermined score by answering successive questions and avoiding going over a nominated limit. By saying 'when', a contestant could freeze a score. The TCN9/Grundy version of *Say When* was a moderate success and remained on air until mid-1964.

One other Grundy's quiz show for TCN9 at this time should be mentioned to round out this account of the early television output. Unlike the others, the programme was fixed term, intended for a young audience, not developed by Grundy from a US quiz-show format predecessor and put very little black ink on the books. This was the *Ampol Stamp Quiz*, which went to air in an afternoon timeslot in late 1964 (Moran & Keating 2003: 49). The programme was devised by the Australian petroleum company Ampol and its advertising agency, which planned to use the company's service stations to offer weekly stamp updates over the thirteen weeks of the competition. Grundy was asked to produce the episodes while TCN9 agreed to broadcast the programme. The packager agreed to produce the series, even though, as will be outlined later in this chapter, there had been a parting of the way between the broadcaster and Reg Grundy Services.

Format-spotting and reverse engineering

Reg Grundy's career-long involvement with television programme formats started in 1959 when he began packaging quiz shows for TCN9. Much later, by the 1990s, this kind of insider industry knowledge became more formally and systematically available to industry professionals as international format marketing became a regular part of television trade fairs in the United States, United Kingdom, Western Europe and elsewhere (Cunningham 2004b: 1183–84; Moran 2009). Over the preceding 30 years, however, this kind of programme knowledge was more difficult to come by and more sporadic in its application. Yet the practice of television programme format remaking was to form the basis of Grundy's television production empire. It is therefore useful to trace the changing circumstances whereby the independent programme packager and would-be format mogul gained advanced access to new television programme ideas from the United States and elsewhere. In turn, this gave him an inestimable advantage over other Australian packaging rivals when it came to pitching new game show ideas to broadcasters.

It is possible to identify four phases in Grundy's access to overseas quiz and game show formats, bearing in mind that these probably overlapped at different times. The first stage was the 'bond store' period, which occurred while Grundy was packaging for TCN9 from 1959 onwards (Grundy 2010: 87–92). The 'bond store' was a mechanism in the programme distribution and licensing chain. The onset of commercial television in Australia from 1956 had resulted in a system of regular contact between Sydney (and Melbourne) television executives concerned with programming, and their counterparts in production and distribution in the United States. There were regular programme licensing visits to the United States to acquire new programmes for broadcast on Australian television, with higher-cost night-time programming, such as drama series, sitcoms, specials and so on, commanding most of the visitors' attention. In shipping canned programmes to Australia following these visits, US distribution agents for the networks and the programme producers included other, less costly 'filler' daytime programming samples in the hope of picking up further licensings. These included quiz shows, children's series and panel and talk shows. The bond store was a kind of 'no man's land' operated by Australian customs, where goods including overseas television programmes were held pending formal importation, whereupon customs duty had to be paid and censorship review had to occur. Alerted by Bruce Gyngell, Grundy soon discovered that, once viewing arrangements could be made, the bond store was an Aladdin's cave for spotting new attractive television quiz-show programme formats for local remaking.

A second stage of accessing quiz-show knowledge occurred a little time later and involved Grundy documenting quiz shows as these went to air on US television. The method was simple and primitive, using whatever means were to hand to document as much as possible of the broadcast programme. Grundy mentions Gyngell, TCN9's programme manager, playing him an audiotape recording of the Goodson-Todman quiz show *Say When* (2010: 87) and leaving him and his company to devise a version of the programme for remaking for the station. Obviously, the visual dimension of such programmes was vital. Here, Grundy's skills as an artist and visual designer would have been useful in helping to recreate the look of a programme. Later, for the US field trips that began in 1966 (Grundy 2010: 99–102), the producer took careful instruction from his employees on how to photograph still images off a television screen so that he would have a visual record as well as an audio recording of the images and sound in a new US quiz programme (Drummond 1995).

Another stage of quiz-show format-spotting occurred a little later, after Grundy had been making regular trips to the United States for the purpose of spotting potential new quiz- and game show formats on broadcast and syndicated channels. By this time, programme recording facilities – even for a more inexpensive form such as quiz and game shows – were falling in price and improving in technical quality (Fang 2004: 2438–40). Grundy arranged for a US programme distributor, Charles Michelson, to send him kinescopes of new game shows as these were broadcast on US television. In his memoir, Grundy recounts receiving two reels of kinescoped programmes at his Gordon home, one of which was the US pilot for *Sale of the Century* (2010: 123–25). He believed the format concept to be excellent and had his company adapt and remake the quiz show, first (as will be seen in Chapter 7) as *Temptation* (2010: 125–29) and later, after the Grundy Organisation had bought the rights (see Chapter 9), as *Sale of the Century* (2010: 231–32). Grundy's access would be enhanced further following advances in broadcasting recording in terms of quality, compactness and efficiency (Odell 2004: 1263–64; Fang 2004: 2438–40).

The final stage of Grundy's format-spotting followed the United States becoming a signatory to the latest revisions of the Berne Convention for the Protection of Literary and Artistic Works (Porter & Mun 2004: 591). The process of international adaptation and format remaking became more regularized and formalized, with a standard fee system in place to govern the assignment of licensing rights to particular companies in specific territories or regions. Bourdin (2011: 163–89) labels this era one of 'open replication' of television programme formats. This stage lasted twenty years from 1979 to 1999, when the 'blockbuster' success of reality television confirmed, once and for all, that trade in television programme formats had become a global business (Wilson 2004: 247–48; Murray 2004b: 1900–02; Blasini 2004: 2226–27; Hoerschelmann 2004d: 2536–37). Even so, the period

1980–95 saw the earlier ad hoc arrangements of genial piracy and occasional licensing fees give way to an orderly system whereby the Grundy company would license adaptation rights for Australia and related territories. Later, such contracts might involve all world territories outside the United States. As we will see in Chapter 9, the company by then known as the Grundy Organisation also began to buy formats, most notably that of *Sale of the Century*. In fact, even in the mid- to late 1970s, Grundy had further facilitated the format acquisition process by acquiring an option on the Goodson-Todman format catalogue, thereby not only securing his company's future in the Australian television market but also opening up the possibility of expansion into foreign territories (Grundy 2010: 211–15).

Format-spotting was only part of the process of adaptation and remaking. Early documentation could be very useful in gaining an advantage over rival Australian quiz-show packagers, such as NLT, DYT and Russell Becker Productions (Moran & Keating 2003: 135–55). On some occasions, such data could also form a pilot of sorts to help convince a station programme manager to go ahead with a programme licensing and production arrangement. Grundy mentions the case of showing Bruce Gyngell, by then the general manager of the Seven Network, his advance copy of the US pilot episode of *Sale of the Century* (2010: 123–25). Gyngell accepted the packager's proposal to produce a local version for the Seven Network, providing that a backer in the shape of the Australia-wide retail chain, G. J. Coles, agreed to sponsor the programme.

However, early format knowledge about quiz and game shows was no guarantee of success in itself. There still remained the matter of adapting that know-how for an Australian broadcaster, whether it existed in the shape of 35mm film, photographs, sketches, audiotapes and broadcast recordings, or even scripts, tapes, written descriptions and set details. The next stage of adaptation involved the careful analysis of such material to identify what made the overall package work. One of the company's early unit managers, John O'Grady, outlined what then took place with this body of data and information:

> Reg would go over to Los Angeles and sit in a hotel room taping US quiz shows, so we had the format. What we didn't have was the blueprint so we'd spend days working out how they must have done it, how to control the program so the big prize didn't go off every time you went to air.
>
> (O'Grady 1995)

Grundy and his staff were engaged in a familiar enough process, one with a long pedigree in the manufacture and maintenance of industrial, military, commercial and digital commodities in hardware and software fields. A common name for the activity is 'reverse engineering'. This is the process of uncovering and understanding the elements of a 'device, object or system through analysis of its structure, function and operation' (Eilam 2005: 1–9). The general activity frequently necessitates dismantling an unfamiliar object into its parts with a view to identifying the components and understanding how they combine in the finished piece (Wikipedia: reverse engineering website). Reg Grundy and his employees, looking at the elements of US quiz and game shows, were involved in a parallel process of reverse engineering, where they sought to separate the components of a new quiz show and analyse its workings in detail with a view to using these to make another version of the programme for one of the Australian commercial television stations.

Personal qualities and company characteristics

Four other features of the company and its principal are worth highlighting as part of delineating the historical and sociological details of this TV format mogul. First, there is the fact that Grundy's early interest in drawing and design at school, art college and in retail now came to the fore in overseeing the quiz shows that he was producing. He mentions that soon after he started producing television quiz shows, 'I was asking for changes to the set, new ways to display prizes, even a new shooting pattern for the show' (2010: 72). In the same vein, he also mentions that with *Say When*, he deliberately chose Asian cooking utensils as prizes because of their distinctive, striking appearance on television rather than their domestic practicality (2010: 76). In other words, Grundy had a sharp eye for the way that a show looked as well as how it worked, and he would pass this on to his senior producers. Related to this ability, there was a relentless capacity for hard work and homework. Later, the then programming manager at ATN7 in Sydney, Glen Kinging, would pay tribute to these capacities as follows:

> He is the most successful in the business by 50%. He has produced more hit shows than all the other packagers put together and it is all the result of doing his homework. The nearest local competitor, Hector Crawford Productions, puts about six hours of drama to air each week. Grundy's 15 hours plus is more even than US giants studios such as MCA Universal.
> (in Penberthy 1980: 13–14)

A third feature had to do with Grundy's growing anonymity so far as the viewing public was concerned, an element of the mogul's character that has been touched on already. Having been a voice, then a voice and a face, Reg Grundy would now retreat into a kind of anonymity as simply a name, although it was one that increasingly would recur on Australian and international television screens for almost the next quarter of a century. Retreating behind his company made good business sense for at least three reasons: it helped to throw the general media spotlight on his programmes; it freed Grundy to concentrate on essential activities such as format-spotting in the United States and elsewhere; and it meant that his company affairs remained in the financial shadows.

Finally, there is the matter of lateral thinking. Grundy's preparedness to protect his fledgling company by taking on other quiz shows immediately after the successful adaptation of *Wheel of Fortune* has already been mentioned. Several other signs of a protective expansionism can also be noted in this period with TCN9. One of these involved circumstances not of Grundy's making, but which extended his industry connections. In the period up to 1964, Reg Grundy Enterprises was a Sydney-based operation, and its sole television client was also based in the NSW capital. Later, as recording capabilities became available first through kinescoping, then in the form of videotaping, it became possible to record elsewhere, usually on weekends when station sound stages became available. Soon, Grundy's production units were on the road, recording quiz and game shows at commercial television stations in Brisbane, Newcastle, Melbourne and Adelaide as well as in Sydney. This pattern suited a major station such as TCN9, which mostly wanted to reserve its own studio space for its more important and higher-budget programmes. Despite the inconvenience of the constant travel, the pattern of television mobility already anticipated in Chapter 2 in the Grundy family's moves between Sydney and Adelaide suited Reg Grundy, who took the opportunity to begin to get to know senior station executives in other cities outside Sydney.

The period also saw an ever-recurring move to diversify the principal's line of business. Three examples can be mentioned. The first saw Grundy produce a board-game version of *Tic Tac Dough*, manufactured and distributed by John Sands Limited in 1960. The second saw the production in 1964 of a pilot film for a would-be television comedy series titled *The Silent World of Buster Fiddess* (Moran 1985: 44). Fiddess was a former Vaudevillian, and the film attempted to capitalize on his capacity to mime and to mug to the camera. The pilot was the brainchild of some of Grundy's staff, who hoped that the company might break into sitcom television output (O'Grady 1980; McCabe 1980). The venture had the backing if not the involvement of Grundy. After all, scripted fiction was a more lucrative area of television production than was daytime quiz-show production. Still, for the would-be mogul, risks were a way to rewards even if, in this case, TCN9 did not commission the production of a sitcom series. The gamble did not pay off.

The third venture had to do with a brief move into recorded music. Altogether, RG Records, a subsidiary of Reg Grundy Productions, marketed four single 45" recordings, featuring the popular host of *Say When*, Jimmy Hannan. One of these songs, 'Beach Ball', rose to no. 2 on the Australian Top 40 charts. The recording initiative soon fizzled out, although 'Beach Ball' had the distinction of becoming a much sought-after recording. It featured the uncredited debut of the British/Australian pop group the Bee Gees, who provided backing to Hannan (Grundy 2010: 91–92). Like the other two initiatives, the music venture finally came to nought, although it underscored the company's ambition to break into new fields and identify new opportunities – an impulse that would later reap rich rewards.

Family business: divorce and custody

A major casualty of the television quiz-show success with TCN9 was the marriage of Reg Grundy and Lola Grundy. As already noted, the television version of *Wheel of Fortune* had proved to be even more time consuming than the radio version. The additional quiz shows being produced for the station meant that Grundy worked seven days a week, with few breaks. The heavy routine led to the couple's business life and domestic life melting into each other (Gillespie-Jones 1995). Tunstall's profile of the media mogul anticipates this kind of development. The couple's home apartment at Double Bay was Reg Grundy Enterprises' first office, with the company's first paid employee using their daughter Kim's bedroom as an office for compiling quiz questions once the child had gone off to kindergarten. Later, the company would rent a vacant apartment in the block as business expanded. As already mentioned, Lola Grundy became *Wheel of Fortune*'s first onscreen hostess. Her real task, however, lay behind the scenes, with contestants needing to be screened before they appeared on the show. As the quiz shows multiplied, this screening work increased. Much driving to and from TCN9 fell her way. By 1962, she was also undertaking another television chore. In early 1960, HSV Channel 7 in Melbourne embarked on a highly ambitious quiz show intended for prime-time broadcast, inspired by recent 'headline' giveaway quiz shows on US network television such as *The $64,000 Question* (Hoerschelmann 2004c: 210–56). The Melbourne quiz programme was sponsored by the nationwide retailer, G. J. Coles, and was titled *Coles £3000 Question* (Moran & Keating 2003: 61; Murphy 1981: 77–82).

The new quiz show was to appear on HSV's Sydney partner at the time, TCN Channel 9. (The GTV9 purchase by Consolidated Press, which caused a realignment of stations over the next three or four years, did not take place until later in 1960.) HSV contacted TCN, which in turn contacted Reg Grundy Enterprises to help ensure that Sydney contestants were correctly screened before being flown to Melbourne to compete in the programme. Lola Grundy became heavily involved in this screening work, and spent time both in Melbourne and also overseas in connection with the show. She and her husband had drifted apart, and Grundy initiated divorce proceedings somewhere around 1964 or 1965.

Few details about the end of the marriage and the subsequent divorce are provided in Grundy's memoir, but it is possible to reconstruct broadly the circumstances of the formal parting. General details of the legal system in which the Grundy divorce was played out were outlined to presenter Damien Carrick on ABC Radio National's *The Law Report* by retired Family Court judges John Fogarty and Austin Ashe in 2006 (Carrick 2006).

At this time in the state of NSW, before the establishment of the Family Court of Australia in 1976 and the instigation of no-fault divorce, there were only three main grounds for legally ending a marriage: cruelty, desertion and adultery. The last claim was favoured by the system as the least problematic of the three. The law was heavily stacked in favour of the husband in a divorce application. Not only was one act of adultery by a wife treated as sufficient grounds for divorce by a husband, but there had to be 'a repeated act of adultery' on the part of a husband before a court might find in favour of a wife. The unstated view was that men could be excused for straying whereas women were expected to remain pure and chaste under all circumstances. There was also a material dimension to this system. Husbands who instigated divorce proceedings would have access to family assets to support the costs of such an action. Unless a wife had inherited her own property, then she was much less able to bear the costs of a defence. As might be imagined, the fault-based system punished the party deemed guilty in both a material and an emotional manner. Sole custody of children was awarded to the aggrieved party, whether or not it was in the interests of the child. And joint family property was also awarded to the same party, often leaving the other party in difficult circumstances (ABC Radio National, *The Law Report*, 19 September 2006).

The upshot of the Grundy divorce was that Reg Grundy became a divorced man and was awarded custody of the only child of the marriage, their daughter Kim, who was then approaching her tenth birthday. Lola Grundy was overseas when the divorce judgment was handed down. She was denied any further contact with the child, and would eventually marry Simon Gillespie-Jones, a Melbourne barrister who she had met in the course of the divorce case. The couple settled in Canberra, and Lola died in 1999. Kim was to grow up estranged from her mother.

Programme cancellations

By early 1964, Reg Grundy Enterprises was the most successful programme-packaging operation in Australian television. Starting with the television version of *Wheel of Fortune*, Grundy had proved himself master of the television quiz show and of commercial television more generally, including the craft of remaking format programmes from elsewhere. He had shown himself to be a reliable packager for TCN9, capable of expanding his company's production capacities to produce up to four shows at the same time, and provide the station with more than fifteen half-hours of programming each week. Reg Grundy Enterprises had assembled a highly competent team of production all-rounders and these, in conjunction with the technical staff provided at TCN9 and other stations with studio capacity, enabled the smooth production of a series of programmes that came in on time and on budget, gathering satisfactory audience numbers to boot. However, although the television quiz-show format mogul had several programmes on air at all times from late 1959 to early 1964, he was vulnerable to business mishaps by dint of the fact that all his programmes had the same buyer. TCN9, in the person of chief executive Ken Hall and programme manager Bruce Gyngell, had encouraged Grundy to work closely with them. He had had little time or opportunity to insure against crisis by selling to ATN7 or newcomer TEN10 in Sydney, or by seeking other television programme buyers interstate. Disaster struck without warning, just as it had in 1953 with the sudden death of Monsigneur Meany at 2SM, precipitating a crisis that triggered Grundy's resignation. In February 1964, the independent television producer was informed that TCN9 was cancelling all his shows then in production (Grundy 2010: 93–96). *Concentration* would end in six weeks, *Say When* in mid-year and *Tic Tac Dough* at the end of the year.

Why did TCN9 drop all of Grundy quiz shows at the same time? The format mogul offers one explanation in his memoir (2010: 93–96): the desire of GTV9 in Melbourne to produce all quiz shows at the southern station for itself and its sister station, TCN9. But such an account makes little sense because the latter was the junior station in the Nine Network, with crucial decisions of this kind being made in Sydney by the company's owner.

A more persuasive explanation relates to a misinformed economy drive at the station, instigated by Frank Packer, the tyrannical and sometimes erratic owner of the network. As noted above, Packer had bought GTV9 in Melbourne in 1960. At the time, there was no cable linkage possible for the transmission of television signals between the two cities. By 1963, a coaxial cable had been laid by the Australian Postmaster General's Department, and Packer was eager to lease the facility to allow programme distribution across the two markets. All the same, as Griffen-Foley (2000) demonstrates, Packer was appalled at the cost of such a rental price and embarked on cost-cutting in his television operation (2000: 312–14). Grundy's quiz shows were already a source of bother to him: he mistakenly believed that the network paid for prizes awarded to winning contestants. In any case, he may have also felt that the promotion on air of companies offering prizes meant they were 'freeloading' on the Grundy quiz shows, denying advertising revenue to the station. This sentiment was common among broadcasters in the United States (Mittell 2004: 1151). Finally, there might have also been a desire on the part of the older media mogul to cut this fledgling TV format mogul down to size. The result for Grundy was not only the cancellation of all his quiz shows on air, but the closure of TCN Channel 9's door to him for almost another six years.

All three Grundy programmes were cancelled, and production would cease very shortly. Almost overnight, Grundy faced the crisis of having no immediate work for himself and his employees. This lack of sales was the kind of thing that happened repeatedly in the broadcasting industry in Australia and elsewhere, where networks and stations are the dog that wag the freelance production tail. Around the same time as the TCN9 cancellations, Hector Crawford and his sister Dorothy, principals of another television programme packaging company, Crawford Productions in Melbourne, faced a similar crisis with no drama series in production following the cancellation of a courtroom drama series (Moran 1985: 64).

For Grundy, the cancellations of his quiz shows were brutal and unwarranted. He would turn 41 at his next birthday, had spent half his life working, had waited almost eight years to get into broadcasting, and had now toiled in radio and television for almost seventeen years. It was too late to think of a career change. Dorothy and Hector Crawford in Melbourne had reached the same conclusion about twelve months earlier. Grundy now dipped deep into his capital in order to hold his staff together while he set about selling new programmes. Although TCN9's door was closed, alongside those of ABC TV and ATN7, the market situation for television quiz shows had in fact improved from the situation Grundy had faced in 1959. The overall Australian commercial television industry was expanding, so other marketing opportunities were becoming available.

Afterword

Reg Grundy came a very long way in the five years covered in this chapter. Highly experienced in the area of radio broadcasting, he took to television like a master, learning how the industry worked not only in the sense of what happened with technology but how a television company conducted its business operations. Many lessons were learnt, especially the need to insure against disaster. In an industry where the seller, the independent television programme packager, is always at a disadvantage compared with the buyer, the television broadcaster, the only long-term way of ensuring that the TCN9 cancellation crisis would not happen again was to expand and diversify. No opportunity could be passed up if Reg Grundy Productions was to survive and expand. Grundy was aware that he must stay on course if he was to become a TV format mogul, and this became his credo for the future. For the present, Reg Grundy had to rescue his company and get it back on its feet. Where, though, were new programme buyers to be found?

Chapter 6

Domestic Consolidation, 1964-70

Introduction

After the bitter lesson of the cancellation of all his shows by TCN9, 1965 saw Grundy and his company start afresh. In fact, the market prospects for a television-packaging company – especially one that specialized in quiz shows – were now considerably better than they had been six years earlier when he had launched his television business. Reg Grundy Enterprises set about recovering its foothold and consolidating its presence in the Australian television production industry. It was soon busier than ever, with an expanding portfolio of productions. There was, though, to be a second financial hiccup in the very late 1960s when it again lost several shows on air. However, the strength of the recovery after 1965 confirmed Reg Grundy's belief that he had a permanent place in the Australian television programme packaging industry, and the mogul bounced back quickly after this second setback. In fact, the period's solid run of programming successes was a foretaste of the uninterrupted rise of Grundy's programming triumphs in Australia and overseas that was to come. This chapter traces Grundy's market strategy, programming successes, staffing, rivalries with competitors and changing relationships with broadcasters between 1964 and 1969. It also refers to the tycoon's private life, following his recent divorce.

Changing context

Television had begun in Australia in an era marked by economic prosperity, political hegemony and social orthodoxy. However, the years 1965–70 saw a different Australia coming into existence (Moran 1991: 82–88; Craven 1989: 1–35). The economy was still prosperous, but other matters were affecting the population. Australia was involved in the war in Vietnam, and this triggered a polarization in society that was exacerbated by political upheaval, dramatic cultural change and increasing social fragmentation.

Television was entering its second decade, so all its teething problems were far behind. The system was mature, financially stable and mostly taken for granted after some of the early moral panics that had accompanied its introduction. Yet, while television was largely thought of as permanent and unchanging, it was undergoing important shifts – some of which were immediately relevant to the fortunes of Reg Grundy Services.

Superficially, the stability of the television system seemed to both reflect and be part of the overall consensus of the society. Between 1965 and 1970, there was a general stability of ownership and management at the commercial television stations (Moran 1985: 22; Cunningham 1993: 19–41). The television system was a triumph of administration and engineering, having progressively been inaugurated in metropolitan, regional and rural Australia between 1956 and 1968, so that almost the whole population of the country was within a broadcast signal. Inside the television industry, it was a somewhat different matter so far as change was concerned. One important departure had to do with the licensing of a third string of commercial television stations in Sydney, Melbourne, Brisbane and Adelaide, which came on air in 1964–65 (Hall 1976; Moran 1985). A long overdue restructuring of the ABC television service to make it more appealing to audiences (Moran 1985; Inglis 1982) and the advent of the 0–10 Network stations meant an increase in competition in the television sector generally (Moran 1993: 569–73).

In-house production on the part of the commercial television stations continued to decline, so independent packagers tended to pick up more programming commissions. The life of a programme packager was not rosy, however. The sector was characterized by a degree of instability: packagers tended to be small and undercapitalized, and often were unable to have more than one successful show in production at any one time. Both Crawford Productions in Melbourne and Reg Grundy Services in Sydney managed to buck this trend, although both went very close to disappearing in the same year. As mentioned in the previous chapter, Crawford's had been in dire straits in 1963–64 before it sold the drama series *Homicide* to HSV7 and then to the Seven Network (Moran 1993: 229–30), while Grundy in 1964–65 faced a desperate struggle in the months between the TCN9 cancellations and the selling of a new local version of *Concentration* to QTQ9 in Brisbane.

Other developments were also afoot in the television industry. The 1964 *Homicide* breakthrough heralded an important change. Commercial television stations had depended on popular US drama and sitcoms, together with in-house variety programmes, for ratings success in the first decade of Australian television (Breen 2004: 188–94). Now the variety show was in decline and would mostly disappear by 1970. The *Homicide* breakthrough heralded the place that a new Australian 'look' in drama contingent on videotape technology and changing economies would have in the evolving television ecology (Moran 1985).

With the rise in the popularity of Australian programmes, there was a shift in the economies of local commercial television. In the first decade of television broadcasting, low-cost import programmes from US networks subsidized the capitalization, equipping and maintenance of new television stations (Moran 1985: 20). From around 1964–65, there was a shift in these economies, with those same low-cost filmed imports allowing Australian commercial stations and networks to underwrite budgets for higher-cost local productions. Now the commercial stations rose or fell in audience ratings on the basis of their Australian programmes (Moran 1985; Cunningham 1993).

Two other changes in the television institution that affected Reg Grundy Services deserve mention. The first concerned an industry-wide rationalization of resources and facilities.

By the mid-1960s, the use of commercial videotape recording facilities in black and white had become general, especially among the major and minor state capital city commercial television stations (Fang 2004). The live-to-air broadcast programme was now mostly a thing of the past, with videotaping ensuring that programmes could be recorded at other times and in other places. This technical development dovetailed with another industry trend, 'runaway' or 'spillover' productions. The system involved allocating spare studio time at a station in a network for the making of a programme that would be broadcast by all affiliate stations in the network. This practice freed up demand for studio time in the major state capital city stations for the production of high-cost Australian programming, which broadcasting executives liked to keep under their gaze (Moran 1985: 12–19). As a lower-cost, high-output form, Grundy's quiz and game shows frequently had to go interstate for their production and recording. Programme hosts, celebrity guests and executive producers were constantly on the move, the first happening because of commissions by stations in the minor state capital cities and the second when production space was found at network-affiliated stations.

The other shift was generic, and related to changes in the structure and form of the television quiz show. Quiz shows in the United States in the early 1950s had tended to extol the authority of high culture and factual, often academic, knowledge in the questions asked of contestants (Fabe 1979: 22–41; Graham 1988: 18–21; Hoerschelmann 2004b: 1871–74). This legitimation was strengthened further in 1954 when the US Supreme Court ruled that quiz-show prize winnings were not a form of gambling, so prizemoney on shows quickly multiplied. In 1958, however, it was discovered that several of the most popular 'jackpot' quiz shows were rigged. The ensuing scandal triggered a shift in the ecology of the US quiz show that immediately affected the kind of formats available to Grundy and other packagers outside the United States. For the most part, the quiz show was no longer programmed in US network night-time slots, but became a feature of daytime broadcasting, and the emphasis on learning and academic knowledge disappeared. Programmes were now called game shows or panel game shows, with tests having more to do with physical contests, gambling and everyday populist knowledge based on consumerism, play and leisure (Hoerschelmann 2004b: 1871–74).

Australian commercial television was not affected directly by the US quiz scandals, and older type quiz shows such as *Pick-a-Box* and *Coles £3000 Question* continued to be ratings winners until well into the 1960s. Yet these once-a-week champions increasingly seemed out of touch with their times. Instead, it was the new Grundy game show formats, recently premiering on US daytime network television, that for the most part seemed subtly more in tune with the new social environment, which included a flourishing pop culture and counter-culture (Hoerschelmann 2004b: 1873). A glance at some Grundy programme titles of the time hints at the context of greater social pluralism within which they were being made and watched. Shows in question included *Blind Date* (1967–70), *Generation Gap* (1969), *The Marriage Game* (1966–69), *Split Personality* (1967) and the magazine programme *Women's World* (1969).

New programme markets

Another major industry development already hinted at involved the coming into being of two new television programme markets. This meant new opportunities for Reg Grundy Services at a time when it badly needed them. The market expansion was not immediately obvious, though – in fact, it took Reg Grundy eight months of idleness before he identified a programme sale possibility outside Sydney, secured a new programme licensing deal and saved his television career.

The quiz-show packager's timing in being forced to look for new markets was very fortunate, even though this seemed not to be the case in 1964. Grundy had been producing television programmes for five years. If he had begun programme packaging in 1956 when commercial television had first started, his company might have ceased to exist five years later when all his game shows were cancelled. The reason was simple: the television programme market was little changed in 1961 over what it had been in 1956. In 1964–65, however, two circumstances combined to extend the commercial television programme market: the creation of a new commercial television network in the east coast state capital cities, and the increased interest of commercial television stations in the smaller state capital cities in licensing lower-cost programmes from packagers such as Reg Grundy Services. Each development warrants closer attention.

The 0–10 Network

The possibility of a third commercial television network in Australia had its beginnings in an engineering decision of the Australian Broadcasting Control Board (ABCB) (Moran 1985: 4–5). In 1955, the ABCB drew up what became known as the Frequency Assignment Plan, whereby frequencies were freed up for television transmission in the Very High Frequency (VHF) Band. Four such frequencies were set aside for television broadcasting in the state capital cities, so in the early 1960s one of these was still available for allocation to a commercial set of broadcasting interests. In 1962, the federal government announced that Sydney, Melbourne, Brisbane and Adelaide were to be granted a third commercial television licence, while Perth was to receive a second. Elsewhere, I have summarized the reasons behind this announcement as follows:

> the advertising industry wanted greater competition; other commercial interests wanted a piece of what appeared to be the profitable television cake … the need to break the media monopoly which was building up with existing metropolitan stations … and the Government's concern that if Labor won the next election it might allow the trade union movement to have the third licence.
>
> (Moran 1985: 22)

Thus, Australia's third commercial group of stations came on the air in 1964–65. The stations were allocated the number 0 or 10 as part of their individual call signs, although later they would universally adopt the number 10 to remove the negative implications of 0. The principal beneficiary of the move to establish the stations was transport owner Reginald Ansett, who acquired new stations in Melbourne and Brisbane (Moran & Keating 2003: 22–23).

Far from proving to be a cash cow, the stations were a drain on collective revenue. They generally came last in the ratings behind the Nine and Seven Networks, which had the advantage of having begun some nine years earlier. In their first five years of operation up until 1970, the 0–10 stations struggled to attract and hold audiences (Jones & Bednall 1980: 29–31; Moran 1993: 369–73). They generally used cast-offs from the existing commercial stations, both before and behind the cameras, as well as in the boardroom and elsewhere. On some rare occasions, the stations would venture into their own in-station productions or else take a chance on new would-be independent packagers, but usually with disastrous results (e.g. see Moran 1985: 100–02). They also commissioned from established independent outside producers, and Reg Grundy Enterprises was to be a principal beneficiary of this commissioning, not only in the area of quiz and panel game shows but also in other forms of light entertainment.

The minor state capital city television stations

It is easy to underestimate the importance of the BAPH (Brisbane-Adelaide-Perth-Hobart) stations in the political economy of Australian commercial television in the period between 1959 when the first of these stations began operating and 1987 when national satellite networking from Sydney extinguished what little programming autonomy still remained (Cunningham 1993: 19–31). As has already been pointed out, television started in the major state capital cities of Sydney and Melbourne in 1956, and it was more than three years before service commenced in Brisbane and Adelaide.

A station licensing inquiry held by the ABCB in 1959 had implications for this second level of television development (Moran 1985: 10). The ABCB looked first at the matter of financial viability so far as stations in the smaller Brisbane television market were concerned. Concluding that the Brisbane advertising market could only support one commercial television station, it recommended the licensing of only one applicant to the federal government. The government was intent on providing network affiliates for the two sets of Sydney and Melbourne stations, however, and rejected this advice. Instead, it directed that the ABCB recommend two applicants who would receive commercial broadcasting licences (Davies & Moran 2012). This pattern was repeated in Adelaide and Perth. With the exception of Hobart, these three minor state capital cities were allocated two commercial television licences, making them junior partners to Sydney/Melbourne stations in what became the

Nine and the Australian (later the Seven) networking arrangements (Moran 1993: 553–55). This intention of junior partnership was reconfirmed in 1962–64, when these cities were given a third commercial licence each to support new commercial licensees in the major state capitals.

Commercial television stations in the BAPH cities were the poor cousins of those in the major state capitals. Their advertising markets were less affluent than those of Sydney and Melbourne, so their economic and political muscle in their networks was less. However, with the exception of the Ansett Brisbane station, they were not owned by Sydney and Melbourne interests so they had a healthy degree of autonomy. The BAPH network stations were to serve several significant functions, both separately and as affiliate stations. For one thing, they could commission programmes and then later sell these to their network partners, including the Sydney and Melbourne interests. They could also serve a talent-spotting purpose in front of and behind the television camera.

More importantly for Reg Grundy Services, they could accommodate 'runaway' productions when the major network stations were too busy to house these in their studios. A pecking order developed so far as this rationalization of production venues was concerned. More expensive, big-budget productions such as drama series and musical specials got preference over more routine, lower-budget, faster-turnaround productions such as women's programming, and quiz and game shows. The former were mounted at stations in the major state capital cities while the latter were very frequently allocated to the BAPH cities. These arrangements made sense on the grounds of finance, control, efficiency and speed.

Thankfully, from the point of view of Reg Grundy Services, these minor state capital city stations also began to commission programmes in their own right from 1965 onwards. Three factors were probably at work. First, the stations already had a short history of producing programming in house, and the move to farm out commissioning to independent packagers was part of a long-term, industry-wide trend. Second, the commissioning took place in lower-cost programme genres such as talent shows, quiz programmes and later current affairs television. Third, the licensing was part of a pattern, whereby BAPH stations asserted local production autonomy and also sought to generate programmes with a high degree of local flavour and appeal. Finally, there was always the prospect of onselling this programming to network affiliates in the other BAPH stations and those in the major state capital cities, making these ventures more profitable. The development of this second-level market, especially in Brisbane, was to be crucial for the company (Grundy 2010: 956; Franco 2008).

Recovery, downturn and comeback

In late 1964, Grundy and his company managed to survive the TCN9 cancellation crisis by selling a programme interstate. The company already had some on ongoing connection with QTQ Channel 9 in Brisbane due to the fact that episodes of the programme *Concentration*, commissioned by TCN9 in Sydney, frequently were shot at the Brisbane station's studios.

Now, out of desperation, Grundy made a bold business move. The run of the Sydney version of *Concentration* came to an end on QTQ9, although it was rating well five afternoons a week. On the first of at least three occasions in his television career, the format mogul was ready to underwrite the bulk of the costs of producing a show. He offered the station a deal whereby QTQ9 would provide 'below the line' resources in terms of studio time and technicians, and would pay Grundy the ordinary licence fee on such a programme. Reg Grundy Services would produce the show and be responsible for 'above the line costs', including the provision of prizes and the transportation of personnel to Brisbane (Grundy 2010: 93–95; Franco 2008). The company would then onsell the recorded programme to other stations in other markets across the country, splitting income derived from these sales. QTQ9 agreed to the proposal and *Concentration* was back before the cameras in early 1965 with up to fifteen episodes being videotaped every third weekend (Grundy 2010: 95). Reg Grundy had survived the most serious crisis that was to befall him in his business career.

By 1966, programming commissions were up and the company was as busy as it had been at the time of the Packer cancellation. This recovery continued over the next five years. Still, the TCN9 cancellation had spelled out an important business lesson to the format mogul: do not become completely dependent on one buyer. Even so, in 1969 there came another calamity, which again involved programme cancellation by a broadcaster (Culliton 1995; 2009; *TV Week* 1971: 7). Though not as grave as the crisis associated with TCN's dropping of Reg Grundy Enterprises' programmes in 1964, nevertheless the 0–10 Network's decision in 1968–69 to not renew contracts on *The Marriage Game* and *Personality Squares* again inflicted a heavy toll on the company.

Identifying the specific period of this second crisis is difficult. Even within a few years, press reports about the organization were unable to cite a particular time, suggesting that the memory of the reversal was already fading. Subsequently, media reports would often claim that the downturn occurred as early as 1968 or as late as 1970 (*TV Week* 1971: 7; Culliton 2009). In his memoirs, Grundy makes no reference to this later bout of cancellations, suggesting that the crisis was more short-lived and less damaging than the TCN9 affair.

To the extent that published television programme guides are indicative, 1970 seems to have been a lean year for Reg Grundy Enterprises. Programme output in this period is discussed in more detail in the next section. Here, though, we might note that although both the Brisbane and Adelaide versions of *I've Got a Secret* continued on air, three other shows being produced by the company came to an end: *The Marriage Game* finished in mid-year, *In Town Tonight* concluded at the end of January and *Generation Gap* ran for just six months. There would have been a lead time on these on-air completions, so that production on both *The Marriage Game* and *Generation Gap* might have ceased several weeks or months earlier. Again, as had occurred in 1964, company employees faced several months of salary reduction before programme commissions on new shows were secured. This time, however, the downturn was more of a hiccup than the calamitous cancellations of 1964. The daytime *Temptation*, based on the US *Sale of the Century*, was already being planned for the Seven Network, and waited only for a potential sponsor – the retail giant Coles – to agree to back it.

Reg Grundy had learnt resilience from the earlier setback, and could be more confident about the recovery of his business. If he had not done so already, he was now entitled to regard himself as a television mogul who was building an empire. In any case, output continuity was maintained with the Brisbane and Adelaide versions of *I've Got a Secret* still in production. The 0–10 failure to renew was a business decision rather than the splenetic and idiosyncratic actions of a powerful, home-grown media mogul and the Network would continue to need new successful packaged programmes. In any case, both the Seven and Nine Networks were also back in the market as far as Reg Grundy Enterprises was concerned. Shortly, the company would be busier than ever, with the 0–10 downfall forgotten.

For Reg Grundy himself, this disappointment was the last that he faced in his career. Its precedents could be traced back not only to the TCN cancellation but also to his resignations from 2CH in 1959 and from 2SM in 1953 – perhaps even to the failure to find a career in graphic art and design in 1939. Instead, his business pathway over the next 25 years would be free from the snags and dangers that he had already survived.

Surge in quiz-show output

Typifying the company consolidation that happened in this period, Reg Grundy Services produced 27 different programmes, the great majority in the genre of quiz and game shows. This was an astonishing increase over the five quiz shows produced in the first period of television programme packaging discussed in Chapter 5. Grundy was back with a vengeance. Of course, the economics of each programme commission varied considerably. The least valuable from a company point of view was a daytime programme broadcast once a week by only one minor state capital city station such as Brisbane or Adelaide, while the most valuable was a programme running five evenings a week commissioned by one of the Sydney or Melbourne stations on behalf of itself and network partners. No licensings quite made it into this second category in this period. Such a commission would come shortly with quiz shows such as *Great Temptation*. For the time being, the company had to be satisfied with *The Marriage Game* and *Personality Squares*, sold to TEN10 in 1967, with the two being broadcast five days a week, with a one-night-a-week prime-time version of these quiz shows also going to air.

Some programmes were short-lived, with shows such as *Split Personality* (1967) and *Missing Link* (1969) failing to run into second seasons. Conversely, other programmes proved to be far more robust, going on to contribute to company coffers for many years. Two state versions of *I've Got a Secret* were highly durable: the Brisbane version played on QTQ9 for nine years (Moran & Keating 2003: 83) while an Adelaide remake ran on one commercial station, SAS9, from 1966 to 1970, when it was cancelled. Grundy had already shown a salesman's flair with cancellations when, after the axing of *First Impressions* by TCN9 in 1964, he had persuaded QTQ9 to pick it up in 1966. He pulled off the same coup in 1970 when he talked one of the other stations in Adelaide, ADS7, into continuing with the production of a South Australian version of *I've Got a Secret* (Moran & Keating 2003: 83). This adroit move of programming salesmanship would be repeated several times in subsequent years including, most notably, with the drama serial *Neighbours*. The result was that *I've Got a Secret* had a second lease of life on Adelaide television, running from 1970 to 1974. Other valuable performers for the company included *Get the Message* (1966–72), *Personality Squares* (1967–69) and *Blind Date* (1967–70).

Rather than examining programmes in isolation, however, it is more useful to investigate the total output of this time. Reg Grundy Enterprises' progress can be gauged in several ways. After almost a year of inactivity after the TCN9 cancellation of all programmes, Reg Grundy Services became far busier than it had been under the TCN9 yoke. 1968 was the busiest year yet for the company, which by that time was producing about fourteen hours of programming each week. As already noted, there were 27 different programming commissions between 1965 and 1970, with several of these programmes continuing into the new decade. The great majority of these occurred in the area of quiz shows and panel games, but there were also two others, *In Town Tonight* (TEN10, 1967–69) and *Women's World* (BTQ7, 1969), which indicated that Reg Grundy Services was willing to try its hand in other areas of television light entertainment programming production, a move that anticipated its diversification into other areas of programme production in the 1970s.

Of course, this jump in the quiz-show productivity of Reg Grundy Services was due not only to the energy and entrepreneurship of the company but also to the steady importation of quiz and game show formats from US network television. Many US game shows playing on the networks and in syndication were raided for formats that could be adapted to provide Australian television adaptations. Thus two recent formats from Heatter-Quigley Productions were remade under their original titles of *Celebrity Game* (CBS premiere in 1964) and *Showdown* (NBC premiere in 1966), while Chuck Barris Productions was the source of *The Newlywed Game* (ABC premiere in 1966) and *The Family Game* (ABC premiere in 1967) (Schwartz, Ryan & Wosbrook 1987: 83, 40–67, 168, 318–20).

Nonetheless, one US quiz-show format source was next to irresistible. This was Goodson-Todman Productions (McDermott 2004: 1013–16). Having started by devising quiz shows for US network radio in the 1940s before moving into television, Goodson-Todman Productions was the most successful quiz and panel show packager in the United States. Network and syndicated versions of Goodson-Todman's many hit formats could be spotted and documented for remaking for the Australian commercial television broadcasters. Thus it was no surprise to discover Grundy producing Goodson-Todman formats from the 1950s, including *I've Got a Secret* (CBS premiere in 1952), *Play Your Hunch* (CBS premiere in 1958), *Split Personality* (NBC premiere in 1959) and *Concentration* (NBC premiere in 1959) (Schwartz, Ryan & Wosbrook 1987: 105–12, 240–43, 366–67, 416–17), as well as some of their more recent formats from the 1960s, including *Numbers Game* (ABC premiere in 1961 as *Numbers Please* (?)), *The Match Game* (NBC premiere in 1962), *Missing Link* (NBC premiere in 1963) and *Get the Message* (ABC premiere in 1964) (Schwartz, Ryan & Wosbrook 1987: 186, 292–95, 302, 322). In fact, Reg Grundy Services derived a third of its overall programme output in the period – nine programme formats in all – from the Goodson-Todman format factory. It is no wonder that the Australian format mogul developed a very high regard for Goodson's quiz-show abilities, which would see him proposing a business merger with the latter in the 1980s, as will be discussed in Chapter 11 (Grundy 2010: 211–13).

Not all Grundy game shows could be sourced to US format originals, however. In some instances, this possibly was due to name changes, indicated by another title appearing in parentheses accompanied by a question mark, as is the case above with *Numbers Please* (?) (Moran & Keating 2003: 104). In this case, there is some doubt about whether the Australian programme had a definite US format source. In any case, Reg Grundy Services occasionally originated its own quiz-show formats. A Brisbane version of *Wheel of Fortune*, probably based on what Grundy had originally devised for TCN9 in 1959, was produced for BTQ7 in 1969 (Moran & Keating 2003: 131). The children's quiz show *Ampol Stamp Quiz* (1964), developed on behalf of a sponsor's marketing campaign, was a minor instance of such a development, and *Ampol Big Game* (1966) was a more striking example (Moran & Keating 2003: 48–49). The latter was a novel football-based game/quiz programme with players from Melbourne's VFL football teams competing in a team-based general knowledge contest that took place on a miniature football field, 'umpired' by a well-known VFL football commentator.

If the United States as a source for quiz-show ideas was important in helping to build the company in terms of size and revenue, so too was commercial television's continuing appetite for new quiz and game shows. As we have already noted, the genre was low-cost and less expensive to produce than other forms of output, such as drama series and specials. This meant that even minor state capital city stations such as those in Brisbane and Adelaide could afford to commission quiz and game shows for local broadcast, while stations in Sydney and Melbourne often tended to order programmes for network-wide broadcast. The 0–10 group was the company's best customer, contracting a dozen different quiz shows, beginning with *The Marriage Game* in 1966–67 for TEN10 (Moran & Keating 2003: 92) and *Get the Message* in 1966–72 for TVQ0 in Brisbane (Moran & Keating 2003: 73) and ending with *The Match Game* in 1969 for ATV0 in Melbourne (Moran & Keating 2003: 93) and *Generation Gap* in 1969 for TEN10 in Sydney (Moran & Keating 2003: 73). In fact, underlying how important the 0–10 Network was to the survival and prosperity of Reg Grundy Enterprises, different members of the new network commissioned almost half of all the programmes Grundy produced in the second half of the 1960s. Eight of these were most valuable, being contracted by TEN10 Sydney for broadcast across all stations in the group. The Grundy company also made programmes on behalf of other stations in the chain, including another network sale to ATV0 Melbourne and three for local broadcast by TVQ Brisbane or SAS10 Adelaide.

This period also saw Reg Grundy Services less constrained as far as licensings to other stations and networks were concerned. Hence stations in the Nine Network constituted another important market for the company, most especially QTQ9 in Brisbane, which had helped keep Grundy afloat after the Packer cancellations and strengthened its balance sheet in the process. Equally propitious was the fact of four programme commissions from the wealthier stations in the Nine Network group. *Ampol Big Game* in 1966 and *The Guessing Game* in 1967 (Moran & Keating 2003: 48–49, 77) marked the company's first programme orders from the Packer-owned GTV9 in Melbourne. In addition, TCN9's decision to buy a daily panel game show, *Everybody's Talking* (Moran & Keating 2003: 67), which ran for the two years 1968–69, could be understood as a more general sign that even the Packer interests recognized the market leadership and talent of Reg Grundy Enterprises and saw that it was time to draw on the company's expertise so far as the station's and network's programming needs were concerned.

Programme commissions from another new customer further contributed to this boom. These were instigated by commercial stations belonging to the Seven Network. Admittedly, most of these came from stations in the minor state capital cities. HSV7 in Melbourne, which had a close and long-standing relationship with Crawford Productions – not only for drama but also for quiz and current affairs programming – bought nothing, however, and did not seem likely to do so in the future. Chapter 5 has already mentioned the total reluctance at ATN7 in Sydney between 1956 and 1969 to commission programme production from outside packagers, an attitude that had militated against Reg Grundy Services selling any shows to that station in the 1960s. However, there was a change of management at ATN7 towards the end of the decade, and that station opened its doors to Reg Grundy Services for the first time in 1969. The programme commissioned was *Pay Cards*, an adaptation of a quiz-show/card-game format of the same name that had premiered a year earlier in US syndication, devised and produced by Nicholson Muir Productions (Schwartz, Ryan & Wosbrook 1987: 347; Moran & Keating 2003: 104). This sales breakthrough with the Seven Network was a propitious sign of things to come.

As the company boomed, so various developments were afoot in Reg Grundy Services. The principal was well on his way to becoming an Australian television production mogul who was both significant and influential. How did he run a rapidly expanding organization that was accountable to no one other than himself? Grundy's juggling of format-spotting, finance, personnel and geography offer useful answers to this question.

Running the business: format-spotting

I have already emphasized the necessity of ensuring a steady supply of new quiz-show formats from US network television. As well as thinking nationally, the company was also just beginning to think transnationally. Grundy has written that he made his first trip to the United States in August 1966 (2010: 99–101). The immediate purpose was to watch new quiz shows playing on network television. No longer linked with TCN Channel 9, the quiz-show maestro now needed to do his own programme format-spotting so that he was well placed to offer television stations back in Australia their own versions of recent US successes. This fieldwork made up a crucial form of his R&D for his television activities. Others pursue invention and innovation in laboratories or engineering workshops; Reg Grundy tracked the same objective by watching US television in his hotel room. He recognized the major importance of this fieldwork, and proceeded to give it priority over almost all his other business operations. On his first US trip, he mistakenly visited New York in order to watch the new network quiz shows and only later realized that stops either in Los Angeles or even Honolulu could have served the same purpose of giving him access to such programmes on cable relay. However, that first trip served its purpose of beginning to acquaint Reg Grundy with the media industry that was US network television. Soon, these trips to the United States and then the United Kingdom would become regular and frequent parts of what it meant to be an Australian television programme packager of quiz and game shows.

Running the business: programme economies

Some of the economies of quiz and panel game shows have been touched upon in Chapter 5, but these warrant further mention in relation to Grundy's situation after 1965. Quiz and game shows were an attractive form of programming as far as television stations were concerned. As previously noted, they could be developed quickly, could provide a relatively fast alternative for a ratings problem in a particular timeslot, might prove to be highly durable and popular on air even though they mostly had a shorter broadcast life than other forms of programming, were usually studio-based and could be recorded at television stations interstate, and were relatively inexpensive to produce with commercial manufacturers and retailers providing most of the necessary prizes (Shaw 1987: 481–501: Mittell 2002: 319–42; Cooper-Chen 1994). In addition, the inclusion of commercial announcements about prizes provided by the quiz-show packager further reduced running time, and therefore studio recording time.

The fact that the packager gathered the necessary prizes without any cost to a commissioning television station would prove to be very important after 1965, as quiz and game shows began to be commissioned not only by the larger wealthier commercial television stations in Sydney and Melbourne but also by their satellite siblings in Brisbane, Adelaide, Perth and even smaller regional cities such as Ballarat and Newcastle. Reg Grundy Services did not sell quiz and game shows to stations on this lower tier, although it would peddle a considerable number of formats to BAPH stations over the next fifteen years or so. Sometimes, these quiz shows were seen only in their city of origin. Often, though, they were sold interstate. As mentioned above, even as early as 1960, the Reg Grundy Services/TCN9 version of *Concentration* was bought by GTV9 in Melbourne, thereby enabling that station to save money by cancelling its own in-house version of the programme.

Reg Grundy Services took more of a hand in distribution as time went by, selling canned or finished programmes to commercial television stations in the major state capitals, the BAPH cities and regional cities. As the costs and availability of recording and playback facilities spread, canned episodes of programmes, including quiz and game shows, could be sold in all these markets. By the second half of the 1960s, this distribution system was in full swing, so that Reg Grundy Services struck an agreement with a distribution agent to pursue such sales (Grundy 2010: 125–26). Although the price that a country station could pay was small by Sydney and Melbourne standards, nevertheless there were as many as 27 such stations, and programmes were often stripped for broadcast five days a week, making the pursuit of sales very worthwhile.

Running the business: anonymity and secrecy

As observed in Chapters 1 and 12, Tunstall's identification of the mogul (Tunstall & Palmer 2001) includes mention of a personal, even idiosyncratic style. So it was with Grundy, although this developed over time. During the years in radio and the early period in television from 1959 to 1964, Reg Grundy had been a well-known voice and presence in broadcasting. But now began a process whereby the television producer and owner of Reg Grundy Services increasingly was becoming a name without a public presence. As already noted, Grundy ceased to compère *Wheel of Fortune* in its last eighteen months on air, as the needs of his many TCN9 productions made increasing demands on his time. The host-cum-producer was also less and less available to newspaper and magazine reporters for publicity purposes as his workload increased. Reg Grundy was also less accessible to some of his own employees. According to John Culliton, one of his quiz-show producers in the late 1960s, Grundy used a backroom office at the North Sydney Arthur Street production office (Culliton 2009). The space was routine and modest, without a view: it represented a workspace for its occupant rather than a showplace to impress visitors. By the early 1970s, to anticipate the next chapter, Grundy had taken to working almost entirely at home. For a time, he had a weekly meeting with a handful of chief executives very early in the morning before other employees had arrived at the office. But soon this practice was also discontinued, so that Grundy executives, television station programmers and others only saw him in his home office (Weston 1995). This process of 'de-Grundification' eventually came to general notice. The Grundy name remained on all the company's programmes, but the voice and face faded in the memory of the public at large and Grundy himself was a void so far as junior company employees were concerned.

Even at this distance in time, several elements are worth mentioning. First, there were few models for this kind of phenomenon of a mogul who had become a name without a face. One figure that was well known in media folklore was Howard Hughes: oil magnate, aviation owner and erstwhile Hollywood film producer. Part of Hughes' career was detailed in the Martin Scorsese 2006 feature film *The Aviator*, starring Leonardo DiCaprio. After a bad plane crash that almost cost him his life, Hughes became increasingly eccentric, with a mania for privacy and secrecy. Reg Grundy's desire for confidentiality and seclusion led several in the Australian media to see him as a local version of Hughes. There was little validity in such a comparison, though. Grundy had plenty of contact and communication with his top executives and producers, even if more lowly employees almost never set eyes on the figure as the company grew in size.

If Reg Grundy increasingly was a name without a face so far as Australian television viewers were concerned, reports of a shadowy existence also began to circulate. This had to do with a widening awareness in the television industry, and eventually among the public at large, that it was no coincidence that Australian versions of US quiz shows were turning up on local television under Grundy's name (Grundy 2010: 104–05). As a later media report put it:

> Grundy's ... productions have been based on ... concepts, many of which were lifted from the US by Reg Grundy in the 1960s and 1970s (according to TV industry legend, Grundy used to lock himself in a Los Angeles hotel room, watch the daytime game shows and return home with ideas for new Australian shows).
>
> (Penberthy 1980: 14)

Running the business: confidentiality and control

There was, instead, a different explanation for the seclusion and privacy. Secrecy and confidentiality were in fact key ingredients in Grundy's business activity. A fellow salesman at 2CH in the mid- to late 1950s mentioned in interview that Grundy always remained silent about commissions arising from selling on-air time, although it did seem that he was doing very well (Morotoff 1995). Similarly, Reg Grundy Enterprises and its corporate successors were private companies that had no obligation to provide annual reports. In fact, even in 1994–95, when plans were afoot to list Grundy Worldwide as a public company, the group applied to the Sydney and New York stock exchanges to have a series of disclosure requirements waived by the Australian Stock Exchange (*Sydney Morning Herald* 1994: 17; *The Australian* 1995: 25; Potter & Kidman 1994: 17). As we will see in Chapter 12, nothing came of this application because a buyer for the company was found instead. Nonetheless, the move was in keeping with a general reluctance on the part of Grundy to disclose details of financial operation not relevant to others.

If secrecy and confidentiality represented one side of Grundy's business operation, another concerned the desire for complete control and mastery of the television production business. Grundy mentions that in 1974 he and Hector Crawford, owner of Crawford Productions, met to discuss a partnership in television programme packaging (2010: 225–27). The two companies – one in Sydney and the other in Melbourne – were doing extremely well at the time, mostly in different areas of television output. Joined into one corporate entity, they could have complemented each other. In 1993, for example, two Dutch television packagers came together in just this kind of marriage to form what became the highly successful television production enterprise, Endemol (Moran 1998: 33–39). Nothing came from the idea of a Crawford–Grundy amalgamation, however. Whatever Crawford's motives for withdrawing from a possible union, it would also have suited Grundy's desire for dominance not to share company control with another.

In fact, there seem to have been only two occasions when Grundy possibly was prepared to cede some business control to another by way of a partnership. This occurred in the United States, most probably in the 1980s, when Grundy suggested to Mark Goodson that they merge their businesses into Grundy-Goodson (Grundy 2010: 211–14). Two reasons can be suggested for this marriage proposal by Grundy. First, the move made some commercial sense. Bill Todman, Goodson's long-time professional partner, had died in 1979, leaving the ageing Goodson (born in 1915) to operate alone (McDermott 2004: 1013–16). In addition, from 1986 onwards, Grundy's US venture in quiz and game show packaging to the networks was not going so well, so combining the two companies might have paid big dividends in terms of quiz-show licensings. Another reason for the partnership suggestion from Grundy was more personal. Ever since the adaptation of *Concentration* and *Say When*, two shows first devised and produced by Goodson-Todman Productions in the early 1960s in Australia, Grundy had held the company in very high esteem. A partnership would signify Grundy's graduation to the top level in the transnational craft of programme format origination. The master's apprentice would finally become an equal of the master. Mark Goodson passed on the offer, however. Instead, when Goodson died in 1992, the Goodson company and format catalogue passed to his son, Jonathan. (Later, coincidentally, as will be seen in Chapter 12, both the Goodson and Grundy format libraries would be swallowed up by the same transnational production conglomerate.) Meanwhile, apart from small percentages given to two top executives and his wife, Reg Grundy remained the sole owner of his company and in complete control of its fortunes.

Running the business: personnel and divisions of labour

Even by the middle of 1962, less than two years after Reg Grundy Services began operations, the quizmaster-producer was claiming that the business was so big that he could not oversee it all and he had been forced to learn to delegate (*TV Week* 1962: 22). Some of this claim was rhetorical, but it was certainly a sign of things to come. For while staff frequently had to pitch in to help each other on whatever tasks were urgent, particular jobs were being delegated to employees who became experts in that domain. Grundy had added specialists to his organization, teaching individuals tasks that he had hitherto had to attend to personally, thus leaving himself free to concentrate on other parts of the enterprise. One of the first tasks that he relinquished was the awkward and sometimes thankless task of prize coordination, while another in 1962 involved finding substitutes for himself to host *Wheel of Fortune*.

Selling shows – or, more precisely, the licensing of programmes for an agreed number of broadcasts – was (and remains) the lifeblood of the television programme packaging industry. Broadcasters need programmes and packagers need to fill their needs. Selling is the name of the game. So who did such selling on behalf of Reg Grundy Enterprises and its successor companies, and how did these deals take place? In Chapter 3, I quoted the words of Reg Grundy to the effect that if one sold socks in a department store one could sell television programmes to broadcasters. Grundy did his own hawking in the early days of his television career. His memoir recounts an interview with senior staff at TCN9 in 1959, when he sold his first television show (2010: 66–70). Ten years later, he was still peddling would-be shows to television station programmers, but could now do this in his home office with a copy of the US version of a format that he was offering to remake for the Australian television broadcaster (Grundy 2010: 123–24). In any case, quiz and game shows were already very attractive to networks and stations, so often little pitching was necessary. As Reg Grundy became very busy, this kind of selling devolved to others in his organization, as much by chance as by design. There was nothing accidental or chaotic about such a process, however. Instead, as Reg Grundy Enterprises later the Grundy Organisation grew in size and capacity, so it developed experience, industry contacts and a substantial track record, which meant that sales often happened in more unexpected ways with more unlikely members of the company. A former accountant with Reg Grundy Services, Barry Weston, offered this account of the sales process:

> All sorts of people used to sell the shows and [they] … used to sell themselves. The television stations were so dependent on Hector Crawford and Reg Grundy that they just used to ring them up and ask them. Brian Treasure, who was program manager at Channel 7 in Perth, wanted a program. [Compère] Tony Barber [had] gone through *Temptation* and *Great Temptation* [and] was in oblivion at a radio station in Perth. Bill [Mason] and I went to Perth … [and we] had in our bag *Family Feud*, a program that we either acquired the rights to or we knew it existed or whatever. We showed it to Brian Treasure who was, at the same time, the personal manager of Tony Barber. He said 'The show would be wonderful but it needs Tony'. We said to Reg 'We can sell the program but the program needs Tony'. Reg said 'Tony's wonderful'. So I said to them 'Lend me a typewriter'. And I typed out a sales agreement on the spot. I said 'Sign this and we are in business'. And away we went.
>
> (Weston 1995)

Running the business: travelling formats

The period 1965–69 saw Reg Grundy Services beginning to set up productions and offices wherever there were market opportunities, in a manner that anticipated its move offshore after 1980. Grundy had called Sydney home since 1939, and the pattern had continued with his company only selling to a Sydney television station up until 1964. From 1965 onwards, this routine changed as the company got back on its feet. Reg Grundy Services ceased to be based exclusively in Sydney, and became a more intra-national entity, selling quiz and other shows to commercial television stations along the east coast of Australia from Brisbane to Adelaide. Of course, the most valuable sales were to stations in Sydney and Melbourne, and over half of all commissions came from these hub cities. Nevertheless, as we have seen, there was also a healthy crop of programme commissions from stations in the minor state capital cities.

A second reason for interstate travel was to use available studio space at affiliate stations in other cities for the making of quiz and other shows, especially when studio space was unavailable at Sydney and Melbourne stations. This frequently happened with strip programming for daytime quiz shows intended for broadcast five days a week. The 'spillover' arrangement meant that Grundy's producers (and often hosts and celebrity guests) were regular air travellers between Sydney, Brisbane, Melbourne and Adelaide. Contra deals with the two domestic airlines, the national Trans Australia Airlines (TAA) and the commercial Ansett Airlines, helped to facilitate this travel (Weston 1995). The fact that Ansett Industries owned both the Melbourne and Brisbane stations in the 0–10 Network suggests that the airline had a vested interest in the continuation of this arrangement.

Additionally, when several productions were occurring simultaneously in the same city, it was logical to open a small office in that city for the duration of such shows. Of course, this was in addition to the company's principal office, now located at Arthur Street in North Sydney, in the heartland of Sydney's television industry (Moran 2010: 343–56). The additional interstate offices could be closed again, with operations reverting back to Sydney once such programmes were at an end.

Family business: daughter, household and new romantic partner

To round out this account of the years 1965–70, it is useful to trace the interconnection between Grundy's business life and his domestic circumstances. We might start by recalling Tunstall's point, mentioned in Chapter 1, that with the media mogul the two arenas often blur into one. As noted in the previous chapter, Reg Grundy had been awarded custody of his daughter, Kim, after his divorce from his first wife. Grundy's mother, Lillian, who had been a widow for over ten years, moved in with her son and granddaughter to help run the household. The most immediate question was where to live. Although Kim attended primary school in the Double Bay area on the eastern side of the city where the Grundy family had lived for over 25 years, it was more convenient for the new household to locate on the north side of the Sydney Harbour Bridge to provide easier access to company offices in Arthur Street in North Sydney, not to mention the commercial television stations a little further north. After renting several apartments, the three-generation Grundy family ended up living in a post-World War II brick house on the upper North Shore, where father and daughter enjoyed an in-ground swimming pool together all year round (Drummond 1995; Culliton 1995; Grundy 2010: 85–86). There was probably little time for any other domestic or social engagements because the tempo of the television work had increased further. With her mother, Lola, gone from her life and her father continually busy with his television production business, the daughter looked to her grandmother as her prime parent. Kim called Lillian 'Mum', and preferred herself to be known as Robin, Lillian's pet name for her husband

Roy Harold in the years before his death (Grundy 2010: 85–86). Lillian and Kim were, in any case, no strangers to the business. Lillian regularly visited the company office to help with sorting mail. Kim, too, would visit after school and during school holidays (Culliton 1995).

A second focal point for the business/family link had to do with the entry of a newcomer. Soon, there was another woman at the company offices and in the family home. This was Joy Chambers, a young Brisbane woman who previously had won a Gold Coast beauty contest and had ambitions to work onscreen in television. In early 1966, she had successfully auditioned before Grundy to become one of the celebrity panelists for his upcoming panel show, *I've Got a Secret* (Grundy 2010: 106–09). As already noted, the programme was a Goodson-Todman US format and was based on its earlier success with *What's My Line?* (McDermott 2004: 1013–16). The game show, which aired twice a week, involved four celebrity panelists attempting to detect the secret of a notable guest. It proved to be immensely popular, and ran on Queensland television for ten years. Joy Chambers was a newcomer to television, but was witty, vivacious and attractive on camera. Rumours of a romance between her and another panelist on the show, entertainer Ron Cadee, were fostered by the company and the station as publicity for the show. Instead, though, there was great surprise when Reg Grundy and Joy Chambers married in late 1971 (Grundy 2010: 110–16).

The marriage not only gave Grundy a romantic and domestic partner, but also gave the company a useful asset. Chambers appeared in every episode of the Brisbane version of *I've Got a Secret*, and also surfaced frequently as a guest on other Grundy panel quiz shows of the time, including the Adelaide version of *I've Got a Secret*, *Play Your Hunch*, *The Guessing Game* and *Queensland's Celebrity Game*. Later, from the mid-1970s, she would also make short-term, recurring but striking appearances in Grundy-produced drama serials from *The Young Doctors* to *Neighbours*. Underscoring the point that she was being given no free ride by Reg Grundy Services, feminist critic Lesley Stern would write appreciatively of Joy Chambers' role as Rita Merrick in *The Restless Years* as follows:

> The only character ... who can use everyone else's secrets as a weapon is the dark and devious Rita Merrick. With style and panache, she reigns over underground empires, maliciously mocks familial harmony, executes blackmail, extortion, murder, revenge. She is an occasional character rather than a resident, she materializes like a deus ex machina not to right the wrongs of the world but to divert attention. Her eruption into the fiction serves to lead us astray, into proliferating plots and action-packed drama.
>
> (Stern 1982: 113)

Afterword

The beginning of the 1970s marked the end of the most crucial decade in Reg Grundy's career. His personal life had settled down after the end of his first marriage, with a new partner ready to give his business career primacy in their relationship. After the previous dozen years in radio, the quiz-show master had recognized the need to move into television if his business interests were not to stagnate. Despite whatever nerves and hesitations he might have suffered, Grundy's career trajectory had been marked by boldness. He presented himself to TCN9 not as a would-be station employee but a contractor who would provide the broadcaster with valuable quiz-show programming. Nor did he have an output ceiling, but would expand his programme production as the station required. Grundy had not been daunted by the TCN9 cancellation of all his quiz shows, but struggled on and recovered. Company success in the period surveyed in this chapter vindicated the bold decision to persevere in quiz-show packaging. There was far less hesitation about continuing after the 0–10 stations' cancellations in 1969. In the 1970s, 1980s and 1990s, Grundy and his company would encounter other business vicissitudes, but none as crucial as those that he had faced and overcome in the 1960s. His career was now permanently outward bound.

Chapter 7

Transnational Ambitions I: First Moves, 1969-74

Introduction

By 1970, Reg Grundy had been working in Australian broadcasting for more than two decades. He had encountered both good and bad times in his radio and television career up to that point, but the next quarter century was to mark a different path of continuing success and company expansion. The bad times largely fell away, and Reg Grundy Enterprises diversified in several ways – although these new initiatives were not always successful. A move into television fiction production turned out to be a triumph, however. The Grundy company was on its way to being a devisor and originator of programme formats, while continuing to import quiz-show formats. More new markets were opening in Australian television, and Reg Grundy Enterprises would expand its operation to help fill that demand. One of its new programmes was entitled *Moneymakers*, and the name characterized what was happening with the company. This chapter investigates the further consolidation and expansion of the Grundy operation. Reg Grundy was now a millionaire several times over, but he was eager to embrace further business openings. The company was beginning to eye off opportunities beyond the Australian market, and Grundy's second marriage had given the producer and company owner a companion as eager for overseas business and social adventures as he was.

Background developments

Before looking at happenings in the Grundy's television operation and the way that it was responding to new business opportunities, it is again useful to outline the broader context within which this development was occurring. This can be approached first in terms of shifts occurring in society at large, and second by examining developments more specific to media industries, especially Australian television. The most significant backdrop had to do with finance. The Australian economy continued to revel in the affluence brought about by the long post-World War II boom, even if that wave of prosperity was coming to an end ('Long Boom' 1998: 399). The good times themselves had not always guaranteed economic prosperity for the working population as a whole. The 1970s saw a downturn in the economy from 1970 to 1971 as well as the first oil crisis in 1974. However, business activity picked up after each of these slumps.

Socially, different ideological currents were washing across the nation (Moran 1991: 82–88). The consensual view of Australian society that previously had been taken for granted was being eroded, and a different view of what constituted the national spirit was being articulated in its place (Moran 1991: 82–88; Craven 1989: 1–35). This was due to a concomitant pluralism, an increasing advocacy of multiculturalism and a greater liberalism – 'a new permissiveness', as the popular media put it. Authority and certitudes came under scrutiny and were in many ways found wanting (Moran 1991: 84–86). Coincident with, or at least linked to, this was an assertion of a more 'nationalist' or 'Australian' outlook, as opposed to both an older British Commonwealth perspective and a more recent 'Americanized' or 'internationalist' perspective (Moran 1991: 89–90). This new nationalism was seen to be tied to the election to government of the Australian Labor Party, a momentous event that ended the reign of a conservative coalition that had been in power since 1949 ('Long Boom' 1998: 311–14).

Change had been afoot since the mid- to late 1960s, and the early 1970s saw its acceleration, including in the field of Australian media. Government support for the Australian feature-film production industry in the 1970s would see it produce artistically significant film on the one hand and commercially viable works on the other (Jacka 1993: 72–85). Television production was seen to be one of the general beneficiaries of this development, with the new feature-film production industry providing investment finance, personnel training and new market opportunities to broadcasters and programme packagers, as well as newly emergent film production companies (O'Regan 1992: 15–44). Two other administrative moves by government also had implications for the television industry. The first was a new readiness on the part of government to take more notice of media in general and television in particular (Hall 1976: 14–21). The overseeing of Australian television was taken away from the Postmaster General's Department and allocated first to a Department of Communications and then to a Department of the Media. In 1972–73, the new government and the Department of the Media, prompted by the apparent failure of the 0–10 Network to achieve profitability, was thought to be considering taking away the licences of stations in this third commercial television network and reallocating them to form a second public-service television network (Hall 1976: 34). This never eventuated, however.

The Australian government did intervene in the area of programme production and broadcasting, by introducing a Points System in 1973 for programmes broadcast by commercial television stations (Cunningham 1993: 25; Moran 1985: 33). It modified an existing program-content broadcast system that had not differentiated between programme types but only required that a certain number of broadcast hours be locally produced. The Points System, by contrast, differentiated by allocating points to different genres of output and required that they meet particular scores or targets; it thus discriminated in favour of specific programme forms. Drama was most valuable under this system, while quiz and game shows secured far fewer points. This had important consequences for a company that specialized in this genre of programming. Increasingly shy of media exposure, Reg Grundy had one of his senior producers, Bill Mason, appear on a current affairs programme to voice the company's opposition. As Mason put it some time later:

> I went on *This Day Tonight* back in those days to argue that the emphasis on Australian drama would represent a severe blow to our company in the game show area. And in fact we reduced our staff from 250 to forty in a period of two or three months. We sunk down to about ten hours (of program output) a week overnight. It was that which forced us into the drama area.
>
> (Mason 1980)

There were other developments afoot in the television industry that also affected Reg Grundy Services. One of these had to do with a stabilization of the Australian television sector as a whole. The wave of television station start-ups that had begun in 1956 had come to an end, with some 98 per cent of the population now able to access the service. No new commercial stations in either metropolitan or regional centres began during this period. In addition, there was also a stabilization of the economies of the 0–10 Network with the enormous ratings success of its soap opera drama, *Number 96*, between 1972 and 1976 that helped move it out of harm's way so far as government intervention was concerned (Moran 1993: 319–29; Moran & Keating 2007: 283; Kingsley 1989: 266–71). Another shift in the industry involved a changing of the guard in terms of senior management, including programme executives. Those in the new generation of executives that came forward were more open to Grundy's salesmanship than some of their predecessors, so the company soon was busier than ever. Another change involved continuing movement away from the system of recruiting major programme sponsorship in favour of the system of 'spot' advertising (Rutherford 2004: 28–32). This system appealed to advertisers because it helped spread their message, allowed stations to charge more overall, and therefore was likely to increase the demand for locally produced programming.

A final shift in commercial television by the early 1970s was the increasing acceptance of programme packagers by commercial broadcasters. The belief of the early to mid-1950s that most Australian content would be produced in-house had given way to another arrangement whereby networks and stations outsourced most of their programming requirements to independent programme packagers. The production of news, sporting broadcasts and other kinds of factual programmes was retained by broadcasters, but they were also happy to farm out quiz shows, drama and some other types of programming to experienced packagers. Reg Grundy Enterprises had been one of the pioneers of independent production, but now the company had many rivals. One last development was the move by the commercial broadcasters towards 'strip' weekday programming, the practice of screening the same show each weekday in the same timeslot – in this instance, in the early evening zone (Moran & Keating 2003: 331–32). The change regularized and systematically varied what was on offer before peak broadcasting started. News and quiz shows were now joined by nightly half-hour current affairs and drama serials, produced by independent packagers. Reg Grundy Services could not pass up this expanding market opportunity.

Company growth: distribution

If Australia – including its television service – was changing, so too was Reg Grundy Enterprises. Various resources were added between 1969 and 1974 that helped turn the group into a fledgling conglomerate with offshore transnational ambitions. These related to programme distribution, the acquisition of more company office space, the addition of more technical capacity and the recruitment of specialist staff. As always, though, there were some initiatives that led nowhere.

By this time, Reg Grundy Services was beginning to think about the systematic marketing of its programmes. The great majority of these were remakes of US quiz and game show formats, so there was little chance of distributing such content outside Australia. Besides, until around 1974, most of these programmes had been recorded in black and white, which further militated against any overseas sales. There was a potential market in regional Australia, however. Around 1971, Reg Grundy hit upon the idea of licensing his programmes to other commercial television broadcasters, whether in the other state capital cities or in regional cities. The commissioning station or network was happy to agree to this arrangement because Grundy would handle this distribution and split whatever revenue was acquired (Grundy 2010: 134–36). In fact, in at least one instance with the highly successful *Moneymakers*, the 0–10 Network was so pleased with the program's performance that it allowed Grundy to retain all fees paid by country stations (Grundy 2010: 132–33).

Reg Grundy Services worked with a freelance Sydney distributor, Max Dutch, who was paid a 15 per cent fee for programme licensings. The company was producing five quiz shows for the 0–10 Network at the time, so that one of the first programmes to go into this kind of syndication was *Blind Date*, which was sold on to Adelaide, Perth and a string of regional city stations (Grundy 2010: 131–33). Altogether, the regional programme distribution was a most successful venture. Not only did it put more black ink on the books, but it also confirmed that valuable transnational distribution opportunities would probably open up once Australian television had moved to colour recording and Reg Grundy Services had drama series and serials to distribute.

Changing locations

As the previous chapter has anticipated, Grundy's offices began to spread as the company's business expanded. The Sydney headquarters changed its address twice, and there was also a need for production offices in three other state capitals. Since 1965, Reg Grundy Services had been increasingly peripatetic, so it took these changes in its stride. In any case, Grundy himself now preferred to work from home while moves were also afoot to establish offices in the United States as part of an extended preparation for entering the US network television market. Chapter 5 noted Reg Grundy Enterprises' move to relocate its Sydney production office to Miller Street in North Sydney. The site was a short distance away from the TCN9 studios and this saved having to cross the Sydney Harbour Bridge from the Double Bay apartment where the company began. After more than ten years at Miller Street, the operation moved to another North Sydney location at Arthur Street in 1971. By 1974, the Sydney operation had outgrown these premises, however. A new drama division, for example, needed to be housed a little further north in the growing retail hub of Chatswood. Reg Grundy himself was working from home so that the office situation caused him little bother. His senior staff found the dispersal to be a problem, however. A suitable building available for sale was found on the Pacific Highway at Artarmon in the geographic triangle of Sydney's televisionland (Moran 2010: 343–56). It was immediately purchased. The compact, two-storey structure was very convenient to all three commercial television stations, and Grundy House came into being – although fewer and fewer ordinary staffers ever saw the company's principal.

Grundy had by then moved with his new wife into a grand old house located some distance north from the company office, on Pittwater. There was little space between Grundy's business and personal life by this stage, so the house functioned as both residence and office, with Grundy devoting a good deal of time to watching his own recent programmes for quality control purposes (Weston 1995; Drummond 1995). A large theatre-like area, complete with projection booth, had been constructed for this purpose. It was soon joined by videotape players and television screens. Business meetings took place in the residence, as did television industry-based parties and other social events.

There were additional Grundy offices elsewhere. The upsurge in local production in Brisbane that had begun in 1965 has already been noted. In the period 1969–74, Reg Grundy Enterprises sold quiz and other programmes to all the Brisbane stations (Beck 1984: 188–91), so there was a continuing need for this production office. The same was true in Melbourne and Adelaide, where Grundy supplied programmes to all three commercial television stations in each city, some for broadcast to a statewide audience and others for national broadcast by interstate members of the particular network. Initiatives were also in train to secure offices in the United States, in both New York and Los Angeles, although this move would not actually come to fruition until 1979. Nevertheless, Reg Grundy had been making regular US visits since 1966 for format-spotting purposes, and was beginning to develop the contacts who would help him set up North American offices for an intended US expansion (Holmes 1980; Weston 1995; Grundy 2010: 104–05).

One of these was Bob Crystal, who originally had worked in the New York music publishing business, followed by seven years with singing star Doris Day's Hollywood company (Crystal 1995). Arriving in Australia on behalf of Dean Martin, Crystal produced several *Tonight* shows starring US entertainer Tommy Leonetti for ATN7. Returning to Los Angeles in 1970, Crystal undertook various entertainment-related activities, including US distribution of the format for a television panel-talk show, *Beauty and the Beast*, which ATN7 had originated (Murphy 1981: 80). By early 1973, Crystal had been introduced to Grundy and had agreed to become the company's West Coast representative. A Los Angeles office of sorts seems to have been established around this time (Grundy 2010: 134–35).

Company growth: OB cameras and van

Another venture of Reg Grundy Enterprises in its bid for diversification was the acquisition of a facility for outside broadcasting. In 1972–73, the company purchased an Outside Broadcasting (OB) van (Day 1980: 58; Drummond 1995; Culliton 2009). The vehicle was fitted out with colour video cameras and recording equipment, supplied by Dutch electronics giant Phillips, and rumoured to have cost more than $100,000 to put on the road (Toohey 1973: 2). Beyond signalling that company coffers were buoyant, it was a little unclear just why the acquisition had gone ahead. Still, the move could be justified. Australian television was still on the black-and-white image system, but a changeover to colour was expected sooner or later (Donnelly 2004: 554–55). After all, television systems in the United States, United Kingdom and Canada had already switched from black and white to colour. The Grundy company was eager to get ahead in the anticipated world of colour television, and was said to be planning a variety series for world release (Toohey 1973: 2). Colour video recording and editing were essential for such a purpose, even though Australian commercial television stations had not yet begun to purchase and introduce colour facilities. Further, by housing such a facility in an OB van, the company also hoped to switch the facility to other uses when it was not in demand for variety and drama production (Culliton 1995, 2009).

These plans mostly came to nought. The facility was sent to Melbourne, where it was involved in filming a one-hour special for the Seven Network, *Keep Smiling*, featuring Tony Barber, the host/star of Seven's very successful quiz show, *The Great Temptation*. A six-month trial contract was also arranged with the Sydney Turf Club and the Australian Jockey Club to videotape horseracing each Wednesday and Saturday for closed-circuit broadcasting at their Sydney and Melbourne racecourse venues (Toohey 1973: 2; Culliton 2009). The horseracing recording contract was not renewed. Plans to record trotting and greyhound racing meetings also did not eventuate. Hence the van was sold and the venture was soon forgotten (Culliton 2009).

Company growth: an abortive merger

Company expansion can occur not only through the acquisition of specialists experienced in new areas that expand business capacity but also through merger with other firms, especially those with complementary capacities (Gomery 2004: 1479–82). In 1974, as foreshadowed in the last chapter, Reg Grundy boldly contemplated an amalgamation that would have made the resulting production company a giant in Australian commercial television. He suggested to Hector Crawford, principal of Crawford Productions, that they merge their companies (Grundy 2010: 226–27). The suggestion made good business sense because Crawford Productions and Reg Grundy Services matched rather than overlapped each other. Crawford had always been based in Melbourne, with a background in music and drama (Moran 2004b: 627–28). In 1974, the company was riding high with four crime series in production, together with a sitcom, a variety programme and a soap opera on air (Moran 1993: 516–19). Grundy was located primarily in Sydney, with its core strength lying in the area of quiz and game shows.

Perhaps the only factor militating against the Crawford-Grundy merger was the fact that the Australian commercial networks might have been wary of such a giant and switched their programme commissioning to other, smaller production companies. The matter was never put to the test, however. Reg Grundy put the merger offer to Hector Crawford but the latter declined the marriage proposal (Grundy 2010: 221–23). Interestingly, as will be seen in Chapter 10, Reg Grundy would make a similar merger suggestion to a US game show devisor and producer, Mark Goodson, almost two decades later (Grundy 2010: 213–14). This later proposal would also fail to come to anything.

Company growth: Sydney recruits

Grundy was bent on expansion and diversification, and had the cash flow to support these ambitions. Rather than developing new capacities from scratch, company thinking was to buy in experienced personnel to speed up the process. Accordingly, in the early to mid-1970s, a significant number of television production professionals were persuaded to join Reg Grundy Enterprises in Sydney. These newcomers were a diverse bunch, overlapping so far as their arrival times were concerned. There were three different groups: a trio of Sydney-based independent producers, a string of former employees from Crawford Productions in Melbourne, and a more diverse Anglo-Australian diasporic collection. Each deserves further mention.

The producers who accepted exclusive personal services contracts with Reg Grundy Enterprises in 1973–74 were Robert Bruning, Roger Mirams and Ron McLean. All three were experienced professionals, who had solid production records both as independents and under contract to other companies (Moran 1993: 524–25, 538–40). Bruning had been an actor, writer and producer, and had appeared as the lead in an ill-fated police series, *The Long Arm* (1970), for ATV0 in Melbourne. Moving to Sydney, he set up his own company, Gemini Productions, producing and appearing in a successful half-hour situation comedy for Nine entitled *The Godfathers* (1971). He then concentrated on production on his next two projects. The first was an ambitious, hour-long police/crime series, Nine's *The Spoiler* (1972), which was axed after thirteen weeks. The second was a *Godfathers* spin-off situation comedy, *The People Next Door* (1973), which proved to be less successful than the original. Thus, the call for Gemini Productions to join Reg Grundy Television came at an opportune time for Bruning.

The other two independents had already produced two drama series together, although they would pursue their own projects while working under the Grundy umbrella. The older, more experienced figure was Roger Mirams. He had been involved in photography during World War II and had moved to Australia from New Zealand, setting up a

Melbourne-based advertising agency after serving as an official photographer at the Olympic Games in Melbourne in 1956 (Moran 1985: 65–71). Various children's television programmes followed, including a colour-film series for Screen Gems, *Adventures of the Sea Spray* (1966), which involved extensive location shooting in the Pacific (Perry 1991: 66). Meanwhile, Ron McLean was primarily a drama series writer, having broken into television in the drama boom that had developed in both Melbourne and Sydney after 1965 (Moran 1985). By the early 1970s, McLean had seen a large number of scripts go before the cameras for series such as *Homicide* and *The Rovers*. Mirams was producer on the latter, and he and McLean decided to work together. Their first venture was *Spy Force*, a World War II espionage series set in the Pacific (Moran 1993: 4334). Paramount Pictures was a major investor, with Mirams acting as producer and McLean churning out scripts for most of the 43 hour-long episodes. The series had a relatively successful airing on the Nine Network in 1971. Then followed another drama series, *Silent Number*, a calculated gamble to cash in on the popularity of crime and medical dramas by concentrating on the doings of a police doctor (Moran 1993: 415–16). The duo used an old company registered to Mirams, South Pacific Productions, to produce the series, with Mirams and McLean acting as joint producers, and McLean writing the episodes. However, the series' production contract with the Nine Network was not renewed after the first thirteen hour-long episodes, and *Silent Number* played off without fanfare in 1974. By then, Mirams and McLean had joined the Grundy company alongside Bruning. These three independents could pursue their own projects under the company umbrella, as well as being involved more directly in company-initiated projects when this suited. Subsequent chapters trace this trio's contribution to the Grundy output.

Company growth: Crawford recruits

Grundy's fiction production was also swelled by a loose group of production professionals who had cut their teeth at Crawford Productions in Melbourne. As early as November 1973, Reg Grundy Enterprises could announce that it had snared script editor and writer John Edwards from Crawford's to head up storylining, script editing and writing for Grundy's first drama serial, *Class of '74*. By then, Crawford's had become a mini-Hollywood programme factory, employing several hundred staff. At the time, it had up to four hour-long crime series, a weekly variety programme and a feature film in production, together with a situation comedy and a soap opera in preparation (Moran 1985: 89109). This made it an excellent training ground for new writers, directors, technicians, assistants, production managers and many others where they learned and refine their craft. A number of these professionals were attracted to freelance work in Sydney from the early 1970s onwards.

Sydney was proving to be the centre of production for the new government-supported feature-film industry (Moran 2010: 343–56). It also acted as a magnet for television drama production, with the outstanding success of *Number 96* from 1972 to 1976 (Moran &

Keating 2007: 283). Grundy's imminent move into drama production also acted as a further inducement to former Crawford employees to journey north. The majority of these migrating professionals simply swelled a Sydney pool of talent into which Reg Grundy Services could dip as various fiction projects got underway. Apart from Edwards, the only other ex-Crawford employee needing mention is Don Battye (Battye 1980), a skilled producer and script editor with experience in drama series and serials who joined Grundy as a contract employee in 1975 and would remain there for the next decade. Edwards and Battye, not to mention Bruning, Mirams and McLean, had numerous contacts among former Crawford employees, so that it was not surprising to find many of them staffing key production roles in the drama series and serials that would soon begin to roll out from Reg Grundy Enterprises.

Company growth: Anglo-Australian connections

Although US network television had been the source of many new Grundy quiz shows over the past dozen years or more, nevertheless the company found it just as congenial and obvious to pursue business opportunities and needs on the European side of the Atlantic. There were close industry connections between UK and Australian television, especially between the BBC and ABC, and between ATV and the Seven Network (Cunningham & Jacka 1996: 121–46). There were also links at the individual and social levels. The colonial connection meant that many more Australians had tended to head to the United Kingdom and Europe rather than to the United States, for work, study or cultural reasons (1996: 121–29). If anything, this flow had increased in the second half of the 1960s, with airlines cutting travel time and an affluent Australian economy making the costs of a plane ticket more affordable. By 1970, there was a sizeable contingent of Australians in London and nearby cities who had backgrounds in journalism, film production, documentary-making and television production, and who might be willing to return to Australia. Alongside these, there were television professionals born in the United Kingdom who might also be lured to Sydney to work on productions for Reg Grundy Services.

One early example of the possibilities engendered by this professional cross-current was the recruitment of John Culliton after his return to Australia from the BBC in 1968 (Culliton 2009). Previously, he had worked as an ATN7 cameraman before becoming a studio director up until 1964, then undertaking a four-year stint at the BBC. He joined Reg Grundy Enterprises, where he remained as producer until 1973. Culliton would also have been a valuable source of information about other experienced Australians working in media industries in the United Kingdom.

Grundy's most important UK connection was probably Bruce Gyngell (Jacka 2003: 1045–48). Gyngell had become general manager of TCN9 in 1966, but had left in 1969 after a falling-out with network owner Sir Frank Packer. Grundy encountered him again as sympathetic general manager of the Seven Network, but Gyngell left Seven in 1972 to join Sir Lew Grade at the ATV Network in the United Kingdom (Pickering 2004a: 1017–19), first as producer and programmer, then as heir apparent in 1973. Gyngell resigned once he realized that Grade had no intention of retiring (Pickering 2004a). He remained in the United Kingdom for the next three years, as a film company manager and freelance producer (Jacka 2003: 101–09). Reg Grundy was in contact with him, and probably shared with Gyngell his company's urgent need to buy in production expertise for its intended move into drama (Toohey 1973: 2; Grundy 2010: 117, 178).

One of these recruits was another expatriate, Ken Hannam. The latter had also been an early employee at ATN7 in 1956, and had been one of the two directors on the first two soap operas produced in-house there. He worked freelance for the BBC, directing *The Troubleshooters, Dr Finlay's Casebook* and *Paul Temple*. Hannan seems to have been recruited by Reg Grundy Services, and was expected to start work in Sydney late in 1973 (*TV Week* 1973: 4). The appointment was not taken up, however. Instead, in 1974, Reg Grundy Services pulled off a recruitment coup by signing another Australian expatriate.

Reg Watson was born in Brisbane in the late 1920s and had planned to become an actor (Watson 1980). Arriving in Britain in the early 1950s, he found himself working in commercial television after the end of the public-service BBC monopoly in 1955. Watson joined Midlands Television, the fledgling ATV commercial television company owned by former theatrical showman Lew Grade, in Birmingham as a writer and then producer. One of his important early credits involved directing personality and actor Noele Gordon in a popular live midday chat show, *Lunchbox*. In 1964, Grade decided to launch an evening soap opera, following the success of Granada's twice-a-week serial *Coronation Street*, which had begun in 1960. Gordon was brought over from the talk show and Watson went too, as producer, director and eventually writer (Gordon 1975: 144). The new serial was called *Crossroads*, and Watson made the crucial decision to produce and broadcast the programme five evenings a week, a pattern already known to the British audience through daily radio serials. Later, the programme ran four nights a week (Hobson 1982: Moran & Keating 2007: 278–79).

Negotiations between Grundy and Watson seem to have taken place in 1973, so that by early 1974 Watson was taking up a new position in Sydney with Reg Grundy Enterprises as executive producer and head of drama serials. Watson did not come alone. One of the senior producers at ATV, Alan Coleman, had trained as a director under Watson and had worked on *Crossroads* for eight years (Coleman 2009). Coleman was recruited as a drama serial director, and joined Reg Grundy Services in mid-1974. The ATV exodus did not end there. Three other freelancers – friends of Watson and members of the same family – also came to jobs in wardrobe and stage managing on Grundy's serials (Watson 1980).

These ATV recruits were the most important new Grundy staff to be garnered from the Anglo-Australian connection. Nonetheless, two other staff signings also deserve brief mention. Ted Morrisby had trained as a journalist in Sydney before going to London, where he worked as researcher for the BBC current affairs magazine programme *Whicker's World* (Morrisby 1988; Pickering 2004b: 2530–37). From 1965 to 1972, he pursued a successful career in independent documentary film production. Bruce Beresford was younger, having been born in Sydney in 1940 (Moran & Vieth 2005: 29). He directed several short films in

Sydney before working as a filmmaker at both the British Film Institute and the Rhodesian Film Unit. The Australian government's decision to establish a feature-film production industry brought him back to Australia, where he managed to write and direct his first feature film, *The Adventures of Barry McKenzie* (1972). Waiting for other film projects to get up, he joined Morrisby in a new documentary production unit that Grundy had just established. Meanwhile, there was plenty of other production occurring in the company.

Grundy quiz shows: casualties and champions

In the early 1970s, and despite a downturn in the Australian economy in 1970–71, there was an expanding demand for programming supplied by Reg Grundy Enterprises. All three Australian commercial television networks were now happy to buy from the company. Stations in the minor state capital cities were also eager customers. Reg Grundy's willingness to become involved in the production of other kinds of light entertainment programme packaging, outside quiz and game shows, had been signalled in the late 1960s when it produced a 'tonight' show, *In Town Tonight*, for TEN10 (1967–68) and a women's magazine programme, *Women's World*, for BTQ7 (1969) in Brisbane. The ambition strengthened within a few years, so an output inventory needs to examine other forms of entertainment programming and a series of ventures into feature-film production, whether for the big or small screen. Additionally, a major new programming initiative was added in 1974 with the debut of Grundy's first evening drama serial.

Quiz and game shows for all three Australian commercial television networks underwrote the costs of these new packaging gambles. As suggested above, the landscape of Australian television quiz, panel and game shows changed considerably in the period between 1969–70 and 1975 (Moran & Keating 2007: 29). Older, more avuncular quiz-show hosts disappeared in favour of more youthful, effervescent and friendlier compères. The two long-running, big prize evening quiz shows, *Pick-a-Box* and *Coles $7000 Question*, with their major sponsorships, came to an end. The way was cleared for the Australian television game show to undergo a metamorphosis, whereby particular programmes could be stripped five times a week, appearing in an early evening timeslot that became known as 'Access Prime Time' (Moran & Keating 2003: 25–28). Such programmes were especially lucrative when shown by the different stations in a national networking arrangement. Reg Grundy Services was particularly suited to take advantage of this development. Having fine-tuned its craft, experience and skill as a quiz-show packager in the 1960s in daytime television, and more occasionally night-time television, the company could now step forward with new, attractive and up-to-date quiz-show formats that already had aired on US network television. It could also reach back for older US quiz-show champion formats, knowing that a change of title, decor, contestant rules, host or prizes might also work wonders.

The result was that Reg Grundy Enterprises shortly became busier than ever. The early 1970s saw it producing up to fifteen hours of quiz shows each week (Toohey 1973: 2–3), while a title check shows that it packaged more than 25 different quiz, panel and game shows in this period. Some of these game shows had only a brief life – often whether they returned less or more profit to the company coffers depended on whether they were produced at a station in a minor state capital city or a major state capital (Moran & Keating 2003: 22–25). Brisbane remained a significant minor state capital city television market, and the company could reach into its own archive to produce new adaptations of old favourites, such as *Wheel of Fortune* in 1970 (Moran & Keating 2003: 131) and *Name That Tune* the following year (Moran & Keating 2003: 98) for daily daytime broadcast on BTQ7. The next year saw the company producing a new format entitled *What Do You Know?* (Moran & Keating 2003: 129) for the same station's afternoon line-up. Some game shows in the major markets of Sydney and Melbourne came and went just as quickly as those in the minor markets had done. Among the latter were the once-weekly *Tell the Truth* (1971) for TEN10 (Moran & Keating 2003: 122), a brief attempt to resuscitate *(Coles) $7000 Question* for HSV7 in 1971 after the programme had shifted from sponsorship to 'spot' advertising (Moran & Keating 2003: 61), *Tell the Truth* for the same station that same year (Moran & Keating 2003: 1212) and *Blind Date* for ATV0 in 1974 (Moran & Keating 2003: 54). *Lucky Seven* also had a 1970 outing for ATN7 (Moran & Keating 2003: 90).

Beyond these casualties, there were more durable programmes, lasting more than a season even if they were not ratings bonanzas. Again, both Brisbane and Adelaide proved to be fertile markets for daytime and evening game show commissions for the company. *Beat the Odds* was made for BTQ7 between 1971 and 1972 as a daily daytime programme, and the children's quiz show *Big Challenge* ran from 1966 to 1971 on the same station (Moran & Keating 2003: 51–52). Meanwhile, Reg Grundy Enterprises' good relationship with QTQ9 continued. *Password* appeared each weekday in 1972–73 (Moran & Keating 2003: 103), while the panel game *I've Got a Secret* continued to appeared twice weekly until 1975. Mention was made in the previous chapter about the supposed 'romance' between two panelists, Ron Cadee and Joy Chambers, but the 1971 disclosure of Chambers' marriage to Reg Grundy did nothing to dampen the Queensland popularity of the programme and of Chambers herself.

Instead, QTQ9 proceeded to commission another panel show, *Funny You Should Ask* (Moran & Keating 2003: 72), which again starred the Cadee Chambers duo and ran from 1972 to 1974. Meanwhile, the company was also busy in Adelaide, where it produced a new version of *Concentration* for ADS7 between 1973 and 1974 (Moran & Keating 2003). Two other game shows were even more notable. The first was the South Australian version of the Goodson-Todman format, *I've Got a Secret*. As Chapter 6 noted, this began on SAS10 in 1966 and was to run until 1969 when it was cancelled. Reg Grundy was not prepared to admit defeat, and succeeded in reselling the panel show to rival station ADS7, where it would continue on air until 1974. In fact, when it could, Reg Grundy Services made a practice of reselling a cancelled show to a rival network or station. It would notably pull off such a coup with the drama serial *Neighbours* in 1986, as we will see in Chapter 10. In the period under review here, it also did it with the quiz show, *Three on a Match* (Moran & Keating 2003). This was an adaptation of a 1971 NBC daytime quiz show, devised by Bob Stewart

Productions (Schwartz, Ryan & Wosbrook 1987). In 1972, Grundy produced an Australian version for Adelaide station ADS7. The contract was not renewed, so the company sold the show to SAS10, which ran it from 1973 to 1975. *Three on a Match* had one other claim to fame because the company was looking to the inauguration of colour transmission, and this programme was its first to be recorded in colour.

In addition to these BAPH city commissions, there were more lucrative sales in Sydney and Melbourne, making a busy company even busier. Again, there were new US formats as well as old favourites. Among the former was *Split Second* for TCN9 in 1972–73 (Moran & Keating 2003: 118). This was a 'pricing' game show format derived from a Hatos-Hall original that had debuted on the US ABC Network a short time earlier (Schwartz, Ryan & Wosbrook 1987: 418–20). Additionally, there was *Gambit*, a combination of a quiz show and the card game '21', also for TCN9, produced in 1973–74 (Moran & Keating 2003: 72) and based on a 1972 format of the same name devised by Heatter-Quigley appearing on US CBS Network in 1972 (Schwartz, Ryan & Wosbrook 1987: 476–77). The unsuccessful *Split Second* had featured long-time Grundy host Jimmy Hannan as compère, but Hannan was to have much more success with another Grundy offering, *Spending Spree* (Moran & Keating 2003: 116). This ran from 1971 to 1974 on a daily daytime basis, and was a revamped version of *Say When* from almost ten years earlier.

As Chapter 5 noted, *Say When* had been a Grundy adaptation of a Goodson-Todman-devised format, and its new outing as *Spending Spree* was only one of several Grundy recyclings of formats deriving from the most successful US quiz-show format originating companies that took place between 1969 and 1975. Several of these formats have already been mentioned: *Concentration*, *I've Got a Secret*, *Password* and *Tell the Truth (What's My Line?)*. Another format from the same stable became the basis of a true Grundy game show champion of this period. This was *The Price is Right*, another 'pricing' show that Goodson-Todman had devised and first produced for the US NBC Network in 1956 (Schwartz, Ryan & Wosbrook 1987: 372–77). Grundy's adaptation for ATV0 in 1973 and 1974 proved to be enormously popular, stripped as a half-hour programme in an early evening time slot as well as a one-hour-a-day version appearing five times a week (Moran & Keating 2003: 109).

Two other quiz-show remakes were even more remarkable. The fact that these came not from Goodson-Todman but from other US quiz-show devisors and packagers highlighted Reg Grundy's genius in spotting promising formats and producing highly successful Australian versions. Grundy draws attention to both formats in his memoir, thereby underscoring their importance to the company (2010: 128–33). The first was *Moneymakers*, a quiz show where contestants chose questions that gave them points on a board that then provided the opportunity to win large cash prizes (Moran & Keating 2003: 96). The programme originally was produced for one of the Brisbane broadcasters, TVQ0, and was based on a US predecessor, *Money Makers*, which had gone to air in syndication having been devised by TeleColumn (Schwartz, Ryan & Wosbrook 1987: 304–05). The Grundy version immediately began making a good deal of money for the packager. It was the first quiz show on Australian television to be stripped five evenings a week, appearing on air in a 7.00 p.m.

timeslot. Within months, *Moneymakers* had become a national show, having been picked up by network affiliate stations in Sydney, Melbourne and Adelaide. It was to run until 1973. More remarkably, Grundy also spun off three further versions for children under the title of *Junior Moneymakers* (Moran & Keating 2003: 86). These versions were produced as 7.30 p.m. Sunday-night specials for TVQ0 in Brisbane, ATV0 in Melbourne and SAS10 in Adelaide.

The other formats spotted by Grundy and remade for Australian broadcast would ultimately become the company's champion of champions so far as quiz shows was concerned. The format began life as *Sale of the Century* on the US NBC Network in 1969, having been devised and produced by Jones-Howard Productions (Schwartz, Ryan & Wosbrook 1987: 396). Grundy saw the pilot for the latter and successfully pitched it to Bruce Gyngell, who was by then general manager at the Seven Network. A major sponsor was acquired and a stripped weekday version went to air (Grundy 2010: 123–30). Various changes had been made to the original, including its visual appearance, title and host. In mid-1970, *Temptation* began on ATN7 and the Seven Network, compèred by breezy, engaging newcomer Tony Barber. It became an immense hit, with various 60-minute specials also appearing, and was to run until 1974 (Moran & Keating 2003: 122). Better still, it also forced its way into the Network's evening schedule. The trigger for this was not only its high daytime ratings, but the fact that ATN7's long-running *Pick-a-Box* came to an end in mid-1971, with the retirement of its producer-host Bob Dyer. To safeguard its early evening timeslot and maintain a quiz-show audience, Seven decided to run a night-time version of *Temptation*, which was titled *The Great Temptation*, retaining Barber as the compère and increasing the value of prizes (Moran & Keating 2003: 76). By mid-1972, the night-time title had been further varied to *$25,000 Great Temptation*.

The impact of all these programmes on the bottom line of the company was immense. Between 1971 and 1973, three Grundy quiz-show giants *Spending Spree* on the Nine Network, *The Great Temptation* on the Seven Network and *Moneymakers* on the 0–10 Network were competing directly with each other on weeknights. In addition, two of these had spin-off programmes in the shape of the weekday daytime versions of *Temptation* and the weekly, one-hour children's special, *Junior Moneymakers*. Reg Grundy Services had no real competition in the area of Australian quiz shows anymore. It needed to look beyond the genre to other areas of programme production if it was to continue growing. Hence, as early as October 1971, it would announce that it planned to expand into the more lucrative area of drama production (*TV Week* 1971: 7).

The drama of soap opera

In fact, it would take a little longer for Reg Grundy Services to pick up a commission to produce fiction television. Nonetheless, the signs were positive. In 1972, a market emerged in Australian commercial television for a new form of drama with the overwhelming success of the soap opera *Number 96* (1972–76) (Moran & Keating 2007: 383). Serial fiction had already been tried twice by broadcaster ATN7, but without success. The sudden popularity of the racy *Number 96* meant not only that a market for stripped drama had been created, but that packagers without a background in fiction production stood a chance of getting into this new arena. In 1973, probably on the basis of its excellent recent track record with the Seven Network, particularly with *Temptation* and *The Great Temptation*, Reg Grundy Enterprises signed a deal to produce an early evening drama serial for stripping five days a week. The company moved a senior quiz-show producer to the new area and, as already mentioned, also managed to lure writer John Edwards away from Crawford Productions in Melbourne to act as script editor for what was to become *Class of '74* (Moran 1993: 117–19). What the company lacked was a senior producer with a background in serial drama who might oversee the production. Instead, existing Grundy producers with backgrounds in the game show genre had to fill the gap for the time being in order to get the new serial off the ground. As I mentioned above, help was on the way in the form of ex-*Crossroads* executives Alan Coleman and especially Reg Watson.

As its name implies, *Class of '74* was set in a high school, and traced the intertwining lives of teachers, general staff, older students and parents. It was earmarked for screening immediately after ATN7's main evening news, and aimed at capturing younger as well as older viewers. The serial was moderately successful, and in its first year on air managed to gain good ratings. Ironically, one of its side effects had been to persuade the Seven Network to cancel *The Great Temptation* to free up the timeslot. This was far from the only occasion when one Grundy programme competed directly against another as its share of Australian television programming across all three networks continued to increase.

Coleman arrived in 1974 and Watson came some months later. These arrivals were in time to help establish a more efficient system of production planning for the programme, which was already in production, but not to influence key decisions that had been made. In fact, whether deserved or not, *Class of '74* was in trouble with the Australian Broadcasting Control Board over what could be said and seen on screen (Moran 1993: 119). The production company and broadcaster decided to make some radical changes to what became *Class of '75* the following year. Many members of the cast were replaced. A decision was also taken to inject more comedy into proceedings. Unfortunately, the changes led to a significant fall-off in ratings and on behalf of the Seven Network, ATN7 cancelled the serial.

Despite its brief time on air, *Class of '74/75* could by no means be dismissed as a failure. A total of 290 half-hour colour episodes were produced, which represented a useful start for Grundy's drama catalogue for international programme distribution. Producers, directors, technicians and others used to working on game shows had made a credible effort in the new genre of soap opera, while Coleman and Watson's arrival meant that Reg Grundy Services was more professionally equipped for the next drama serial commissioning. Programming casualties were a fact of life in the commercial television industry, so Reg Grundy Services had a reasonable expectation that other drama commissions would come its way. As the next two chapters will show, these sales did indeed materialize for a company that would soon show itself to be a master of the genre.

Feature films: pilots, documentaries and *Bazza*

The Grundy group also became involved in feature production, primarily intended for overseas as well as local media markets. The move was aimed at testing possible new business opportunities and gave rise to three separate ventures. The first was entirely incidental and involved television features or telemovies that had originated as two-hour drama series pilots. First cabs off the rank were *The Martins & the McCoys* and *Two-Way Mirror* in 1974. Neither pilot resulted in series commissions. Even so, they had been produced as telemovies in colour, so they became part of a growing Grundy drama catalogue. Before long, that fiction catalogue – including a larger bunch of pilots – would be available for licensing to broadcasters outside Australia.

The second venture was a short-lived documentary feature unit. It was headed by Ted Morrisby, who would work as producer with Bruce Beresford as film director. On joining Reg Grundy Services, Beresford wrote and directed the first of a planned series of feature-length documentary films, *The Wreck of the Batavia*. It was filmed off the West Australian coastline, and edited in Sydney at a reported total cost of $58 000 (Toohey 1973). A second documentary feature, *Poor Fella Me*, which Beresford both scripted and directed, then followed.

As producer and head of the documentary division, Morrisby set about the task of distribution. In late 1973, he was reported as visiting 21 countries to seek licensings for *Wreck of the Batavia* and to announce a further nine documentary projects, including *Poor Fella Me* and one concerning the early Australian convict colony of Port Jackson. *Batavia* was reportedly sold to Canadian, Mexican and Finnish television stations (Toohey 1973). It was becoming clear, however, that while the Australian Television Points System encouraged the production of documentary film for the home television market, the one-off nature of these made it difficult to distribute such films internationally. Morrisby seems to have left Reg Grundy Enterprises a short time later and resumed his overseas travels, writing and filmmaking (Morrisby 1988). The Grundy documentary unit was quietly disbanded.

The third venture was even more ambitious, and also involved Beresford. It was a feature film destined for cinema rather than television release. The film in question was a follow-up feature film to Beresford's very successful debut feature, the comedy *The Adventures of Barry McKenzie* (1972), which was based on the comic strip in the UK magazine *Private Eye*, depicting the comic adventures of a hapless Australian at large in London. Beresford had written the script with the co-author of the cartoon strip, expatriate Barry Humphries, and directed the film with Humphries appearing as one of his many comic personae, Edna Everage. The film was a popular and commercial success in both Australia and the United Kingdom, so Reg Grundy Enterprises was keen to finance a sequel.

Entitled *Barry McKenzie Holds His Own* (1974), the spin-off was scripted by Beresford and Humphries, with Beresford again directing (Pike & Cooper 1981: 425–26). The farce followed the hero from Sydney to London, Paris and Transylvania, and included a large contingent of actors of UK-based Australian origin or British actors who had worked in various Australian productions. Filming began in Sydney in late 1973 and continued there, as well as in London and Paris, with a premiere in late 1974. *Barry McKenzie Holds His Own* was reported to have cost $450 000, provided by Reg Grundy Enterprises, and did well at the box office. However, the company decided that, by and large, it was economically safer to stick to television production where broadcasters and not packagers bore the burden of the financial risks. There would be only one more venture into feature-film production, discussed in Chapter 8.

Other programmes

Finally, there was a string of other shows, further increasing the saturation of Australian commercial television with Grundy programmes to the point where they were competing against one another. In the last years of Australian black-and-white television transmission, the company made variety, specials, human-interest and advice, children's and music programmes alongside its quiz shows and drama serials. These were produced not for the major state capital city stations but for broadcast stations in Brisbane, Adelaide and even Australia's regional cities. A 1973 feature story about Reg Grundy Services suggested the existence of a variety show division producing some of these programmes (*TV Week* 1973: 14). A tally of these shows is as follows: *Anything Can Happen* (1972–73, ADS7), *Emergency Line* (1973–74, ADS7), *ESP and All That* (1971, BTQ7), *Heartline* (1971, BTQ7), *Hotline* (1970, BTQ7), *Hypnotism and All That* (1971, BTQ7), *Ideal Fun Day* (1970, QTQ9), *Martin St James* (1971, TVQ0), *Penthouse Club* (1972–75, ADS7), *The Ron Cadee Show* (1970, QTQ9) and *Travellin' Out West* (1972–79, NBN3).

The last of these warrants a little more detail, highlighting as it does the company's willingness to take on any production that was likely to generate profit. *Travellin' Out West* was an hour-long music show that featured bush music and country music and followed in the wake of forerunners in the 1960s (Smith 1984: 104). In fact, this music show was the only television series ever commissioned by Australia's 24 regional city commercial stations through their 'network' association, Australian Television Facilities (ATF) (Culliton 1995). With the imminent election of a federal Labor government in 1972, the regional television commercial stations had a need to re-emphasize their connections to their local audiences, even beyond replaying programmes produced in the state capital cities in such genres as news, quiz, variety and drama (Culliton 1995). Two episodes of *Travellin' Out West* were recorded each fortnight at NBN3 in Newcastle, the largest of the regional stations and 100 miles north of Sydney. Twice a year, one of the Grundy's producers would go on the road with a live version of the show. Regular performers supplied the music for these concerts. The Grundy RG label was revived so that LP records of parts of the concerts could be sold off through deals with the local regional television stations. These state tours were also important for Grundy's producers in terms of maintaining contact with local stations and audiences (History of Country Music website).

Family business: marriage and estrangement

A final disengagement between daughter and father happened somewhere during this time. There seems not to have been any initial disaffection. Grundy's memoir records that Kim was an eager assistant in helping to secure a dress for Joy's marriage to her father in late 1971 and that she attended the ceremony alongside her grandmother, Lillian (2010: 115). By then, Kim was in secondary school at the Sacred Heart College at Rose Bay in Sydney's eastern suburbs. This was a significant distance from where the Grundys lived, but the enrolment was maintained because Kim would have had many long-standing friends at the school who had, like her, come from the college's feeder primary school where her mother, Lola, had also attended school.

By 1974, larger changes were afoot in the Grundy domestic arrangements. After a second marriage ceremony with Joy in London as part of an around-the-world trip, Grundy had bought a fine stone house, complete with jetty, on Pittwater on the narrowing peninsula of Sydney's northern beaches. Kim was in her last year of secondary school and may have boarded at the Sacred Heart College during the week. The following year, Kim began an Arts degree at Sydney University. Her study included German. Coincidentally, that was one of several school subjects in which Reg Grundy had shone at St Peter's College almost 40 years earlier. Kim lived in one of the residential colleges, and visits to 'Bayview' became less and less frequent (Drummond 1995). In 1980, a business profile of Grundy and his group of companies noted that 'Kim, is a talented linguist, and teaches languages in Double Bay' (Penberthy 1980: 15). Meanwhile, Lillian Grundy had moved back to the old family apartment at Double Bay and later acquired a live-in nurse/companion. Reg Grundy's mother died in early 1984.

Afterword

The years 1969 to 1975 were propitious for Grundy and his organization. His career turned two important corners. He now sold to all three Australian commercial television networks, so his star was no longer tied to the vagaries and eccentricities of television station owners and managers, as had often been the case in the previous decade. Additionally, his company had added a second even more financially profitable area of television production expertise to its quiz-show capacity in the form of drama. The new know-how made Reg Grundy Enterprises even more secure in the Australian television programme production marketplace. Never again would Grundy face the peril of having no programmes in production. Television drama serial production would prove even more lucrative than quiz shows, so that Grundy was in an increasingly prosperous position to bankroll new schemes for further development. Reg Grundy Enterprises was already the largest programme production company in Australia, with greater profits and more program-hour output than any of its competitors. Further business opportunities could only be pursued offshore. Grundy's second marriage would not stand in the way of such a development; rather, it would be facilitated by the fact that both partners were intent on following their own careers.

Chapter 8

Transnational Ambitions II: Retooling for Domestic and Offshore, 1974-79

Introduction

Colour television transmission was introduced in Australia at the beginning of 1975, and the change triggered a new financial bonanza in commercial television. Advertisers immediately were attracted to the potential boost in sales that colour television might generate. Although the economy reeled from the shock of the first oil crisis and would suffer a second shock in 1979, nevertheless the television viewing population rapidly invested in new colour television receivers, and production revenues and industry profits soared. Reg Grundy Enterprises was already the busiest producer of quiz shows and other forms of live entertainment programmes, and the company now set about dominating the production of scripted fiction of all kinds. It soon displayed overwhelming mastery in this new area of output. This strength was to turn it into a significant international producer of programming, the largest in Australia and larger than many US programme production companies. Hitherto, Grundy's programme distribution had mostly been confined to the Australian market. Now, the colour fiction output that had been accumulating rapidly since 1974 dictated that sales should be pursued offshore. Reg Grundy Enterprises was at a crossroads, as was Australian television production generally. Long an importer of programming know-how, the Grundy Organisation, as it retitled itself, began to export programmes. At first it concentrated on distributing such fare as the documentary features, the Barry McKenzie film and some light entertainment specials. Soon it also had drama series and serials to license to overseas television stations. By the end of the decade, a handful of overseas Grundy offices had appeared. Moves were afoot to make the Grundy Organisation a transnational presence in the television production business. This chapter analyses the last years of Grundy as an exclusively Australian operation. The period 1975–79 saw the company putting the finishing touches to its local operation, which would in turn equip it for the transnational challenges ahead. Reg Grundy was now over 50 years of age, but he had no thoughts of retiring. Australian television was about to enter its third decade, with colour giving it an astonishingly new lease of life. Reg Grundy's business would undergo a parallel reinvigoration that would make it eager to seize the market opportunities that lay ahead.

Circumstances big and small

There was no very neat point at which the general Australian concerns of the last chapter ended and a new set of issues took their place. In fact, it is as well to start here by underlining a few of the continuities of social issues between the first and second halves of the decade (Moran 1991: 82–88). Society remained prosperous in the wake of the 'long boom' ('Long Boom' 1998). However, the second oil crisis of 1979 conjured up the twin demons of unemployment and inflation, meaning that soon the post-war partnership of government and business would be swept aside in favour of liberalization and deregulation (Sterling 2004a: 688–89). Everyday ideas remained, as always, in flux. Social pluralism still seemed to be the order of the day, but consensus was less in evidence as marginalized groups – including women, gays, Aborigines and the disabled – increasingly drew attention to their relative powerlessness. If there was a residual consensus, there was also an emerging field of conflict and competition. These different and competing ways of seeing were associated with a kind of atomization of the people into an often darker particularism and individualism (Moran 1991: 85–86).

If trade and thought were changing, so too was television. The 0–10 Network would be reinvigorated thanks to the purchase of ATV Channel 0 Melbourne from Ansett Industries in 1978, and TEN Channel 10 Sydney from United Telecasters in 1979, by Rupert Murdoch's News Limited (Gonzerath 2004a: 1558; Moran 1993). After spending almost twenty years waiting to gain control of a commercial television network, News Limited finally got its way. Murdoch was determined to increase the network's ratings and Ten's programme budget rose considerably, leading to a string of commissions in the areas of miniseries, telemovies and drama serials.

A second public-service network, SBS TV, began in 1980, operated by the Special Broadcasting Service. A third structural change was the establishment of the Australian Broadcasting Tribunal (ABT) and the abolition of the Australian Broadcasting Control Board (Moran 1985: 20; Cunningham 1993: 23). The change was part of a new approach to broadcasting by the state, which was generally moving in the direction of deregulation (Sterling 2004a: 688–89). Under the ABT's reign, commercial licensees were given control of such areas as programme standards and advertising, although the stations were meant to be publicly accountable for their practices. Australian content levels remained regulated under the Points System, although stations lobbied vigorously to be allowed to set their own content levels. One other gain for program-makers and audiences was the introduction by the ABT of the C classification for children's programmes in 1978 and a C quota in 1984 (Moran 1985; Cunningham 1993).

Finally, a more visible change for the industry as a whole at this time was the changeover from black and white to colour (Donnelly 2004: 544–55). Colour broadcasting was introduced at the beginning of 1975, and was to prove a bonanza for Australian television as a whole (Hall 1976). Electrical retailers experienced a boom in the sale of expensive new receiving sets; advertisers were eager to display their wares in colour in commercial breaks; station and network finances rose significantly; and audiences increased as the public turned back to watching television. In turn, the new television environment helped trigger a rising slate of programme commissions so that independent packaging companies also shared in the bonanza. Let's look at the Grundy output in this period.

Output: light entertainment and game shows

Reg Grundy Services had set about producing exportable content from the early 1970s onwards. Even so, quiz and other live audience-participation programmes were still important for the Australian television market, both to help retain Grundy's pre-eminent position and to finance present and future operations offshore. Nevertheless, the real key to its plans lay in producing new, original and novel content based on formats of its own devising, with more lavish budgets. Thus a tally of its output between 1974 and 1980 needs to take account of several genres in which it was active. These include a host of light entertainment and game shows, three soap operas, four drama series, a clutch of telemovies, several documentaries and another feature film for hard-top cinema release. As always, there were winners and losers among programme types and between programmes themselves. And as always, the company was ready to learn from these results by concentrating on strengths and turning away from disappointments.

As we saw in Chapters 6 and 7, Reg Grundy Enterprises had shown itself ready to make programmes outside its safety zone of quiz shows. This continued to be the case between 1975 and 1980, when it produced three 'live musical' light entertainment programmes alongside its efforts in quiz shows and fiction of all kinds. Such productions helped put black ink on the books. *Pot of Gold* was a daily daytime excursion into the arena of the talent show for ATV0, and ran between 1975 and 1978. *Bandstand* was a revival of a highly successful 1958–72 TCN9 forerunner, itself a remake of Dick Clarke's *American Bandstand* (Bordowitz 2004). It was made as a Saturday-night feature for TCN9 in a vain attempt to counter the popularity of the ABC's *Countdown* (Inglis 1982: 459–60). After two seasons on air, it was clear that the old magic was gone and the show was cancelled. The last of the trio was *National Star Quest* for the 0–10 Network, an amateur musical contest with heats and finals, broadcast between 1975 and 1978 (Hall 1976: 154).

It was game shows that put meat and potatoes on the Grundy table, however. In 1976, in her study of Australian television, critic Sandra Hall recorded her visit to studios at ATN7 in Sydney to watch the recording of the pilot for a new Grundy game show. Her wry account detailed discussion among members of a would-be studio audience as they endured a long wait before videotaping began on the pilot for a game show that was new to Australia. The show was *High Rollers* (Schwartz, Ryan & Wosbrook 1987: 206–07), which was intended as a daytime programme on weekdays on the Seven Network (Moran & Keating 2003: 78). Unfortunately, the Grundy adaptation was not renewed for the following year. Of course, quiz and game show production had a high casualty rate. As already noted, they were inexpensive to mount, quick to produce, could plug a programming gap and were capable of achieving solid popularity. The fact that all or almost all Grundy game show productions were based on mostly recent US formats also helped reduce the time taken to first get them on air.

High Rollers exemplified this pattern: it was based on a format devised by US game show packager Heatter-Quigley, which had debuted on NBC in 1974. The Grundy version appeared in 1975. It was one of at least half-a-dozen company game shows that came and went within a year. The casualty list included *One in a Million* (TVQ0) and *Name That Tune* (ATN7) in 1975, *Super Seven* (BTQ7) in 1976, *Let's Make a Deal* (TCN9) in 1977 and *Celebrity Tattletales* (ATN7) in 1980. They were all based on US game show format originals from such devisor/packagers as Ralph Edwards, Goodson-Todman, Hatos-Hall and Merv Griffen Productions, and had debuted on US network television as early as 1953 and as late as 1974.

Happily, there were quiz and game shows that put real cash in the Grundy coffers. Those that managed to return for second or third seasons included *The Better Sex* (TVW7) in 1978–79, *Casino 10* (TVQ0) in 1975–77, *The Celebrity Game* (TEN10) in 1976–77 and *Second Chance* (TVQ0) in 1977–78. Another trio were ratings triumphs: *Celebrity Squares* (TCN9) between 1975 and 1978, *Family Feud* (TVW7/GTV9) from 1977 to 1984 and *Graham Kennedy's Blankety Blanks* (TEN10), broadcasting from 1976 to 1979. As always, these were not originals but represented clever adaptations of US-devised formats.

Graham Kennedy's Blankety Blanks deserves further mention. The Grundy show was a very successful adaptation of the Goodson-Todman-originated programme *The Match Game* (Moran & Keating 2003: 75; Grundy 2010: 190–96), which had run on daytime network television for almost twenty years from 1962 onwards, and had also given rise to an evening programme in syndication from 1975 (Schwartz, Ryan & Wosbrook 1987: 292–97). The Australian version featured Graham Kennedy, the durable superstar host of various variety *Tonight* shows (Docker 2004: 1247–48), overseeing a group of television celebrities who attempted to match a panel's missing phrase word even while the game itself constantly took a back seat to humorous interplay between host and celebrities. It ended after four years but only because the host grew tired of the routine.

Graham Kennedy's Blankety Blanks had a second claim to fame. It was the only Grundy programme in Australia ever to carry the name of the host in the title, just as some nine years later *Bruce Forsyth's Hot Streak* was the only overseas Grundy quiz show to carry the name of its compère. Programme producers have always been reluctant to feature the name of a master of ceremonies in a program's title because it diminishes the importance of the programme itself, and can result in a program's cessation should that host decide to leave. Between 1959 and 1962, Reg Grundy himself had attempted to have his first quiz show on TCN9 known as *Reg Grundy's Wheel of Fortune*. While this logo was inscribed on a second wheel stand constructed at TCN, and subsequently featured on screen and in many publicity photographs, the fact is that TCN, television guides and the public at large only knew the programme under the title of *Wheel of Fortune*. TCN's owner and management would not have tolerated the more elaborate title on the show.

Output: soap opera successes

After the uncertain start in drama production with *Class of '74/75*, the company now launched three soap operas that were almost immediately popular with Australian broadcasters and audiences. *The Young Doctors* (1976–82) was part of a 1970s wave of television fiction that set out to snare young viewers along with adults. The Nine Network conceived the idea for the serial and then commissioned Reg Grundy Television to produce an initial thirteen weeks of episodes (Grundy 2010: 176–77). As the title suggested, the subject of this early evening drama was life at a large public hospital, featuring romance and other relationships between doctors, nurses, other staff and patients (Moran 1993: 496–97; Coleman 2009: 159–70). Sex and other possible problem issues were off limits, whereas bombings, murder and dangerous psychopaths could and were used to solve various storyline problems. Nine announced that it was trialling the serial alongside Crawford's *The Sullivans*, although both serials ultimately were commissioned to go into regular production (Moran 1993: 497).

Barry Weston, who was company accountant at the time, has suggested that Reg Grundy himself paid for a further thirteen weeks of episodes to help the programme build audience (Weston 1995). This made business sense, even if it was not a common industry practice. *The Young Doctors* was only the second soap opera produced by Reg Grundy Television, and the first to be devised and originated by import Reg Watson. A failure with this production venture would have seriously stalled the company's attempt to add drama to its production output. Parallels can be drawn, however. For instance, as Chapter 11 observes, Grundy again broke his own rule of never engaging in deficit financing of a show when in 1991, in the United States, he almost single-handedly underwrote the production costs for *Dangerous Women*, a kind of sequel to another Grundy soap opera, *Prisoner* (Grundy 2010: 247–48). In addition, as noted in Chapter 13, Dutch TV format mogul John de Mol was desperate to get the first series of *Big Brother* on air in the Netherlands in 1999 and agreed to pay half its production cost. Back in 1976, Packer's or Grundy's judgement proved to be sound. *The Young Doctors* ran until 1983, amassing a library of 1400 colour half-hour episodes that made it the company's longest-running drama serial before *Neighbours* eclipsed its record (Moran 1993: 497–98).

Another successful Grundy serial followed the next year. Late in 1977, devisor/producer Reg Watson had a second hit serial with *The Restless Years* for the Ten Network (Moran 1993: 379–80). Again, the aim was to capture younger as well as older viewers, so the fiction involved the emotional struggles of school leavers, teachers and parents. As Grundy puts it in his memoirs: 'So *Class of '74* begat *Glenview High* which begat *The Restless Years*' (2010: 185). The serial ran until 1981, amassing a total of 781 half-hour episodes, making it a success although not an overwhelming triumph. It had a way to run before fulfilling its full potential, however. Nearly a decade later, as detailed in Chapter 11, *The Restless Years* was to serve as the basis for two European adaptations, which at the time of writing are still in production and on air.

The next serial also proved to have a good deal of audience interest, commercial longevity and even critical respect. This was *Prisoner* (Curthoys & Docker 2004: 1825–26). It would be retitled *Prisoner: Cell Block H* for international distribution, to avoid confusion with the 1967 ITV series *Prisoner* that starred actor Patrick McGoohan (Berger 2004: 1829–30). The Australian soap opera was the second serial commissioned by the Ten Network, and was intended for a later time slot than *The Restless Years*. Concerned with life in a women's prison, its fictions dealt not only with the prisoners but with the male and female guards, as well as families and others on the outside. Its principal attraction lay in its representation of women variously affected by institutional forces, and their efforts to cope with and even triumph against these (Moran 1993: 365–66). *Prisoner* ran from 1979 to 1986, and resulted in a total of 692 hour-long episodes. It generated cult audiences in Australia, the United Kingdom, the United States and elsewhere, and led to a series of adaptations and spin-offs in Australia, the United States and the Netherlands (Curthoys & Docker 2004: 1825–29; Moran 1998: 91–107).

Finally, mention should also be made of a serial that had a much briefer life. This was *Until Tomorrow*, a singular, even experimental, outing. It was produced and broadcast in 1976, and put to air by the Seven Network. Part of its curiosity lay in the fact that it had been made in Brisbane, the only Australian soap opera ever to be produced outside stations in Sydney and Melbourne. Moreover, it was conceived as a venture into the genre of the daytime soap opera, a subgenre in which US network television had long excelled. *Until Tomorrow* was made on a shoestring budget, and this showed in its mise-en-scène, which featured a small handful of characters and no outside settings (Coleman 2009: 190–92). Similar economies operated behind the camera, with a skeleton crew being employed, including a writing team of two or three (Moran 1993: 472–73). Although the programme ran on all network stations, its licence was not renewed.

Output: the telemovie upsurge

Almost as remarkable as the drama serial output was the company's success in the area of telemovies. Indeed, after its brief flirtation with feature-film production for the big screen, Reg Grundy Services swapped the uncertainties of cinema release and distribution for the certainties of television broadcast deal-making involving telemovies. Now it added the equivalent of more than 25 telemovies to its distribution catalogue for commission sales in Australia and overseas. The telemovie itself was a made-for-television feature, shot on either video or film, and designed to fill a two-hour slot in the broadcasting schedule of networks and stations. It was a relatively new genre that had first appeared in the United States around 1964, with its market origins lying in the corporate need to supplement the supply of recent cinema feature-film releases available for television broadcast (Evans 2001: 586). Its inception at Grundy can be seen as part of the mood of innovation and diversification at work there in the 1970s. Three elements triggered the Grundy crop of telemovies: the drama series output, the television market situation and the circumstances of one-off productions.

US network television had seen the development of series with episode on-air running times of 120 minutes, and the form was obviously a sibling to the telemovie. In 1976, Reg Grundy Productions produced the legal series *Case for the Defence* for the Nine Network. It was (and still is) the only series with episode lengths that fell into the 'long-form' category, which enabled episodes to be broadcast as equivalent to feature-length movies. The series had to do with complicated and engrossing legal cases involving an idealistic barrister, allowing plenty of screen time to delve into events before and after its courtroom scenes (Moran 1993: 102–03). *Case for the Defence* was produced in 1976, although Nine was to wait until 1978 before it aired its nine feature-length episodes. In the meantime, the series was listed in the Grundy distribution catalogue, where it was available either as a series or as one or more telemovies.

The second group of Grundy telemovies was the Gemini Movie Package, which consisted of eleven titles. A chronological listing of these in terms of the years of their production runs as follows: *Is There Anybody There?* (1975); *Mama's Gone a-Hunting* (1976); *The Alternative* (1976); *Gone to Ground* (1976); *The Night Nurse* (1977); *Plunge into Darkness* (1977); *Death Train* (1978); *Demolition* (1978); *Image of Death* (1978); *The Newman Shame* (1978); and *Roses Bloom Twice* (1978). The distribution catalogue would later describe the package as 'covering various subjects from action dramas, psychological/mystery thrillers to family adventures and human emotional dramas' (Leong 1994: 29). As several of the titles suggest, their recurring subject was murder and their characteristic genre was suspense and intrigue. Two of these telemovies, *The Alternative* and *Roses Bloom Twice*, broke the pattern by concentrating on women protagonists and feminine issues.

The Gemini Movie Package was the brainchild of independent producer Robert Bruning. As we saw in Chapter 7, Bruning had been a key recruit to Reg Grundy Enterprises in the first half of the 1970s. Gemini Productions had already had various television sitcom and crime series to its credit, and Bruning had set about producing a slate of feature films for television. With investment support from the new Australian film authorities as well as two of the Australian commercial networks and even US giant Paramount contributing to the first telemovie in 1976, Bruning surrounded himself with a regular production group so that a steady output of television dramas was maintained. Budgets were tight, although there were sufficient dollars to lure minor Hollywood star George Lazenby into appearing in *Is There Anybody There?* (1975) and *The Newman Shame* (1978). The latter was the penultimate Gemini telemovie; after these productions, Bruning left Grundy to produce a long-cherished feature-film project.

The last part of the Grundy telemovie package came about in a more sporadic way. *All at Sea* was a comedy telemovie set in a tropical island resort, with an ensemble of characters trying, variously, to take advantage of each other, often with farcical or slapstick consequences. The telemovie was commissioned by the Ten Network and starred the cast of *The Celebrity Game*, which Reg Grundy Enterprises was producing at the time for the same buyer. The telemovie came together in record time when the network found that it had studio downtime on its hands and a series of celebrity performers under contract (Weston 1995).

Grundy series pilots were produced in the form of two-hour, self-contained episodes so that they too could be listed as telemovies. These included *King's Men* (1975), *Chopper Squad* (1976) and *Glenview High* (1978). There were also two telemovie pilots for series that never happened. The first was *Billion Dollar Baby* (1976), in which a naif falls in love with a woman robot; it was intended to lead to a sitcom spin-off (Grundy 2010: 188). The Grundy Organisation also had a hand in helping to produce the telemovie *The Lion's Share* in 1977, along with Colin Eggleston Productions, for a series that also failed to go ahead. The telemovie was written, directed and produced by Colin Eggleston and starred his partner, Briony Behets, in a drama concerning a wealthy family, ruled by a patriarch with a shady past, with a son and two daughters caught up in a power struggle over family wealth (Murray 1996: 101).

Two other pilots shot as telemovies did result in series commissions. *Jackson High* (1976) was the second pilot for what became the series *Glenview High*, while *Secret Valley* (1979) led to the commissioning of the Grundy children's series of the same name. The latter was produced by Roger Mirams, another of the independent drama producers that Reg Grundy Services had contracted in 1973–74 to help boost its fiction output (Moran 1993: 404–05). Although he had to steer around the unexpected burning of the program's bush set just before pilot filming began, Mirams working with a team of cast and crew that he had assembled over the years completed the pilot and went on to secure a slate of international backers for the series production. Mirams was extremely busy at this time, having produced the telemovie pilot for another Grundy series, *Chopper Squad*, in 1976. He also found time to produce another one-off telemovie for the company. This was *The Scalp Merchant* (1978), which was shot in Western Australia. The telemovie featured another minor Hollywood star, Cameron Mitchell, in the role of an investigator trailing stolen money hidden in a remote timber town by prison escapees (Murray 1996: 186).

Output: four drama series

In 1975, when colour broadcasting was introduced, fiction series had been a staple of Australian television for more than a decade. Yet there were signs that network interest in the form was waning in favour of continuing fiction (Moran 1985: 44–46). Ongoing serials, with their open-ended storylines, had emerged as a viable programming form in 1972, leading to an upsurge in the commissioning of soap opera. By 1978, another form of continuing stories had also arrived in the form of the television miniseries, with over 100 being commissioned between then and 1995 (Murray 1996: 169–253). This general programming shift needs to be borne in mind when considering the relatively small amount of Grundy drama series output in the period 1975–79. Four series constituted the cycle.

King's Men was a short-lived venture into the genre of the police crime series (Moran 1993: 249–50). After Crawford Productions' great success with the genre over the previous dozen years, Grundy and Nine gambled that the type could be reinvigorated by relocating its setting to Sydney and focusing on a veteran detective inspector. This ambition was compromised by the perceived need to also cater for younger viewers by featuring youthful detectives. Thus, despite some spectacular action scenes, *King's Men* gained only ordinary ratings and was not renewed after a thirteen-week outing.

The second series, *Chopper Squad*, was an action adventure series that ran to 26 one-hour episodes and premiered in 1978 after a pilot had been produced in 1976 (Moran 1993: 115–16). This time, there was no confusion about the program's intended appeal and dramatic situation. It depicted the work of a Sydney surf rescue squad and offered good colour photography, exciting stunt work (particularly involving the helicopter used in the series) and generally solid performances from the leading cast of young males, already known to audiences through other crime and adventure series.

Case for the Defence has already been mentioned. It was a courtroom drama that featured an idealistic young barrister and his female partner caught up in complicated cases involving crime and murder. As already noted, each of its nine episodes had the running time of feature films, and while this made for interesting, engrossing fiction that was handsomely mounted, the series played off in late timeslots. The upshot was that *Case for the Defence* was largely overlooked by viewers and was not renewed by the Nine Network.

Finally, *Glenview High* (1978) was another attempt to draw audiences along the path of *Class of '74*, *The Young Doctors* and *The Restless Years*. The series was set in a secondary school in a tough, working-class Sydney suburb, and was centrally concerned with an idealistic young teacher, his fellow staff (including a headmistress), as well as students, parents and others (Moran 1993: 197–98; Grundy 2010: 152–54). *Glenview High* was commissioned by the Seven Network, and each episode managed several storylines as well as touching on various social issues. Ron McLean, one of the three independent producers who had joined the company in 1974, was centrally involved in its production, writing many of its 39 scripts as well as producing the series. It was his first real opportunity to pay off on the gamble that Grundy had made in acquiring his services. Unfortunately, *Glenview High* did not settle into the long-running series that the Seven Network and Grundy had hoped for.

Output: documentaries including *ABBA: The Movie*

As we saw in Chapter 8, the documentary film feature was one of the new areas of programme output that the company had embraced briefly earlier in the decade. However, the documentary film whether intended for the small or big screen was commercially elusive in terms of profit. Unlike the routine patterns of production that could be established with other genres of television output, such as quiz shows and drama serials, documentaries were time-consuming, costly to underwrite and often struggled to achieve topicality and interest. By 1975, the documentary unit was being allowed to shut down. Even so, a small, mixed bag of documentary films did appear under the Grundy name between 1975 and 1979. Kevin Arnett's *World of the Supernatural* (1977) was a television special that harkened back to a string of similar features that Grundy had produced in the early 1970s, such as *ESP and All That* (1971). Another 1977 documentary feature, *Confessions of Ronald Biggs*, focused on the Great Train Robbery escapee, at the time living in Brazil, and was an independent production in which the company invested and distributed. Next came *Killers of the Great Barrier Reef* (1979), a nature documentary produced for a US company, Gold Key (USA).

A better illustration of Grundy's increasingly transnational reach was its brief engagement with the European pop group ABBA and the production of two documentary-like features, a television special, *ABBA: Down Under* (1976), and a feature film for cinema release, *ABBA: The Movie* (1977). As previously noted, Reg Grundy Services had begun packaging a new version of the popular Australian television music series, *Bandstand*, for the Nine Network in 1976, after Nine had cancelled the original series in 1972. 'ABBA mania' had not yet happened, so Nine and Grundy were able to sign up the group to appear on *Bandstand* and other television programmes (Grundy 2010: 1567). The Grundy company, the Nine Network and RCA Records co-organized an ABBA promotional tour of Australia in March 1976. A television special, *The Best of ABBA*, was produced as part of *Bandstand*. It turned out to be very popular, was aired four times, and was later sold to twenty overseas territories under the title of *ABBA: Down Under*.

Arrangements for a feature film had already taken place before an ABBA concert tour took place early the following year (Baker 1979: 24; Grundy 2010: 156–58; Palm 2002: 188–97). Reg Grundy Services was the driving force behind the film, and put up 25 per cent of the budget, with ABBA's record company, Polar Music International, providing the rest (Palm 2002: 328). *ABBA: The Movie* was shot in an improvised cinéma vérité style by its Swedish director, Lasse Hallstrom (Palm 2002: 341). The feature premiered in Sydney at the end of 1977, and did sufficient box-office business to be declared an international success, with Polar and Grundy recouping their investment (Weston 1995). Warner Bros distributed the film outside Australia, New Zealand and parts of Europe, although 'ABBA mania' was waning by then (Palm 2002: 370–71). Curiously, there is no entry concerning the film in Pike and Cooper's (1981) canonical account of Australian feature films produced between 1901 and 1977. In any case, the ABBA film was to be Grundy's second (and last) venture into feature-film production intended for hard-top cinema release. It would mostly concentrate on television series and serials from this point on. As this survey of output, ranging from light entertainment and game shows to documentaries, has suggested, this was the side of the screen industries that Reg Grundy Services knew best. But what of the company's own business activities outside the area of programme production? The rest of this chapter concentrates on elements of the Grundy operation between 1975 and 1980.

New company offices

This period saw changes occur with the Grundy group of companies itself: the opening of new company offices, additional business initiatives, the development of international programme licensings and the re-corporatization of the business entity. These subjects follow and the chapter ends with a more synchronic account of the company as it launched itself as a transnational operation.

First, though, the matter of location. The acquisition and establishment of the Grundy office at Grundy House in the heartland of the Sydney television industry was outlined in the previous chapter. New offices in other centres were added between 1975 and 1980. This was in line with the practical view of opening (and closing) such venues as they were needed for new company productions in other places. But animating such developments more broadly were the interrelated philosophies of parochial intranationalism and parochial internationalism. The first idea was illustrated in Chapter 7, and both are explained further in the next chapter. Here, it is enough to note that the two are opposite sides of the same coin, dictating that programme formats should be customized so that locals are involved in production and attracted as audiences. To this end, two Australian interstate offices were in full swing at this time. The first was in Brisbane, where Grundy's quiz shows for local commercial stations included *I've Got a Secret, Super Seven, Second Chance, Perfect Match* and *Pyramid Challenge*. Similarly, by 1977 the company had opened another interstate office, having set up a production of *Family Feud* in Perth for TVW7 and the Seven Network, which would continue in production until 1984. The same office also saw the making of another game show, *The Better Sex*, at STW9 for national broadcast on the Nine Network, with the programme running for two years. Perth also served as production base for the making of two of the offerings in the Bruning/Gemini telemovie package, *The Newman Shame* and *The Scalp Merchant*.

A much more ambitious offshore development was also taking place. As noted in Chapter 6, Reg Grundy had been visiting the United States since 1966, in order to acquire new quiz and game show formats. At some point, he had resolved to turn his operation into a transnational one by becoming an independent television producer in the US market. Indeed, in late 1977 the Australian office of the company announced a 'big film being set and filmed in New York with big US stars' (*TV Week* 1977: 1). In fact, the announcement was probably premature because no such film eventuated. Nevertheless, concrete plans were afoot to secure business and production bases in the United States. The same announcement mentioned that the company had set up a New York office. In 1978 79, the group registered a US company, Reg Grundy Productions, which was incorporated in November 1979. A Los Angeles office was also established around the same time, a vital step for Grundy's first transnational production venture.

Re-corporatization

As we saw in Chapter 5, Reg Grundy had found that in order to act as an outside producer of quiz shows in television, beginning with *Wheel of Fortune*, he needed to corporatize himself as a business entity. Accordingly, in 1959 he had set up the private company Reg Grundy Enterprises. Over the next twenty years, several other linked, private entities had come into existence, with Reg Grundy Services acting as the group name. In 1977, coincident with Ian Holmes – the former managing director of TEN-10 – joining the group, the decision was taken to set about a restructuring of the total operation (Moran 1985: 143–50). By 1979, Grundy House in Sydney could boast that there was a new business name for the overall entity. Why did such a reorganization take place? There seem to have been at least four reasons why Reg Grundy Services was recast as the Grundy Organisation.

First, there was the administrative fact that the Grundy companies had tended to grow in an ad hoc fashion over the twenty years since the founder had begun his television production business. As noted in passing, various company activities had adopted such names as Reg Grundy Enterprises, Reg Grundy Services and Reg Grundy Television. And, just as the move into Grundy House had centralized the company's physical operation in Australia under one roof (apart from state offices elsewhere), so the creation of a new corporate entity was to have a parallel effect as far as the business organization was concerned.

An additional trigger for the creation of the Grundy Organisation may have been related to the recruitment in 1977 by Reg Grundy of Ian Holmes as chief administrative officer. Holmes had a technical background in Melbourne commercial radio, then television. He worked at GTV9, where he rose to the position of programme manager, before joining TEN10 in Sydney as managing director. Holmes played a major role in commissioning *Number 96*, the first successful drama serial on Australian commercial television, which improved the fortunes of the 0–10 Network and also changed the programming landscape of Australian commercial television for the next twenty years. The creation of the Grundy Organisation formalized a new set of key administrative changes, with Ian Holmes becoming president of the new entity and Reg Grundy becoming chairman of the board. It also signalled new geographic spheres of operation, with Holmes overseeing Australian operations while Grundy pursued business opportunities in the United States (Holmes 1980; Grundy 2010: 205).

Mention of Reg Grundy acting as 'overseas salesman extraordinare' (Penberthy 1980) suggests a further reason for the organizational change. At the time, it was explained that the divisional changes and new executive titles were prompted by the desire to help make the group more organizationally intelligible to US executives in broadcasting and related fields (Moran 1985: 149–55). In seeking to create a more international administrative identity, the Grundy group was reaffirming its ambition to develop a transnational operation. It possibly was also facilitating the official establishment of a US branch, which also occurred in 1979, when the Grundy Organisation formally came into existence.

A final reason for the business reorganization seems to be the most compelling one, even if the details are obscure and hard to come by. It is related to the move offshore of the Grundy operation's legal and accounting matters (Weston 1995). Various other companies that had originated in Australia were pursuing the taxation advantages to be had in such offshore arrangements at the time (Braithwaite 2005: 36–40). Grundy decided to relocate its legal and accounting offices to the principality of Monaco on the shores of the Mediterranean. At the time, Monaco – together with other European sites such as Lichtenstein and Switzerland – was one of the oldest tax havens in the world (Cromie 1989: 62–70: Fung 1989: 45–50). It also had the business advantage of being close to Cannes, where the MIP television market was held each year (twice yearly from 1983). More to the point, relocating the business and legal affairs there probably created various financial savings and efficiencies.

Further business initiatives

The newly announced Grundy Organisation was very impressive as an Australian business conglomerate, at least on paper (Cunningham & Jacka 1996: 81–87). The new entity had a business logo in the shape of a transparent 24-sided clear crystal, which featured the name 'The Grundy Organisation' in such a way that the consecutive letters 'RG' in the word 'Organisation', were shaded inside the clear crystal. Such oblique symbolism appealed to the company's principal (Weston 1995). The multiset of sides was seen to represent the many activities in entertainment and consumption industries in which the Grundy Organisation was involved. As managing director Ian Holmes put it: '[Grundy's] business was anything to do with leisure' (Moran 1985: 142–58). The Grundy Organisation was, to all appearances, an extremely active set of individual business initiatives, financed from core activities in television production that were moving the company in new trading directions.

Television production remained its core activity, as the above account testifies. And while plans were also afoot for production in the United States, no programme recording had yet taken place. Five additional areas of trading activity were highlighted as part of its commercial horizon, however. These were fun or theme parks; fast-food franchising; group tours and travel; product presentation; records; and film-product merchandising (Penberthy 1980: 13). Some of these initiatives were short-lived, while others were even more chimerical. Records, for instance, had been a passing involvement in the early 1960s, briefly revived with the *Travellin' Out West* series, even if this activity was now back on the agenda.

For that matter, Grundy Travel was not in the business of selling travel tickets to the general public (Weston 1995). Instead, the facility had been established to overcome a financial difficulty encountered by the parent operation in flying senior production personnel, on-camera performers and, more occasionally, game show contestants to destinations in the different Australian state capital cities. Previously, television-packaging companies had received free travel from Australia's two domestic airlines in return for on-air promotion of their services. As mentioned, Ansett Industries exemplified this connection between elements of the Australian transportation and communication businesses, owning both an Australia-wide private commercial airline and Channel 0 commercial television stations in Melbourne and Brisbane. However, the two national airlines Ansett and Trans Australian Airlines (TAA) had curtailed this contra deal arrangement, leaving television programme packagers to face the cost of such travel. Grundy's financial services department discovered that travel agencies were entitled to substantial airfare discounts, however (Weston 1995). Even more importantly, there were no financial or administrative obstacles to setting up a travel agency. The result was a new phantom business operation established under the umbrella of the Grundy Organisation that operated as Grundy Travel. Its function was to achieve economies for Grundy's Australian air travel rather than to sell airline tickets to the public.

Other business involvements of the new Grundy Organisation were more straightforward, even if some failed to deliver the financial bonanzas expected. The most costly of these commercial gambles was that involving Grundy Leisure and its first theme park, which opened at Surfers Paradise on the Queensland Gold Coast (Moran 1985: 150; Grundy 2010: 228–30). Inspired by the example of US theme parks, including those associated with Disney and Warner Bros, and even importing a former Disney theme park executive to head up the venture, Grundy's Surfers Paradise Centre was a children's fun park that also planned to snare parents to its rides and games (Penberthy 1980: 14). The Centre included a pizza parlour, Chuck E. Cheese, with the Grundy's business becoming a franchisee of this New Jersey computer-animated figure. The latter led a string of puppet characters in a mechanical cabaret, which was supposed to entertain customers as they ate pizzas. Buoyed by business optimism, the Grundy Organisation announced plans to open other fun park outlets in Sydney and Melbourne, even including the pizza franchise. Unfortunately, the crowds stayed away and this disastrous venture was quietly unloaded (Grundy 2010: 230).

Other undertakings were more profitable. One such venture was an involvement in the management of the new Sydney Entertainment Centre. Joining with a group of Holmes' long-term associates in the broadcasting and entertainment industries, the Grundy Organisation bought into Arena, a management company contracted to run the Entertainment Centre, and derived good long-term returns on a modest investment (Weston 1995; Grundy 2010: 230). Altogether, these ventures probably evened out on the Grundy account books. All the same, the making of television programmes could never be a 100 per cent safe business. Reg Grundy was sufficiently entrepreneurial to know that it was worth backing other ventures in the hope that one or more might prove to be a significant commercial success.

Transnational programme distribution

As we have already seen, the pattern of Grundy's development as a production company involved the successive opening of additional markets for his shows. In 1959, the new vendor was television itself so the producer could take his radio quiz programme to Sydney's TCN Channel 9. By 1965, two further markets had come into being in the shape of the 0–10 Network and the minor state capital city commercial stations in Brisbane and Adelaide. Reg Grundy Enterprises spotted further sales opportunities around 1970, when a changing of the programming guard at Sydney's Channel 7 and Channel 9 allowed it to begin selling significant numbers of shows to the Seven and Nine Networks. In 1974–75, a much larger market opportunity began to open up with the demise of black-and-white television broadcasting.

The advent of colour television transmission in Australia in 1975 brought the domestic industry into line with television systems elsewhere in the developed world. There had been no overseas markets for black-and-white Grundy quiz shows, and this would still be the case with colour versions of the genre. A neighbouring television industry, such as that of New Zealand, would either produce its own quiz shows, based on imported or home-grown formats, or else import programmes with high production values from the United Kingdom or United States. Fiction was another matter, with early colour-film series produced in Australia, including *Adventures of the Sea Spray* (1967) and *Skippy* (1968), achieving relatively wide international circulation and recognition. Crawford Productions had already licensed large blocks of its early black and white courtroom and police drama series for airing in such markets as the United Kingdom and New Zealand. With Grundy's double moves into both colour and drama from 1974, the door opened for the overseas distribution of large batches of its high-volume, low-budget drama serials and series. In fact, the licensing of Australian television programmes into other territories became a significant financial matter for Australian television stations, and for Australian packaging houses generally (Macken 1989: 9; Cunningham & Jacka 1996: 16–29).

Under standard licensing agreements between programme packagers and Australian television networks, each party was entitled to a percentage of fees when programmes were licensed for broadcast in other parts of the world. This was, in most cases, additional profit for the production company and the network so that fees could be varied from one territory to another, generally being set by the size of the territory's viewing population as well as the degree of affluence of that particular market. Hence, to use a later example, the licence fee for the broadcast of an episode of Grundy's long-running drama serial *Neighbours* (1985 on) in the United Kingdom was far more valuable to all concerned than the return yielded in a place such as Mauritius, even if both yields helped put some black ink on the books.

Equally critical was the percentage breakdown of these residual rights in a programme. The core business of the Australian television networks was domestic broadcasting. For the most part, the broadcasters did not see themselves as being in the business of overseas programme distribution, and were not willing to establish the infrastructure necessary to buttress such sales. Instead, they left this to their partners, the packaging companies, while deriving a share of the overseas distribution profits. Usually, the television networks collected approximately one-third of these overseas fees while the packaging companies had a larger return commensurate with being partners in the initial production venture and being the main driver of transnational sales.

The last link in this distribution chain was the overseas representative or organization that dealt with the actual marketing of programmes, including publicity, handling and shipping. Paramount Pictures had a series of connections with Australian commercial television, thanks in part to Adelaide-born executive Bruce Gordon (Mauger 2006). Hence, in 1975 or thereabouts, Grundy decided to have Paramount act as its agent, an arrangement that was in place until the early 1980s.

Personal style and company style: professionalism and specialization

With the Grundy Organisation on the verge of becoming a transnational operation, it is useful to end this chapter by looking backwards as well as forwards to characterize the company's business practices and modes of operation. Many incidental hints have already been offered, and it is worth spelling out just how TV format mogul Reg Grundy shaped his company. Four characteristics were important: professionalism, quality control, delegation of responsibilities and programme sales.

Reg Grundy almost invariably hired from within the television industry, often learning about a potential employee by working alongside them at a television station on a Grundy quiz production and then offering them a job with the company. Key executives recruited in this way included Lyle McCabe as executive producer from TCN9 in 1965, Bill Mason as producer from BTQ7 in 1969 and Ian Holmes as managing director from TEN10 in 1977. As Grundy's memoirs suggest, this same pattern continued to be applied later in such settings as the United States and United Kingdom (2010: 266–70, 274–75, 279). In making these and other key appointments, Grundy was developing the personnel that would allow him to fine tune his operation as a highly professional organization imbued with the same commercial outlook as the television industry in Australia and, later, the United States, the United Kingdom and elsewhere. Thus, while audience entertainment and show-business values pervaded the subject matter and style of Grundy programmes, these were underwritten by a professional approach to economy, efficiency and craft (Cunningham & Jacka 1996: 81–87).

As his team of employees grew in number, so Grundy began to concentrate on key areas of the organization, delegating or allowing others to undertake particular roles and responsibilities. Shortly after he began producing television quiz shows, Grundy realized that he could waste a lot of valuable time visiting the studio floor of a production of one of his shows (Grundy 2010: 78–79). He decided to concentrate on quality control by watching recorded episodes of these shows in his office. As less cumbersome recording facilities became available, Grundy increasingly was drawn to viewing these recordings in the quiet privacy of wherever he was living. Extended notes were made about the episodes being reviewed, and executive producers would receive long, detailed memos and phone calls concerning his analysis. This quality control on Grundy's part seemed to persist until the mid- to late 1970s. By then, the development of his US operation was his main concern, so the Australian quality control fell increasingly to other executives.

Other key tasks also eventually fell to others. One of the most important was selling the idea for a new programme to a commercial broadcaster, whether this idea was based on an overseas show (mostly the case with quiz shows) or was an original creation (invariably the case with a fiction series). Reg Grundy's memoirs recall several examples of his triumphant pitching of shows to broadcasters, such as his account of coming across the US format for *Sale of the Century*, successfully demonstrating this to the then general manager of the Seven Network and the two then proceeding to successfully woo a major sponsor for what became *Temptation* (2010: 123–27). This was in 1969–70. Within a decade, much of this kind of selling was falling to others. Reg Grundy corroborates this delegation of sales duties in his memoirs. He notes, for example, that in 1979 he was mostly hard at work in the United States, so it was his Australian general manager, in conjunction with the programming head of the Nine Network, who decided to revive the *Sale of the Century* format, including paying a licensing fee to its US owner (2010: 231).

Personal style and company style: privacy

Grundy ran his company along professional organizational lines. As the number of employees grew, he withdrew from a frontline managerial role in the organization in favour of delegating to his executive officers, who then had more to do with middle-range executives and those on the lower rungs of the organizational ladder. To sustain the time demands of the tasks that he had set himself, Grundy budgeted his days and hours, preferring to meet his top executives early in the morning; eventually, he had them meet him at his home. Many junior employees never set eyes on the company's owner and chief executive, even if the various company names never allowed anyone employed by the company to forget who really called the organizational shots.

The cool, impersonal professionalism of the Grundy company can be highlighted further by considering the way that a major Australian rival in the field of commercial television production went about its business during the same period. This was Melbourne-based Crawford Productions, which has already been mentioned. Crawford's had begun in 1945 as a radio programme production company, which in 1957 began producing fiction and other kinds of shows for television (Moran 1985: 89–109). It was a family company owned and operated by Hector Crawford, his sister Dorothy and nephew Ian, with many long-term employees regarding both Crawford and the family in general as the guiding spirit of the company. Like an old-fashioned family business, Crawford Productions operated in a hierarchical fashion that ran from Hector Crawford down to the most junior employees. Indeed, Crawford Productions consciously operated a production apprenticeship system at this time, recruiting inexperienced hands who later would become production technicians, directors, unit managers and so on. By contrast, Grundy was always less centralized and more 'horizontally' organized. Although it eventually employed many hundreds of workers, Grundy operated no trainee system, preferring to recruit more experienced personnel where possible. There is no record of Crawford Productions ever recruiting experienced independent producers to operate under the company banner, along the lines already discussed in Chapter 7. Finally, and not surprisingly, there was also a significant contrast between the public presentation of the two company owners. Framed photographs of Hector and Dorothy Crawford always adorned the different lobbies of their headquarters over the years. On the other hand, no Grundy portrait was ever displayed to employees and company visitors at any Grundy office.

Personal style and company programme funding

Lastly, it is worth noting another business rule of the company, which was breached on just two occasions by the owner himself. This involved underwriting the cost of a programme production by the independent production company or packager rather than by a broadcaster. In Australian commercial television, the practice had been one where broadcasters met all production costs, both by providing 'below-the-line' facilities and resources at a television station and by paying an 'above-the-line' fee to the packager. This finance model was by no means universal. In Paraguay from 1995 to 2000, the Grundy company would produce a version of *Sale of the Century, La Venta del Siglo*, free of charge under a 'barter' system for broadcaster SNT Canal 9, whereby the producing packager could then sell time to advertisers within the broadcast programme. Chapter 11 provides more details. It also discusses the case of a Grundy drama serial in the United States in the early 1990s where the company met most of the production costs. As noted in Chapter 7, this had a precedent in the making of *The Young Doctors* in 1976–77 (Grundy 2010: 176–81). Apart from these variations, the iron rule was that the broadcaster paid the costs of a program's production.

Afterword

The years 1975 to 1979–80 saw the Grundy company emerge triumphantly as the largest television programme producer in Australia. In late 1977, for example, it was making seventeen hours of game shows each week and some twelve to fifteen hours of drama. There were no further challenges left in the Australian television marketplace, so if Grundy wanted to expand further, then it was time to think of entering larger, more robust and more lucrative markets overseas. This chapter has analysed company activities during the second half of the 1970s at a time of overall buoyancy in the Australian economy and in the Australian screen industries in general. The year 1979 marked two decades of Grundy activities in Australian commercial television. Within three years, some of the company's production personnel would be making Grundy's first programmes in overseas markets. The Grundy Organisation was about to become a transnational operation.

Chapter 9

Transnational Ambitions III: Australia, the United States and South-East Asia, 1979–85

Introduction

The years from 1979 to 1985 were a time when many Australian-originated companies were becoming transnationals by building on strong foundations first established in the home market. The Grundy Organisation was one of these. It continued to call Australia home but now looked outwards. Its domestic operation proceeded strongly, with a clutch of programmes proving to be very profitable in their own right and promising greater potential as formats. Australian profits also helped to underwrite the overall transnational expansion on which the company was now embarking. After an extended period of industry stability, coinciding with 'the long boom' in the economies of many western territories, television systems were beginning to expand under the impact of new technology, changing regulatory practices and emerging financial pressures. The Grundy Organisation recognized this shift, but mostly concentrated its overseas efforts in the United States. Reg Grundy spearheaded this development, and by 1985 he could point to notable achievements after more than ten years of effort. There were incidental disappointments, however, so the footing gained was by no means secure. This chapter follows the story of Grundy's activities in the early 1980s, a time that saw the company making television programmes in Australia, the United States and, briefly, South-East Asia. There were gains and losses, and these would serve as a prelude to further growth later in the decade.

The Australian framework

Once again, broader social developments need to be noted before we examine the activities of the Grundy Organisation. In the case of the home market, three interconnected areas are important: the economy, the culture of ideas and the media industries – especially the Australian television sector. The changes from 1942 onwards, surveyed in previous chapters, were glacial compared with the shift that was now happening. The years 1979–85 represented a decisive period, one that saw a significant break with the economic and political certainties that had, by and large, been in place for more than 30 years. The second oil crisis of 1979, followed by sharp rises in both unemployment and inflation, helped trigger a change that Cunningham & Jacka (1996), drawing on work by British economic geographers Askoy and Robbins, describe as a move from Fordism to a post-Fordist world-view (1996: 33–37). The larger contours of the change saw a move away from a Keynesian framework that emphasized government activity in the economy as a means of fostering a welfare state and a social democratic agenda, in favour of seeing the market as a more efficient mechanism for allocating goods and services (Pusey 1992: 1–22). With strident, right-wing governments coming to power in the United Kingdom and United States after 1979, an Australian federal Labor government, elected to office in 1983, found itself unable to resist some of the winds of deregulation and anti-statism that were blowing strongly overseas (Davison, Hurst & Macintyre 1998: 389).

The changes in Australia's financial and political landscape did not occur overnight, and in any case were more muted than developments elsewhere. Nonetheless, in the period under consideration, there was a gradual dissolution of the Keynesian partnership of private capitalist interests and public statist imperatives. Australian federal governments, whether from the conservative or progressive side of politics, found themselves attempting to negotiate the contradiction between a commitment to social democracy and a strong welfare programme on the one hand, and a swing towards laissez-faire capitalism on the other (Cunningham & Jacka 1996: 3–29). An overall partial deregulation emerged, one that went further in areas such as telecommunications and less in others such as broadcasting (Curtin 2004: 993–97; Sterling 2004a: 688–89). In fact, intense internationalizing tendencies came into play from 1983, when the new Labor government deregulated the financial system (Pusey 1992: 14–29; Cunningham & Jacka 1996: 65ff). Various home-grown Australian companies in such areas as mining, banking and media took the opportunity to transnationalize their operations if they had not done so already. Hence, for example, media owner Rupert Murdoch abandoned his Australian citizenship in 1985 in order to become a US citizen, a move that was vital to his ability to carry on media business in the United States and elsewhere (Shawcross 1992: 480, 512; Gonzerath 2004a: 1558–60, 1646–48). Similarly, from 1983, Reg Grundy was another Australian mogul who chose to develop the transnational reach of his operations.

Within the arena of Australian television broadcasting, less apparent change was evident. Mostly it was a matter of business as usual, especially after the brief economic downturn of 1979–81. The bonanza of advertisers, broadcasters and producers associated with colour programming continued (Moran 1985: 21–29; O'Regan 1992: 16–21; Cunningham & Jacka 1996: 38–68). I have already mentioned two significant changes that occurred in the Australian television system at this time: Murdoch's News Limited success in gaining control of the 0–10 Network in 1978–80 and the inauguration of a second public-service television broadcaster in the form of SBS TV in 1980. Neither of these changes expanded Grundy's market opportunities, however. One other development in the Australian screen industries environment also had little impact on the company's Australian operations. This was the introduction by the federal government of generous tax incentives to stimulate film and television fiction production after 1980 (Jacka 1993: 72–87). The scheme led to a significant increase in Australian feature films and television miniseries, although Grundy was more interested in producing local programmes in overseas television markets (Moran 1985: 143–58; Cunningham & Jacka 1996: 81–86).

The Grundy Organisation succeeded in producing its first programmes outside Australia in 1983. This was the culmination of more than twenty years of effort in the United States. Reg Grundy had been honing his sense of television industries elsewhere since 1959, and for at least a decade had nursed ambitions to make television shows offshore in the world's most lucrative television market. That ambition now became a reality. The survey of production output that follows in this and succeeding chapters therefore takes account of programme production in Australia and in other national television industries. The content tally for the home market comes first.

Australia: the quiz shows

Australia was the engine room for the Grundy international expansion that was now underway. Game shows, drama series and soap operas were crucial to this drive, and these three areas are examined in this and the next two sections. By the early 1980s, the Grundy Organisation had over two decades' worth of experience in producing quiz and game shows for the Australian commercial television networks. Its knowledge and expertise in remaking overseas formats in this genre were without equal in the home market – even if the networks did, on some rare occasions, venture into commissioning quiz or panel shows from other packagers, or even producing in-house. Despite such disappointments, the Grundy Organisation forged ahead in its production of quiz shows, offering an extensive catalogue of game show formats, mostly derived from US companies, with Grundy now systematically optioning clearances for Australia, and often for Oceania and/or South-East Asia as well.

Many of the shows were familiar to Grundy, the networks and viewers, even if they sometimes came and went quickly. Frequently, these adaptations for Australian television carried their original names, such as the 1984 remake of *It Could Be You*, which had first been produced by Ralph Edwards Productions for NBC in 1956 and had been immensely successful on Australian television between 1960 and 1966 (Schwartz, Ryan & Wosbrook 1987: 228–29; Moran & Keating 2003: 80–81). Sometimes a new game show was a Grundy reversioning of a format that was closer to home in its origin. One example was Grundy's adaptation of Bob Dyer's *Pick-a-Box*, the radio and television quiz show that had run from 1952 to 1972. This was updated as *Ford Superquiz* for the Nine Network, with celebrity husband and wife team Bert and Patti Newton substituting for Bob and Dolly Dyer (Moran & Keating 2003: 71). Unfortunately, this revived version was not to viewers' liking, and the programme appeared and disappeared quickly in 1981–82.

A handful of other format adaptations had no better luck. In 1980, Grundy revived *The Marriage Game* from a decade earlier. The programme was retitled *Celebrity Tattle Tales* and licensed by the Seven Network, but only lasted for one season (Moran & Keating 2003: 58). The following year, Grundy produced an adaptation of *Personality Squares* (Schwartz, Ryan & Wosbrook 1987: 229) for the Ten Network. This was an updated revival of a very successful 1970s format, which itself was based on the Noughts and Crosses scorecard. It too lasted only one season (Moran & Keating 2003: 106). A third Grundy game show casualty occurred in 1982, in the shape of *$10,000 Moneymakers*. Its predecessor, *Moneymakers* (Schwartz, Ryan & Wosbrook 1987: 304) had been very successful for the Ten Network between 1971 and 1973, but this new version for the same network barely made inroads into the ratings against another Grundy programme on a rival network, and was dropped after a year (Moran & Keating 2003: 96).

Balancing these short-run game shows were six others that put plenty of black ink on the books. Two were moderate successes. These were *Matchmates,* an afternoon game show that helped give TCN and the Nine Network a quota of children's programming from 1981 to 1983 (Moran & Keating 2003: 99), and *Play Your Cards Right*, a BTQ7 game show based on the NBC Barry-devised format *21* that ran for three years from 1984 until 1986 (Schwartz, Ryan & Wosbrook 1987: 476; Moran & Keating 2003: 106).

Four other game shows proved to be an enormous bonanza for the Grundy Organisation. None of these was a new format, signalling that the company's genius lay not in any originality or novelty attached to the formats, but rather in deciding which formats to pitch to network buyers and what to inject into these, so far as their look, sound and pace were concerned. Two were to have solid runs on air, leaving the company and commissioning networks delighted with their performance. *The New Price is Right* was a revamp of the Goodson-Todman format that had debuted on NBC network television as early as 1956 (Schwartz, Ryan & Wosbrook 1987: 372–77) and given rise to a cycle of remakes on Australian commercial television in the intervening years (Moran & Keating 2003: 108–10). As its name implies, the game element in *Price* was a costing or guessing game involving items for the home and elsewhere, and now enlivened by the very active encouragement of and participation of the studio audience as well as the contestants (Schwartz, Ryan & Wosbrook 1987: 372–77). *The New Price is Right* was produced for the Seven Network and proved to be very popular, running from 1981 to 1984 (Moran & Keating 2003: 99–100). Meanwhile, the format predecessors for *Perfect Match* included *Blind Date* and *The Dating Game*. Grundy proceeded to update elements of these for the Ten Network. The resulting programme gave the network a solid hit that ran from 1984 to 1987. In fact, a rival network paid indirect tribute to Grundy's and Ten's success with the format by producing its own in-house version of *Blind Date* under the title *The Love Game*, although the rival adaptation lasted only six months on air (Moran & Keating 2003: 104–05).

The last two game show adaptations were even more successful and durable. *Wheel of Fortune* was to run on the Seven Network from 1981 until 2002 (Moran & Keating 2003: 131). The programme had debuted on US daytime network television in 1979, and had been created by Merv Griffin Productions, despite the coincidence of having the same name as the quiz show that Reg Grundy had devised first for radio in 1957 and for television in 1959 (Schwartz, Ryan & Wosbrook 1987: 499–502; Becker 2004b: 2527–28). Unlike the latter format, this version of *Wheel of Fortune* was based on the parlour game of Hangman. More importantly, talk show host Merv Griffin had copyrighted the title of the programme, so that even if he had wanted to, Reg Grundy could not remake his first quiz-show format under its original title. Still, that was of no consequence in the world of commercial television broadcasting. Griffin's *Wheel of Fortune* had turned out to be enormously popular and successful on NBC daytime. By the mid-1980s, its host and hostess had achieved celebrity status. The Grundy Organisation's adaptation of *Wheel* would turn out to be comparably successful, although its late-afternoon timeslot and the need to pay licensing fees to the Griffin organization would mean that it was less lucrative for the company than another Grundy favourite, *Sale of the Century*.

Sale of the Century would prove to be the most important quiz-show format of its type, both for Australian commercial television and, as we will see below, for the Grundy transnational operation (Moran & Keating 2003: 138–39). Chapter 7 has already dealt with an unlicensed adaptation of the format that Reg Grundy Enterprises had produced for the Seven Network under the titles of *Temptation* and *The Great Temptation* in the early 1970s. In 1979, Ian Holmes sold a new version of the format to the Nine Network (Grundy 2010: 231–38). The company licensed the Australian rights and could now revert to the quiz show's original US title. Later, as I mention in the next section, the Grundy Organisation would buy all rights for the format. *Sale of the Century* began on air in mid-1980, and was an immediate ratings success, running five evenings a week in the early evening prime-time programme slot of 7.00 p.m. (Moran & Keating 2003: 113–14). The programme set an all-time record for quiz-show longevity in Australian television that is unlikely to be surpassed, running in that slot until 2002 before being revived in 2005 as *Temptation* and continuing until 2009 (Moran & Keating 2003: 113–14). Even more satisfying from the Grundy Organisation's point of view were the lucrative returns that the Australian adaptation generated, thanks to an early five-nights-a-week timeslot and the fact that the company now owned the format.

Australia: fiction series

Four different areas of programme output can be highlighted here. The types were drama series, children's series, continuing serials and quiz shows. There were only a handful of programmes in the first two genres, but more in the last two. As always, there were disappointments as well as triumphs. Chapters 7 and 8 mentioned the three experienced Australian writer/producers recruited to bolster company drama output. By 1980, Bruning had already put together a package of eleven telemovies before leaving Grundy. Writer/producer Ron McLean's major drama series project, *Bellamy*, went into production in 1980 and began on the Ten Network in 1981 as 26 one-hour episodes (Moran 1993: 76–77). McLean had written for the Crawford police cycle, and this was his second attempt to resurrect the genre after the ill-fated *King's Men* for the Grundy Organisation. *Bellamy*, which he mostly scripted and produced, proved to be one-dimensional and highly repetitive. It veered heavily in the direction of tough, violent action, with the principal figure of the title constantly beset by a rogues' gallery of mad, psychotic killers. The programme was intended for a later prime-time evening slot but it only evoked a lukewarm viewer response and caused the network to play off the remaining episodes in an even later slot. McLean and the Grundy Organisation then parted company.

The Grundy Organisation fared much better with experienced producer Roger Mirams in the area of children's series. The introduction of the C classification by the Australian Broadcasting Tribunal meant that there was now a solid domestic market for children's programming that could be bolstered by having international production investors. Mirams had a long and successful record in producing adventure series. Securing international finance for such ventures had often eluded him, but working as an independent under the Grundy banner was to change all that.

Mirams was to see three interconnected projects reach successful completion in the period 1979–85. The first of these was a telemovie. Not afraid to repeat a series idea from his own past, Mirams put together a successful telemovie series pilot, *Secret Valley*, which was also shown as a four 25-minute episode series (Murray 1996: 137–38, 199). Released in 1980, it depicted a group of children who turn a former ghost town into a holiday resort. The pilot kick-started a series of 26 half-hour episodes that continued the story, with the group banding together to derail the plans of a devious property developer attempting to evict an old man from his property, partly by transforming a derelict ghost town into a holiday camp. Mirams had secured various European broadcasters as investors in *Secret Valley*, and the series was shown extensively there before a very successful debut on the Ten Network in 1984 (Moran 1993: 404).

The ever-resourceful Mirams was also responsible for another children's telemovie that appeared in 1981 while *Secret Valley* was still in production. Using the same production crew and cast of young actors, he had his writers vary the formula of young children banding together to defeat an adult enemy. Thus *Runaway Island* was historical, set in Sydney in the 1840s. The story was familiar but different, about a group of children attempting to foil a villain's efforts to become governor from their base on a secluded coastal island (Murray 1996: 135; Moran 1993: 396). The *Runaway Island* quartet of half-hour episodes had the advantage of being able to be run off as part of *Secret Valley* or shown as a 100-minute, standalone telemovie. Although it had taken Mirams some time to bring his projects to fruition, there was no doubt that he and the Grundy Organisation were good for each other (Grundy 2010: 271–73).

Australia: soap operas

This period saw the Grundy touch sometimes go astray so far as serial drama for the Australian commercial television market was concerned. As the previous chapter indicates, Reg Watson had brought a great deal of know-how and professional experience to the development of Grundy's soap opera output when he joined in 1974, and this had resulted in some immediate successes in the shape of *The Young Doctors* and *The Restless Years*. These serials, as well as other successful serials from Grundy's main drama rival Crawford

Productions in Melbourne in the form of *The Sullivans* and *Cop Shop*, whetted the appetite of the networks for other drama ratings winners. Over the six years being considered in this chapter, no less than seven Grundy serials were commissioned and went to air. As ever, though, there were hits and misses so that the networks were again reminded that not even the Grundy Organisation was infallible. Nevertheless, it is necessary to take account of the failures as well as the successes because the two went together for a company with the resources of Grundy: failures, paradoxically, increased the eventual chance of success, while success offset and overcame the cultural and commercial fallout of failure.

The period was ushered in by Grundy scoring another winner for the Ten Network after the triumph of *The Restless Years*. The serial in question was *Prisoner*, which began broadcasting early in 1979 (Moran 1993: 364–66; Curthoys & Docker 2004: 1825–26). Although set in a women's prison, its drama had to do with relationships, both inside as well as outside the prison, which frequently turned on continuous power struggles among the regular characters. The programme proved to be a smash hit, remaining in production until 1986 and accumulating a total of 692 hour-long episodes. This library helped ensure that *Prisoner* would sell well in overseas markets like the United Kingdom and United States, where it was to achieve cult status. Later, as will be discussed in Chapter 11, the serial would also help provide the format for a US adaptation or spin-off.

One such local remake was soon at hand. This was *Punishment*, which Reg Watson set in a men's prison. The serial went to air in early 1981 (Moran 1993: 371–72). On the premise that a fiction set in a women's prison had succeeded on air, the Ten Network hoped for another hit with the new serial. The move to a men's prison proved to be a mistake, however, with most of the prisoners and their guards being completely unsympathetic characters. There was little to engage a female audience. The network cancelled the series, and only 26 hour-long episodes were produced. Worse was to come for the Grundy Organisation. Over the next five years, its soap opera track record was severely dented, with a succession of ratings casualties. Before examining these, it is worth noting the one other unqualified success that was achieved in the early 1980s. This was *Sons and Daughters*, which was commissioned by the Seven Network (Moran 1993: 486–87). The serial was to result in 972 half-hour episodes, and was in production from 1981 to 1986. As its name implies, *Sons and Daughters* was a family drama that began with melodramatic sensation by having adopted boy and girl twins falling in love, only to learn that they are the sibling offspring of a manipulative mother, who then proceeds to cause further domestic chaos. Although never quite as popular as *Prisoner*, *Sons and Daughters* would still prove to be very important in the company's ledger books, first distributed internationally as a finished programme, and then deployed as a format for subsequent productions elsewhere in the world.

Offsetting these successes were four drama serials that turned out to be rating casualties for both Grundy and the Nine Network. In 1981, it had several successful programmes with the Nine Network and was called in to produce a soap opera that had been initiated independently. The serial in question had the unintelligible title of *Taurus Rising*, and concerned the business and domestic machinations of members of a wealthy, fictitious

Sydney family engaged in building the Taurus Towers, which was to be the tallest building in the city (Moran 1993: 448; Grundy 2010: 186–87). The US prime-time drama serials *Dallas* and *Dynasty* were at the height of their US and international popularity at the time (Brower 2004: 649–52; Mazzarella 2004: 771–73), and Nine believed that *Taurus Rising* might repeat their success locally. Grundy began production in late 1981, and Nine began broadcasting in mid-1982, only to cancel because of poor ratings with 21 hour-long episodes in the can.

By this stage, a second Grundy serial was already in production for the network. Eyeing off the work-and-home dramas of police in *Cop Shop*, which Crawford Productions was making for the Seven Network, Nine ordered *Waterloo Station*, another soap opera set in a suburban police station (Moran 1993: 490–91). Grundy's new programme went to air early in 1983, but had disappeared by mid-year. Nine's soap-opera miseries were intensifying. A third Grundy serial, *Starting Out*, set among a group of young university students, had begun in April as a five-evenings-a-week programme (Moran 1993: 434–35). It too fared badly, with production being cancelled after 85 episodes had been made. A brief respite for Grundy and Nine followed. However, in early 1985 another soap featuring romantic intrigue and melodrama began production. Following in the wake of *Sons and Daughters*, the dramatic starting point for the Nine Network's *Possession* was the turmoil into which the lives of two young women are thrown when one of them learns of tangled parentage (Moran 1993: 359–60). The programme did poorly on air, whereupon Grundy had 52 hour-long episodes for its distribution catalogue, and Nine would go elsewhere for its fiction programming.

Parochial internationalism and its variants

Before turning to Grundy's offshore operation, it is worth framing this development in the light of the idea of 'parochial internationalism' (Cunningham & Jacka 1996: 220–24; Grundy 2010: 303–07). This was a phrase coined by Reg Grundy to characterize the licensing and adaptation of television format programmes across borders, with consequences for the marketing, production and audience appeal of format programmes in different television markets. Thus, while a television programme format inevitably will be devised and developed in a particular national market, it is distributed as a cultural commodity in a larger, global marketplace. In this sense, it is an international cultural commodity that is understood as being capable of being adapted and remade in any particular national industry setting. It has a footloose, 'go anywhere' dimension, assumed to be capable of bypassing differences of language, culture, history, religion and ethnicity when adapted and remade in any national setting anywhere. It can, in short, be 'parochialized'.

This parochial capacity is presumed because at least four sets of elements are called into play in the process of adaptation and remaking (Moran & Malbon 2006: 64–69). These are human labour, textual strategies, audience appeal and subsequent distribution. The first comes into play with the involvement of production personnel in the particular remaking of the programme format. These are, for the most part, local professional and industry employees. While the company licensing the programme format to a local television production or broadcast company in a particular national industry setting may provide the services of a consultant or 'travelling' producer someone familiar with the remaking of the format elsewhere on a short-term basis to help guide these employees, it is assumed that local employees will soon take over full responsibility for the programme remake. For the most part, the adaptation and remaking of the format programme will be undertaken by locally based workers employed by the company licensing the programme. The second element of this local remaking involves the customizing of programme content so that it looks and sounds as though it originated locally. As media researcher Jeremy Tunstall puts it:

> Most people around the world prefer to be entertained by people who look the same, talk the same, joke the same, behave the same, play the same games, and have the same beliefs (and worldview) as themselves. They also overwhelmingly prefer their own national news, politics, weather, and football and other sports.
> (Tunstall 2008: xiv)

The third element confirming the parochialization of the programme relates to the local or national audience. Responding to the textual customizing that has taken place, recognizing and accepting the familiar representations and references at work in the program's images and sounds, the audience accedes to the programme. This is frequently (and mistakenly) accompanied by the assumption that the programme is home grown and of national origin. The last way in which the parochial dimension registers is through the practice of mostly not attempting to distribute the remade programme in other national television industries, out of a belief that it is far too culturally specific to appeal to another audience. In short, the format is international while any finished programme version is seen as more circumscribed and parochial.

This formula of 'parochial internationalism' can be seen as applying to Reg Grundy's activities as a television programme producer from 1959 onwards, in terms of his practice of using programme ideas first devised and used in programme forms in the United States. He assumed – correctly, as it turned out – that quiz and game shows originally developed for the US market could successfully be adapted and remade for the Australian television audience, to the point where Australians assumed that the programme was home grown.

However, if this interchange between a kind of television programming 'them' and 'us' can operate at a national/international intersection, it can also operate at other levels. Two of these deserve mention in connection with 'parochial internationalism'. The first can be labelled 'parochial intranationalism', and concerns format programme adaptation and remaking at a national-regional level. Here, we can recall Grundy's company remakings of quiz and game shows for stations in the Australian minor state capital cities, such as Brisbane and Adelaide – something that has been mentioned in the past three chapters. There was a continuous record of such programme format remakings between 1965 and 1997, and for the most part such productions appeared on air only in the region, whether statewide or even just citywide. Clearly, in Grundy's case, the stage of parochial intranationalism can be seen as a kind of anticipation or preparation for the flexibility and mobility that would be required by parochial internationalism.

Another tier of format adaptation and remaking within which the company would be active can be labelled 'parochial supranationalism'. This practice of format reworking is connected with the advent of cross-border satellite delivery of television programmes. In 1994, Grundy joined with a Swedish production company to produce a pan-Scandinavian version of its game show format extravaganza *Man O Man* (Moran 1998: 83–90). The programme was distributed to Sweden, Norway and Denmark in their respective languages. Buoyed by this experience, the Grundy company produced another pan-national version of the format in South America in 1997. Using satellite delivery once again, the new adaptation of *Man O Man* was broadcast to three of the countries in the Mercosur group Argentina, Uruguay and Paraguay (Moran 1998: 83–84). Altogether, then, this three-tier model of format remaking allows us to draw closer connections between the Grundy company's activities in Australia and those offshore. I now turn to these latter ventures.

The United States: getting started

In restructuring Reg Grundy Enterprises as the Grundy Organisation in 1977, Grundy and his executives were doing more than changing the name of the group. Reorganization heralded moves to facilitate new operations inside and outside Australia. As I have already noted, the move to establish Grundy as a US television company had been in train since the early 1970s. A Los Angeles Grundy representative, Bob Crystal, had been secured around 1974, while a West Coast office was set up in 1979. This was necessary because the company had a growing catalogue of finished programmes for US licensing, including many hours of long-running Australian drama serials, and would soon have a revamped and very successful Australian version of a US original quiz-show format, *Sale of the Century*.

Three factors triggered the move into the United States: the lack of further market opportunity in Australia, the value of the US market, and a strong personal ambition on Reg Grundy's part. The first of these has already been mentioned. The Grundy Organisation was at its peak in Australia, and unless new broadcasting channels were created, there was little opportunity for further growth in sales output. If the company wanted to continue to expand, then it needed to look offshore. In 1979, few business openings were available in parts of the world where television operated under either a public-service or a state-controlled model. The dominance of these models, with their tendency to originate programmes in-house, meant that there was little opportunity for expansion into such television markets as the United Kingdom, Western Europe, Eastern Europe and even neighbouring New Zealand.

By contrast, the US commercial television industry was market-based, and therefore more open to newcomer entry and competition (Anderson 2004: 87–91). US television was one of the most lucrative broadcasting systems on the planet. It was also one of the largest, comprising three distinct but interconnected sectors: network, syndication and cable. Licensing deals with broadcasters in any of these especially the network sector would be very lucrative.

One other reason for the US move should also be mentioned. A successful entry into this industry must have represented a personal ambition for Reg Grundy for quite some time. Australian media, entertainment and culture generally had decisively been impacted by such social vehicles as US journalism, films, advertising, radio broadcasting, television, jazz and rock 'n' roll. This trend had begun around 1900, grew in strength in the 1920s, escalated during wartime and blossomed in the post-war era. By the early 1970s, this cultural flow was further augmented by the extension of US fast-food franchising to Australia. The time seemed ripe for some kind of contra flow. In the media realm, Rupert Murdoch's News Limited had already proven this to be the case; now it was Reg Grundy's turn.

The idea of establishing an arm of the Grundy operation in the United States can possibly be dated as far back as 1959, when Reg Grundy realized the overwhelming importance of television quiz-show formats originating in the United States for Australian commercial television. This contact had been stepped up over the next two decades. From 1966, Reg Grundy made regular visits to the United States – often several times a year – in order to view new US quiz shows shortly after they began on network television. A West Coast representative had been secured almost ten years earlier. Bob Crystal became a kind of advance scout for the US spread of the company, knocking on doors, making contacts and preparing for Grundy's more permanent coming. Other US officers were also engaged. These included Charles Michelson, a US programme distributor, who was charged with the task of sending recordings of the new US game shows back to Australia (Grundy 2010: 123). Now the master's apprentice was keen to show off what he had learned, and the US television industry was the place to make such an impact.

As it turned out, 1979 was an auspicious time for Grundy to establish its first foreign production office. The US television networks were on the brink of an era of crisis and transformation that has continued down to the present (Attallah 1991; Anderson 2004). Three years earlier, the networks that had dominated television broadcasting since the inception of networking in 1946 – NBC, CBS and ABC – experienced a peak of broadcast television viewing. Thereafter, the total network audience size began to contract, and by 1992 it was estimated that the networks had lost about a third of the audience that they had attracted in the halcyon year of 1976. Many new competitors emerged in the 1980s and 1990s. Industry deregulation, coinciding with the advent of Reagan as president, also helped drive this transformation (Anderson 2004: 87–91; Lucas 2004: 343–46; Sterling 2004a: 688–89; Fletcher 2004: 2247–48). Each of the networks changed ownership, and new fledgling commercial networks attached to the major Hollywood companies such as Fox, Warner and Paramount came into being (Hilmes 2004: 1109–11). However, it was the national satellite delivery of cable television, beginning with Ted Turner's Channel 17 in 1980, that proved to be the main drain on the network television audience (Strover 2004: 389–97). Newer sectors such as the computer hardware and software groups and the telephone companies were also eagerly eyeing the television market (Grant 2004: 705–06). The promise was that viewers in large urban centres would have a choice of 500 channels in the not too distant future.

With Ian Holmes heading up the Grundy Organisation in Australia, Reg Grundy devoted all his time and money to establishing the US operation. A New York office located in the centre of US corporate power, including the headquarters of the US television networks, had opened two years earlier and was now joined by a Los Angeles production office. About the same time, the Grundy Organisation registered an American subsidiary company, Reg Grundy Productions Inc., for its US operation. Reg Grundy was already a regular attendee at the annual get-together of the US television industry, the National Association of Television Programming Executives (NATPE), which had begun in 1964 and provided an excellent opportunity to get to know the field of domestic broadcasters and producers (Cunningham 2004b: 1183–84; Taub-Pervizpour 2004: 1168–71).

Following his own philosophy of 'parochial internationalism', Grundy also brought in US personnel to staff his operation (Grundy 2010: 231–43). Four are worth noting: Bob Crystal has already been mentioned; he now became part of the new West Coast operation. US television industry veteran Tom McManus was appointed to head up the Los Angeles office, and in 1981 Grundy also brought another industry veteran, Bob Noah, on board. If the company was to license quiz shows to broadcasters, then it would need to devise new formats in-house. Noah was an excellent choice to partner Reg Grundy at the format-devising coalface, having had a long history in US quiz-show production, working for the most successful companies such as Goodson-Todman and Quigley-Hall (Cooper-Chen 1994: 211; Grundy 2010: 231–32). Finally, the Australian also needed an executive with a good deal of high-level industry clout. By around 1980, he had secured the services of New York entertainment lawyer Richard Barovick (Grundy 2010: 2079). Barovick was a senior partner in a New York law firm, and he agreed to become Grundy's legal representative and head up Grundy's New York office. Barovick would be valued for his skills as a negotiator, and especially for his ability to open doors at very senior corporate levels.

The United States: a drama serial 'calling card'

Grundy had one advantage in attempting to break into the domestic US television production market: the library of programmes and formats it had developed in Australia. As it was out of the question that the big three networks would license a drama serial that had Australian accents, faces, places and situations, Grundy steered towards the 'second-network' syndication market for the re-broadcast of drama originally commissioned for broadcast in Australia (Fletcher 2004: 2247–48). It soon achieved a breakthrough. In 1979, it sold the serial *Prisoner* to independent station KTLA in Los Angeles, and within a year had sold the show in 38 other markets, with fees based on on-air performance (Cunningham & Jacka 1996: 170–78; Grundy 2010: 206–10). KTLA was owned by the media interests of the former Hollywood singing cowboy Gene Autry, but the station management and programmer were left alone to run the operation. The Australian serial was renamed *Prisoner: Cell Block H* to avoid confusion with a UK drama serial of the 1960s entitled *The Prisoner* (Berger 2004: 1829–31). KTLA gave it extensive promotion and aired it at the rate of two episodes a week. It achieved excellent ratings and was to become an international cult serial, beginning in the United States.

The following year, Grundy persuaded KTLA to take their association further by building on the *Cell Block H* foundation. Under Reg Grundy's instructions, Reg Watson produced scripts for pilots of two new serials (Grundy 2010: 210). *Starting Over* was reported as being an adaptation of *The Restless Years*, which had successfully debuted on the Seven Network in Australia in late 1977 and was still in production in 1980 (Moran 1993: 434–35). The story centred on a group of youths at a refuge, an interesting anticipation of another popular serial, *Home and Away*, which the Seven Network would produce and broadcast beginning in 1987 (Moran 1993: 226–27).

Reg Grundy makes no mention of these possible connections when discussing the evolution of *Starting Over* in his memoir (2010: 206–10). There is also some confusion with the other pilot script intended as a kind of follow up to *Cell Block H*. A report at the time referred to this script pilot as 'Willow B: Women in Prison', suggesting that it was a close reversioning of *Cell Block H* (Day 1980: 58). Grundy, however, refers to it as depicting men in prison and carrying the title of *Punishment* (2010: 201–12). Pilots were certainly made of both scripts. The *Starting Over* outing was recorded at KTLA's Golden West studios with locations mainly on Sunset and Hollywood Boulevards, according to Grundy (2010: 208). The pilot for the prison serial was shot at Channel Ten in Sydney, on the basis that costs were lower even though the look and style of *Prisoner: Cell Block H* could be achieved at US locations. Unfortunately, KTLA passed on commissioning a season of either *Starting Over* or *Willow B: Women in Prison*. For the time being, Reg Grundy Productions Inc. had played its best shot in drama but without any success. Luckily, it had other expertise on offer.

The United States: quiz shows

It would take two further years before the company was making programmes for a US buyer. In hiring Bob Noah to help him devise quiz shows, Grundy knew that his own past had mostly caught up with him so far as quiz-show formats were concerned. For more than twenty years, his company had capitalized on adapting quiz-show formats first devised by others for the US network market. The Australian company had itself devised a handful of game show formats over time, but these had not been memorable or durable. The hope for this new market lay in the drawcard of a US quiz-show format that had been improved by adaptations in Australia and elsewhere. One was to hand, and this became Reg Grundy's quiz-show 'calling card'.

The format was *Sale of the Century*. The quiz show already had an impressive track record: the original US version had run on the NBC network from 1969 to 1973, and a further year in syndication (Schwartz, Ryan & Wosbrook 1987: 396), and it had given rise to the very successful *Temptation* and *The Great Temptation* in Australia from 1970 to 1974 (Moran & Keating 2003: 76, 122–23) before reviving on Australian television under its original title in 1980 and breaking all quiz-show popularity records (Moran & Keating 2003: 113–14; Grundy 2010: 231–43). Grundy offered the show to CBS, which declined it. NBC was more interested, and was persuaded to dispense with the usual trial run-throughs and three pilots in favour of viewing a recent Australian episode as a kind of down-payment for what Reg Grundy Productions Inc. would do with a US network version. NBC accepted *Sale of the Century*, and the quiz show began on weekday daytime television in early January 1983 (Hyatt 1997: 371). Reg Grundy Productions Inc. became the first overseas company to make a programme for NBC. *Sale of the Century* was to run until 1989. It was extremely profitable, not least because the Grundy Organisation had by then bought the format rights from the original devisor and owner.

Soon, three other daily quiz shows were on air alongside *Sale of the Century* on NBC daytime. From this point on, all US Grundy quiz shows had to be devised from scratch. The first was *Scrabble*, ostensibly an adaptation of the famous board game licensed by its owners but actually a fast, simplified version that could be played by two contestants. It began on air in mid-1984, and would run until 1990 (Schwartz, Ryan & Wosbrook 1987: 400; Hyatt 1997: 390; Grundy 2010: 266–70). The company had less success with the other two game shows. The first was *Time Machine*, yet another programme made for NBC daytime that involved contestants guessing about people and events of the past. It began early in 1984 and lasted less than four months on air (Schwartz, Ryan & Wosbrook 1987: 456; Hyatt 1997: 433; Grundy 2010: 274–77). Equally disappointing was *Bruce Forsyth's Hot Streak*, a 1986 outing for the ABC Network (Hyatt 1997: 73; Grundy 2010: 278–80). The format had two teams compete by having to describe features in 40 seconds, with their partners then having to guess the object referred to by the clues. In a highly unusual move in game show production generally, Reg Grundy Productions agreed to feature the host's name in the programme title in order to secure the services of a well-known UK programme compère. It made no difference and the programme disappeared after sixteen weeks on air.

While several of these formats were unsuccessful on US network television, that was far from the end of their value to the company. They were company property and might be commissioned for remaking by a broadcaster in another market. This did not happen with *Time Machine*, but it did occur with *Hot Streak* in Germany, as we will see in Chapter 11. One other format devised for a network commission that never materialized should also be mentioned. This was *Keynotes*, a musical knowledge game show in the tradition of the early 1950s classic *Name That Tune* (Grundy 2010: 270). It was devised by Grundy himself and a US producer, first for ABC and then for NBC. Both networks funded pilots but neither commissioned production. Grundy felt that the format carried a demographic problem with different generations of viewers having quite different musical knowledge. Be that as it may, the *Keynotes* format also went into the company's international programme format catalogue, and versions of the programme later appeared in Australia and the United Kingdom, although with only limited success (Evans 2001: 334; Moran & Keating 2003: 87). Despite these setbacks, Reg Grundy would have been pleased with progress, by the mid-1980s, in the most difficult of television markets. *Prisoner: Cell Block H* had achieved cult status in syndication; *Sale of the Century* and *Scrabble* were doing well; even the unsuccessful quiz-show formats might have a broadcast life elsewhere. Meanwhile, another overseas market opened briefly.

South-East Asia: game shows

The Grundy Organisation's move into South-East Asia that took place in these years looks, in retrospect, more like a spillover or afterthought of the Australian operation rather than a long-term move towards Asian transnationalization. Even in the early 1980s, television in South-East Asia and Oceania was mostly a domestic matter. Satellite broadcasting did not yet exist in this part of the world, so television broadcast signals and national borders mostly coincided with each other. Television had begun in the city state of Hong Kong in 1967 as an entirely commercial affair, broadcasting to a population of over six million on the island and in the southern Chinese province of Guangzhou and mostly using either Cantonese Chinese or English (Gwinn Wilkins 2004: 1129–32). Hong Kong laid a heavy emphasis on private enterprise and free trade, so programmes that promoted these values were likely to receive favourable consideration from programme buyers. In 1981–82, Grundy's Sydney office was contacted by the Australian CEO of a new Hong Kong broadcaster, RTV, who had formerly worked in Perth television (Mason 2010). The CEO had decided that RTV needed a 'headline' programme such as a local version of *Sale of the Century* to begin making headway against established rivals. However, costings indicated that the latter would be too expensive by itself. Thus Grundy made available another format quiz show, and a Grundy executive producer who had already worked on the Australian version of *Sale of the Century* was dispatched to Hong Kong to oversee the making of the two quiz shows. The shows were broadcast in Cantonese, compèred by native-born hosts, used contestants drawn from the domestic population and employed a clutch of locals in more junior production roles. The first of the two programmes was *Dai Pai*, which was based on a US format that had first appeared on the US NBC Network in 1978. *Card Sharks* had been devised by Reg Grundy's favourite US quiz-show originator, Mark Goodson Productions (Schwartz, Ryan & Wosbrook 1987: 76–77). Unfortunately, the Hong Kong version only ran for one season before it ceased production.

The Grundy Organisation had more luck with the Hong Kong adaptation of the *Sale of the Century* format. It was entitled *Dai Sou But*, and ran on air in 1982. The programme format was already well on the way to becoming the company's most valuable format ever, with very high ratings on the Nine Network in Australia, which itself repeated the format's earlier success when it played as both *Temptation* and *The Great Temptation* on the Seven

Network. *Dai Sou But* was the second adaptation of *Sale of the Century*, and Grundy's first remake in another television market; it was a precursor to a successful US outing that would appear the following year and a prelude to the twelve other remakes that would occur in the next dozen years across the world (Moran 1998: 75–83).

One other South-East Asian quiz-show production also happened at this time. The format remaking occurred in another island state located between Malaysia and Indonesia to the near-north of Australia. Brunei was a protectorate of a half a million people, ruled by an oil-rich constitutional monarch who had initiated television in 1975, not least to overcome the local saturation coverage by Malaysian television (Sen 2004: 2145–49). The monarch was not only a political leader, but also a religious one, and television assumed an Islamic audience in the kingdom. Again, it was an Australian television executive who initiated the Grundy involvement. The executive worked in programme distribution on behalf of Grundy and a rival, Becker Fremantle. He contacted Grundy's Sydney office, and two senior quiz-show production executives were dispatched to Brunei.

Gambling was not encouraged under Muslim rule, so the format choice was restricted (Mason 1980). Grundy was already producing a children's game show, *Matchmates*, for TCN9 back in Sydney, so Brunei TV was offered and accepted a local adaptation of the programme. Like *Dai Sau But* in Hong Kong, this format remake did well on air and both shows ran until 1986.

This South-East Asia excursion had been interesting, and probably modestly profitable. However, Grundy's quiz-show personnel, led by senior producers, had been confronted by two problems that would continue over the next ten years. The first was language, particularly the difficulty of communicating with local production personnel; the second concerned the production routines and organization employed by Grundy. The company's quiz shows were intended for programming on air five days a week, and this required production at high speed with batches of five programmes being made together. If and when the company made programmes elsewhere, it would probably also need to demonstrate to television personnel in such places that more high-speed and low-cost Australian production routines and practices needed to be adopted. This was still a little way in the future, however.

Family business: relocating to Bermuda

The period 1979–85 saw no new structural developments so far as the Grundy company was concerned; instead, it was domestic location matters that were rearranged. Reg Grundy took the decision to locate his home residence offshore in parallel with the outward-bound ambitions of the Grundy Organisation. In 1984, Grundy and his wife set up a permanent home on the south shore of the small island of Bermuda. Why this move? The short answer would seem to be for tax-related reasons.

There are many tax havens across the world, including Monaco and Bermuda. These shelters differ considerably in terms of the conditions that they offer companies and individuals for rearranging their tax affairs. Personal and corporate tax is not payable in Bermuda, or in some other centres, thus giving these locations an immediate advantage over tax havens elsewhere (Cromie 1989: 62–70; Fung 1989: 51–55; Hogan 1994: 45–50; Hooke 1992: 1–11). Other factors also probably came into play in relation to the Grundy domestic residence decision. As a British colony, Bermuda uses the system of British common law, as do countries that formerly were British colonies (including Australia and the United States) and present-day British colonies and dependent territories. Trusts have become an important tool in the offshore tax-planning industry, particularly in the domain of personal income arrangements. The recognition of trusts under the common law system gives adherent jurisdictions a further advantage over those that adopt the civil law system found in Europe, such as Switzerland, Monaco and Luxembourg.

Communication is also facilitated in a location such as Bermuda. English is the common tongue of the island, and this overcomes the barrier that verbal and written exchange between home company and an offshore company might encounter elsewhere. Allied to this is the high standard of the banking facilities and professional services to do with tax planning that have developed on the island since the late 1940s, when early tax refugees such as English musical comedy star Noel Coward first arrived there. Secrecy and confidentiality represent another face of this service, with particular disclosures constituting a legal offence.

Civil order is yet another important factor in the decision of many wealthy figures to bring their tax problems to Bermuda. Unlike some of the newer tax havens located in such regions as Africa, Oceania and Asia, the British colony offers little threat of the political instability and social unrest that can severely disrupt business activities. Political upheaval can also bring about adverse changes in business and tax laws, but the ordered society of Bermuda offers no hint of such an upheaval. In other cases, government red tape, political scandals and a lack of government credibility can also nullify benefits offered by a tax haven. Thus, Monaco has recently suffered as a tax destination because of the widespread presence of Russian businessmen. Yet another benefit offered by Bermuda – one that it shares with many other tax havens – is the fact that it does not have exchange control restrictions so that private capital funds can be moved about without impediment.

Added to all these advantages are several physical factors that possibly clinched Reg Grundy's decision to live in Bermuda from 1984 onwards. The island is in the Atlantic Gulf Stream and enjoys a pleasant climate for most of the year. There is access to attractive land and sea settings, with cities such as New York and London easily reached by air and sea. Finally, the tone of well-to-do society in Bermuda is chic but conservative, and its general affluence, civil order and physical setting have attracted a distinct set of genteel celebrities from such realms as politics, entertainment, sport and business. It was and is therefore a most attractive setting in which to live and from which to run an international enterprise.

Afterword

In 1983, Reg Grundy's mother was being looked after in her Sydney apartment home by a full-time nurse/carer. She liked to relax in the evening by watching her son's programmes on the Australian commercial television networks. There were plenty for her to choose from, requiring constant channel changing to keep up with the flow of Grundy programmes in the early evening. The array included the drama serial *Prisoner* and quiz show *Perfect Match* on Ten, the soap opera *Waterloo Station* and quiz show *Sale of the Century* on Nine, as well as the children's drama *Runaway Island*, the drama serial *Sons and Daughters* and quiz shows *The New Price is Right* and *Wheel of Fortune* on Seven (Grundy 2010: 263–65). This even spread of programmes across the networks suggests how well the Grundy Organisation was doing with Ten, Nine and Seven. As it had done for over twenty years, Grundy was continuing to provide the commercial sector with popular and entertaining programming that was, for the most part, attracting sizeable audiences, even when one company programme was pitted against another by rival network programmers. Under the capable stewardship of Ian Holmes, Grundy's head of Australian operations, more than twenty hours of television programming was produced each week for the three networks. This meant that the Grundy Organisation stood head and shoulders above any other packager working for Australian commercial television. The ongoing domestic success was also very profitable and ensured that the group would continue to be able to underwrite the transnational activities of its various companies. Grundy's first 'breakout' production activities had now occurred, and it was time to renew and extend these to other overseas television markets.

Chapter 10

Transnational Ambitions IV: Australia, the United Kingdom and the United States, 1985-89

Introduction

Good times, bad times: shortly, this couplet was to become the name of both a Dutch remake and then a German adaptation by Grundy of an original long-running company soap opera first produced for Australian television. The name could equally have been applied to the company's changing fortunes ever since it had launched a series of overseas ventures beginning in the late 1970s. It had been Reg Grundy's policy since his entry into the world of television programme format production back in 1959 to protect one television operation with another. The thinking was that if one game show programme was cancelled, then having another in production would buffer this effect. Selling programmes to all three Australian commercial networks provided such insurance, as did the introduction of drama production, which helped shield the quiz-show output. In turn, overseas expansion further sheltered the overall operation, with good returns from one territory helping to offset disappointing proceeds from another. This master pattern was displayed vividly by company operations in the period 1985–89. These years saw general financial tumult in Australia and elsewhere, which helped trigger upheavals in the television industry. There were programme cancellations in the domestic market and in overseas markets, but there were also commissions for new shows. Transnationalizing the company was an audacious move, but there was no going back if further growth was to be achieved. Even so, it was far from certain by 1989 just how successful the move would finally turn out to be. This chapter is divided into four sections. The first examines overall developments in and general strategies of the company at this time. I then concentrate on Grundy's activities in three key markets. As usual, the emphasis falls on programme output, including the shows' origins and network commissions. Collectively, these licensings put more revenue in the business war chest for developments that still lay ahead.

Background, company restructuring and operation

The Grundy company was to experience enormous expansion over the next ten years, thanks not only to launching a transnational operation oriented to world market possibilities, but also by doing so at a most opportune time. Television markets in many parts of the globe were undergoing significant change and expansion. The general background to this development has already been indicated. Since the early 1980s, the television landscape of national markets across much of the world had begun transforming under the impact of new technologies, commercialization of public-service broadcasting, deregulation of broadcasting policy and privatization of many existing broadcasting channels (Weiten, Murdock & Dahlgren 2000; Strover 2004: 389-97; Curtin 2004: 993-97; Sterling 2004a: 688-89). The advent of cable, satellite and other delivery capacities saw a significant jump in the number of television channels on the air. This development coincided with government decisions that, because broadcasting was no longer a scarcity, the provision of broadcasting should be left to market forces rather than to the state. The new, expanded services turned towards an advertising-supported model of television that was commercial, populist and oriented to entertainment (Moran 2005: 291-307).

Reg Grundy was keenly aware of these changes and opportunities, and was busy putting his company's operation in order accordingly. Even while programme output outlined to this point was happening, other behind-the-scenes developments were also in train, affecting the business empire's future (Cunningham & Jacka 1996: 16-20, 81-86; Moran 1998: 55-73). In 1985, Grundy established offices in Europe as part of an anticipated push into new markets. In 1988, the third (and what proved to be the last) corporate reorganization of the Grundy group took place. As the Australian Taxation Office noted at the time, many home-grown companies were incorporating themselves offshore. The Grundy company was one of these (Braithwaite 2005: 1536). Like its owner, the new business entity secured its own place in the Caribbean sun by basing its parent body in Bermuda (Cromie 1989: 62-70; Fung 1989: 51-55; Hogan 1994: 45-50; Hooke 1992: 1-11). Copyright ownership of the company's programme formats was registered in the nearby colony of Antigua, while legal and financial matters continued to be handled in Monaco.

The parent company, the Grundy Organisation, remained as the Australian branch of the business entity. By this time, over 40 international Grundy companies had been established in different parts of the world. Some, such as those in Australia and the United Kingdom, were very busy while others were not yet active. Nevertheless, planning was afoot for a transnational empire so that key regional Grundy offices had been or were being set up in such key markets as Germany and France, Singapore and Chile. The intention was that these might, in turn, spawn smaller offices in particular national markets. A series of company vice-presidents ran many of these entities.

A new corporate entity, Grundy Worldwide, was established to oversee the transnational operation, the progress of which was increasingly impressive. In less than ten years, for example, the revenue stream from operations across the world had jumped from A$9.5 million to A$140 million, with production and distribution contributing about 70 per cent of the returns (Cunningham & Jacka 1996: 83). Grundy's programmes sold in more than 70 countries across the world. These activities as well as its global productions brought about the increase in revenue, with the company claiming in 1989 to be the second largest light entertainment producer on the planet and one of the world's largest independent production organizations (Cunningham & Jacka 1996: 84). Four years later, it was reported that Grundy Worldwide was making 45 hours of television programming each week (Macken 1989: 9).

As the company expanded internationally from 1979 onwards, three kinds of local involvement or orientation became the norm. The first was the establishment of an independent Grundy office in a new television market as a prelude to local production of programmes for that market. This kind of Grundy production office was set up in the United States, the United Kingdom and Monaco. A more common pattern was to enter into a joint-venture arrangement with an established domestic production company. Examples of this second type of setup included Grundy/JE in The Netherlands and Grundy UFA in Germany. A third strategy for international reach was to license a Grundy format to a local broadcaster or production company where the small size of a market did not warrant either the independent or the coventure arrangements. This kind of sublicensing was to be the case with Grundy-owned format productions in Israel, Indonesia and Greece.

Television programme format access

Central to all this was the company's lifeblood, in the form of television programme formats. Australia media commentary at this time often suggested that Grundy Worldwide's format catalogue consisted of programme ideas and knowledge first developed in Australia, which were now fuelling the production of adaptations in other overseas television markets (*Broadcasting Abroad* 1989: 10–13; Gerrie 1992: 98–100; Nicholson 1994: 44–46). There was some truth in this notion, but a number of riders also need to be added. As we will see in the next chapter, Grundy was to have significant success in both The Netherlands and Germany by remaking soap opera formats that it had first devised in Australia. Several of these drama serial formats also gave rise to other adaptations elsewhere, but with less success. On other occasions, Grundy devised original drama serials in other markets, including Germany, Italy and New Zealand.

The company was in a less advantageous position in international markets when it came to game show formats. From the time Reg Grundy Enterprises began to package quiz shows for TCN9 in Sydney, Australia, up to the moment when Grundy Worldwide was sold, the production entity made more than 100 different game shows, with several of these being revivals or spin-off versions of others. As we have seen, the majority of these quiz and game shows were based on formats imported from the United States. Thanks to the constant appearance of new game show formats on US network television, there was never any pressure on the company in Australia to devise new game show formats or even to buy them outright, although Grundy had originated a small number of game shows in Australia over the years, including *Wheel of Fortune* (1959, 1969) and *Ampol Big Game* (1966).

After 1980, things changed. As already noted, the United States had signed the Berne Convention on Copyright, so US game show devisors led by Mark Goodson Productions were now systematically licensing their libraries of US game shows around the world

(Bourdin 2011). As a new transnational production player, Grundy enjoyed none of the territorial advantages with US formats that it had in Australia over the previous twenty years. In Europe, for instance, Grundy was in competition with US production companies, private national production companies and public-service broadcasters, all of whom were pursuing licensing deals with US format owners. As we saw in Chapter 9, Grundy had bought world rights to the *Sale of the Century* format from its US owner, and also took out options on the German game show *Man O Man* for all territories other than Germany.

In addition, it also had another source of programme formats. Reg Grundy Productions in the United States was busy devising new game shows for the network and the syndication markets in attempts to gain commissions and put shows on the air. Sometimes these efforts were successful; however, others failed to be commissioned after development. In any case, such formats were company property and could end up being licensed to broadcasters in other television markets, including in Europe and Australia. Among the quiz and game show formats that Grundy devised, purchased or licensed at this time were *Sale of the Century, Pot of Gold, Going for Gold, Time Machine, Hot Streak, Matchmates, Keynotes* and *Stoppers*.

Format circulation: the case of *It's a Knockout*

On several occasions in this book, I have drawn attention to the US origins of programme formats being adapted and remade by Grundy. It is worth adding the important qualification that the historical movement of programme formats across borders was frequently a more complicated matter than the revolving door of export/import between a national television market and the US one. Take the Grundy production of *It's A Knockout*, produced for the Ten Network in Australia between 1985 and 1987 (Moran & Keating 2003: 82). *It's a Knockout* was a comedy sporting game involving three teams of adults competing in a series of zany contests in what has been described as 'school sports day for adults', with the contests being officiated by well-known sporting figures and sports broadcasters. The format seems to have its origin in an early French broadcast, *Intervilles*, designed to foster friendly rivalry and cheer between French and German teams in the 1950s. In 1965, the format was revamped as a pan-European comedy sporting show, *Jeu Sans Frontieres* (*The Game Without Borders*). It was to run from 1965 to 1999 under the auspices of the European Broadcasting Union, and involved friendly, zany competitions between different European nations. A UK version of the format began on the BBC in 1966, and would continue with different UK broadcasters until 2001. The UK version was entitled *It's a Knockout*, and was designed partly around the heat sequence that would provide the UK participants for the European-wide *Jeu Sans Frontieres* (Vahamagi 1996: 149). A US network version entitled *Almost Anything Goes* ran for two seasons in 1975–76, featuring a competition of small towns across the country. A children's version, *Junior Almost Anything Goes*, then ran for a season between 1976 and 1977, and was followed by a syndicated celebrity version, *All Star Anything Goes*, which appeared between 1977 and 1978 (Schwartz, Ryan & Wosbrook 1987: 10–11).

With the existence of two English-language versions of the format, there was plenty to choose from when it came to adapting the format for remaking in Australia. A 1970s Grundy rival production company, Willard King Productions, had been quick off the mark and licensed an Australian version for broadcast on the 0-10 Network. *Almost Anything Goes* aired from 1976 to 1978. Filmed in Melbourne, each season featured one or two complete competitions, with the 1977 finale also involving a New Zealand team (Moran & Keating 2003: 48). The Grundy Organisation got its chance to see what it could do with the format in the mid-1980s. Its version was an adaptation of the UK version titled *It's a Knockout*. It ran on the same network now renamed Network Ten as its programme predecessor, appearing between 1985 and 1987 (Moran & Keating 2003: 82). But the US example was also pertinent, in that an 'all star' version of the programme, *Celebrity It's a Knockout*, also appeared in 1986 (Moran & Keating 2003: 57). *It's a Knockout* did well on air, but complaints by neighbours about its filming, together with recessionary forces at work in the Australian economy, generally convinced the network not to renew its licensing.

Neighbours and cross-subsidization

On some rare occasions, the Grundy company engaged in the subsidization of a programme. We noted this in Chapter 8, when Reg Grundy carried the costs of the production of an early thirteen-week stint of the serial *The Young Doctors*, and the same exceptional situation will be met again in the period covered in Chapter 11. Here, it is worth recording the additional financial sacrifice that the Grundy Organisation was prepared to make in order to help keep *Neighbours* on air on the Ten Network in Australia in the late 1980s (Crofts 1995: 98–102; Cunningham 2004c: 1623–25).

By 1989, *Neighbours* had become a British soap opera to all intents and purposes. Once *Neighbours* had been sold to the BBC, Grundy's storyliners had begun to set parts of stories in the United Kingdom to broaden the appeal of the serial (Crofts 1995: 98–108). Story segments were recorded in the United Kingdom to cement this connection, and having a UK Grundy production office was helpful in providing logistical support for these periodic ventures. At the same time, back in Australia, the future of the programme was in increasing doubt in the general situation of economic recession and the parlous financial situation of the Ten Network's new owner, Northern Star.

Rather than have the latter cancel the serial for budgetary reasons, the Grundy Organisation agreed to reduce the price of the soap opera for its Australian broadcast, effectively cross-subsidizing *Neighbours'* production costs. It was vital that the programme remain on air on the BBC, in a much bigger and wealthier television market. Besides, the fee being received from the BBC more than offset the loss on the Ten Network broadcast.

The economics of *Neighbours* brightened even further in the next year or so. By around 1990, all three Australian commercial broadcasters were struggling to meet mortgage repayments on their 1987 network purchases (Cunningham & Jacka 1996: 58–66). The

Grundy Organisation bought residual rights to all the programmes that the Ten Network had commissioned over the years. This resulted in a 35 per cent increase in revenue to the company from the international sales of its various drama programmes, including *Neighbours* (Grundy 2010: 260–61).

International distribution

A further facet of company operation concerned the licensing of existing Grundy programmes especially fiction in overseas markets. Programme distribution has been touched upon several times in this book, first with the circulation of Grundy's quiz shows in regional Australia and second with the cross-border licensing of fiction programmes produced in colour in other parts of the world after 1974. Now new distribution arrangements were put in place as part of an overall company restructuring. Initially, the international licensing of canned or finished programmes had been handled by Paramount Pictures; however, in the early 1980s this relationship had lapsed in favour of the appointment of a series of marketing representatives in different territories, coordinated by a principal agent based in New York. However, these arrangements always involved substantial commission fees for the intermediate party.

Therefore, in 1989 Grundy Worldwide set up its own distribution branch, Grundy International Distribution. This entity was headquartered at Grundy's production office in London, although warehousing and dispatch occurred from a plant in the Netherlands (Moran 1998: 55–56). There was a strong demand for Australian television fiction thanks to the expansion of television markets in Europe and elsewhere (Macken 1989: 9). Hence, it was not surprising that other programme producers sought to avail themselves of the Grundy distribution facility. The growth of its programme sales meant that Grundy International Distribution handled not only its own fiction serials and game shows, especially those produced in the English language but also various US game shows based on Mark Goodson formats, as well as other programmes such as the Australian Broadcasting Corporation's (ABC) legal drama series *Janus/Criminal Justice* (1994–95). Its functions would be taken over by Pearson Television's distribution section after a buyout of Grundy in 1995. This buyout is dealt with in Chapter 12. Here, we review Grundy's output in three transnational markets, beginning with the Australian operation.

Grundy's advantages for public-service broadcasters

Before leaving this matter of the company developing relationship with public-service broadcasters, it is worth pointing out two specific ways in which Grundy Worldwide had a useful edge so far as potential rivals were concerned. For European broadcasters and others used to a public-service model of broadcasting, Grundy was an attractive supplier as these broadcasters attempted to negotiate an industry environment now shifting towards post-Fordism. Its attractions were twofold. First, Grundy was used to working in a streamlined, high-speed, low-cost way on contract systems that saw the production of a week's supply of programming in one marathon production session. Second, while the company firmly adhered to commercial values of entertainment, nevertheless Grundy was not a US company and therefore could be preferred on occasions when it mattered to operators hailing from across the Atlantic (Macken 1989: 9; Gerrie 1992: 98–100; Nicholson 1994: 44–46).

Australia: an unsettled time

The late 1980s were not kind to the Grundy Organisation's domestic operation. The economic crisis of 1987 led to inflation and growing unemployment. By 1990, none of the commercial television networks had money in their coffers (Cunningham & Jacka 1996: 82–86). The new cross-ownership media rules introduced by the Australian government in 1987 had resulted in the sale and purchase of the three commercial networks at highly inflated prices by entrepreneurs who subscribed to the old idea that owning a television station was like having a licence to print money. Events soon proved otherwise (Cunningham & Jacka 1996: 38–76; Moran 2004a).

Businessman financier Christopher Skase bought the Seven Network. Struggling under the weight of debt plus management fees to himself and other executives of $100 million in 1989 alone, Skase made an astonishing bid of $1.2 billion, which he then raised to $1.5 billion to purchase the US-based MGM/UA movie studios and film library. The bid failed and Skase's company, Qintex, later went into receivership. The Ten Network was bought by Frank Lowy through his company Northern Star. Lowy was one of Australia's most successful businessmen, specializing in retail centre development under the banner of Westfield. He was persuaded to diversify his financial interests by moving into television broadcasting. This proved to be a costly mistake, and he sold a controlling interest in Ten in 1989. Developer businessman Alan Bond had bought the Nine Network from Kerry Packer, but defaulted on his debt so that ownership reverted to the Sydney media mogul. Collectively, the new owners had found that their television cash flow from advertising was insufficient to pay the financial loans that had bankrolled their purchases (Moran 2004a).

All three cut back on the commissioning of new programmes, with dire consequences for independent programme producers such as the Grundy Organisation. This straitened market situation was immediately obvious in the area of programme output. In the period in question, the Grundy Organisation was mostly unable to match its output success of the previous decade. A number of notable programmes remained on air, however. These were joined by another, which was to establish its own record for broadcast longevity in succeeding years. Still, the period was conspicuous for the reduction in output of the Australian programme production operation, even if the Grundy Organisation continued to be profitable thanks to a small handful of programmes that have already been identified as stalwarts. Let us examine these in the game show and drama output.

Australia: the quiz shows

The period 1985–90 saw the Grundy Organisation continuing to produce for all three networks, but in a market where there was less revenue overall to be spent on programming. Indeed, the company might have found the going much tougher had it not been for the continuing success of certain of its quiz-show champions. *Wheel of Fortune*, the Merv Griffin-owned US daytime quiz-show format (Becker 2004b: 2527–28), which was making it tough for competitors in the US game show production business – including Reg Grundy Productions continued its successful run on the Seven Network, pouring further revenue into Grundy's Australian coffers (Newcomb 2004; Moran & Keating 2003: 131–32). Equally, *Sale of the Century* continued its enormous success on the Nine Network, with Grundy producing several summer replacements, including a couples game, *The Newlywed Game*, in 1986–87 and a student general knowledge quiz, *Crossfire*, in 1987–88 (Moran & Keating 2003: 63). However, a third Grundy champion from earlier in the 1980s, *Perfect Match*, itself a successful revamp of two earlier game shows, *Blind Date* and *The Dating Game*, came to an end in 1987, leaving a gap in the Ten Network's early evening programming (Moran & Keating 2003: 106–07).

There were no new overwhelming successes, however. The only attempt to break out of the mould and introduce new elements into the game show genre seems to have been *Press Your Luck*, produced for the Seven Network between 1987 and 1988 in an early evening timeslot (Moran & Keating 2003). The programme was the first Australian remake of a recent 1983 game and quiz show on the US CBS Network involving buzzers, Q&A and prize spins (Schwartz, Ryan & Wosbrook 1987: 370–71). The intention was to build on the triumph of *The New Price is Right*, but the show had little success.

Otherwise, it was mostly a matter of old wine in new bottles. *It's a Knockout* has been discussed above. Revivals of classic game and quiz shows in the form of *Blankety Blanks* in 1985 for the Nine Network and *Superquiz* in 1989 on behalf of the Ten Network also occurred (Moran & Keating 2003: 53, 120). However, the first failed to reproduce the success of *Graham Kennedy's Blankety Blanks* of nearly a decade earlier, while the latter went no distance towards matching the long-running *Pick-a-Box* in popularity. Other familiar light entertainment formats also surfaced just as briefly for the Ten Network in 1987. One was *Pot Luck*, a once-a-week night-time version of a daytime talent show, while the weekday *You've Got to Be Joking* was an update of *Candid Camera* (Moran & Keating 2003: 103).

In short, Grundy's game shows survived this difficult period of downturn that had a drastic effect on the Australian television networks. Two of the company's most lucrative quiz shows managed to remain on air, and this helped to smooth out the more disappointing results and returns from the short-lived programme casualties just noted. The same spotty scorecard was evident with the company's fiction output.

Australia: drama serials, children's fiction and *Neighbours*

In fact, there is even less to say about this tally compared with the quiz-show output. After the run of soap opera casualties, especially those for the Nine Network noted in the last chapter, the Grundy Organisation seemed to be heading down the same path with a new drama serial, *Neighbours*. This soap was originally commissioned by the Seven Network to run in an early evening timeslot (Crofts 1995; Moran 1993: 312–14; Cunningham 2004c: 1623–25). It began on air on the Seven Network in early 1985. After the gender intensity of *Prisoner* and the melodramatic excesses of *Sons and Daughters*, Grundy in the person of its chief drama producer, Reg Watson, had decided to err in the direction of ordinariness in the new serial. The locale of the drama was a fictional Ramsey Street in a middle-class Melbourne suburb, with the internal and external interactions of three families forming its point of dramatic departure. The families were nuclear and non-nuclear, and the sense of neighbourliness included these as well as several other residents and modest-sized businesses, school and other small local institutions. Like most soap operas, *Neighbours* focused on a variety of relationships family, romance, friendship and community.

However, the programme failed to build the audience that the Seven Network expected. Late in 1985, the network indicated to Grundy that it did not intend to continue commissioning the programme. Grundy had shown a salesman's flair before when faced with a program's imminent cancellation. For example, back in 1964 when TCN9 had axed the game show *First Impressions*, Reg Grundy himself had persuaded QTQ9 to pick it up two years later, while in 1970 he had talked one of the other stations in Adelaide, ADS7, into continuing with the production of a South Australian version of *I've Got a Secret* after its axing by SAS9. Other instances of this adroit salesmanship have also been noted in these pages. Now it was the turn of *Neighbours* to be rescued from oblivion.

The Grundy Organisation persuaded the Ten Network to pick up the programme. *Neighbours* was refurbished in terms of its look, storylines were redrawn and Ten reprogrammed the show in a prime-time slot at 7.30 p.m. on weekdays, beginning in early 1986. Audience enthusiasm was initially lukewarm, so Ten supported the programme with extensive publicity later in the year. By early 1987, however, *Neighbours* had begun to boost its ratings and soon became a hit serial, with performers such as Kylie Minogue and Jason Donovan catapulting to celebrity status (Grundy 2010: 52–61; Crofts 1995: 98–108; Moran 1993: 312–14).

For its part, the Seven Network realized that it had made a big mistake in not persisting with *Neighbours* during the show's infancy. Unfortunately, it did not return to Grundy for a new drama serial; instead, it produced its own *Neighbours* clone, *Home and Away*, set in a fictional NSW seaside town populated by different generations of people, including a similar group of young adults to the one that had reached stardom through *Neighbours* (Moran 1993: 226–27; Craven 1989: 15–20). *Home and Away* was a more immediate success, and this served to bolster and reinforce the dominance of the Grundy serial. *Neighbours*' triumph in Australia would shortly help open doors for the Grundy Organisation elsewhere in the world.

This was just as well because the astonishing decade of soap opera success achieved in the Australian television market was now almost over. After a disastrous series of new drama commissions, the Nine Network had a hit series with *The Flying Doctors* (Cunningham & Jacka 1996: 95–100), produced by Crawford Productions, and did not seem ready to commission any further serials from Grundy. *Sons and Daughters* had come to the end of its run on the Seven Network in 1987, and with the in-house success of *Home and Away*, Seven was also not in the market for more soap operas.

Ten was interested, however. It commissioned what became *Richmond Hill* (Moran 1993: 383–84; Cunningham & Jacka 1996: 85) from the Grundy Organisation. The intention was to have the programme follow *Neighbours* and its main evening news each evening, so that it was not surprising that the new serial was again set in an ordinary suburb with such locales as a police station, boarding house and pub. *Richmond Hill* began on air early in 1988. A total of 91 one-hour episodes were produced, out-ranking the output of less successful Grundy serials such as *Taurus Rising, Waterloo Station* and *Possession*, and suggesting that the soap had taken off so far as broadcaster and audience were concerned (Craven 1989: 30; Moran 1993: 383). This proved not to be the case, however. The Ten Network, by then grappling with dire financial problems, cancelled the serial in favour of the more youth-oriented *E Street* (Moran 1993: 154–56).

All this left the Grundy Organisation with only one hit drama serial on its hands. All the same, to gauge the full success represented by *Neighbours*, we need to look offshore – although before doing so, it is useful to note one other Grundy Australian success of this period. This was the children's drama series, *Professor Poopsnaggle's Steam Zeppelin*, produced by Roger Mirams who had continued working under the Grundy business umbrella. The story concerned a boy teaming up with a famous scientist to build a flying machine designed by his professor grandfather, to search for amazing megasteam minerals (Moran 1993: 369–70). The series debuted on Australian television in late 1985 with the rest of its 26 half-hour episodes appearing in 1986.

The Grundy Organisation, then, had its share of ups and downs in the Australian television market between 1985 and 1989. Fortunately, the parent company had what would turn out to be a changing series of often highly successful operations elsewhere. One of these – the South-East Asian initiative – had already ended, but a brand new operation was getting off the ground on the European side of the Atlantic.

The United Kingdom

If the United States had been the principal arena of Grundy's offshore ambition in the first half of the 1980s, the paradox was that the company had its biggest international impact on the other side of the Atlantic in the second half of the decade. Again, its Australian fiction programme 'calling cards' got it through the door of the UK broadcasters, while format programme adaptations helped to keep it there. In following this route, Grundy was taking advantage of the long-established ties between Australian and UK television that were mentioned in Chapter 7. Since the 1950s, there had been a sustained history of British television production involvement and investment in Australia (Cunningham & Jacka 1996: 122–42; Steemers 2004: 140–57). The first television series to be made in Australia, *The Adventures of Long John Silver*, was filmed there and in the Pacific in 1956 (Vahamagi 1996: 61). The Australian public-service broadcaster, the ABC – founded in the likeness of the BBC in 1932 – was an early borrower of formats from the British organization, and they were involved in their first co-production venture on a one-off drama in 1966 (Inglis 1983: 390). All Australian television networks, most especially the ABC and the Seven Network, bought large amounts of British programmes over the years, and indeed the early regulation of Australian content on commercial television between 1960 and 1974 further encouraged this by allowing broadcasters to count British programmes as Australian content (Cunningham 1993: 26; Moran 1985: 30). Nor had the programme flow been one way. Rather, there was a history of Australian black-and-white drama series such as Crawford's *Homicide* and *Division Four* being sold in the 1960s and early 1970s to UK regional stations in the ITV network, this trade being a forerunner to the wave of Australian drama serials on British screens in the 1980 (Solomon 1989: 1).

There were other signs of this congruence. Popular domestic soap opera did not emerge as a viable programming form on Australian commercial television until 1972, with the success of *Number 96*. British television writers working in Australia had a good deal to do with the program's popularity (Hall 1976: 89). In turn, as we saw in Chapter 7, Grundy established a drama serial production unit, and in 1974 enticed Australian-born Reg Watson to return from Britain to head up the unit, as well as persuading several other British-born professionals to join the company.

The Grundy Organisation's timing in entering the UK television market was fortuitous. British television was the oldest system in the world, but the late 1980s found it in a state of considerable upheaval (Bryant & Alvarado 2004: 322–27; Blumler 2004: 330–37). Under the Conservative government of Margaret Thatcher, economic rationalism was the order of the day. In 1987, the government passed a declaration that 25 per cent of British programmes on the BBC and ITV should come from outside independent producers, a measure that was later ratified in the 1990 *Broadcasting Act*. There was strong pressure to disaggregate the vertical integrated duopoly of both the public-service BBC and commercially regulated ITV. The BBC began downsizing and disaggregating its operation, and started outsourcing production.

Meanwhile, Grundy was eyeing off the UK programming market. A number of its drama series, such as *Glenview High*, *Case for the Defence* and *Chopper Squad*, were sold to UK regional stations in the late 1970s. It was its soap operas that were to make Grundy a household name, however. In 1984, it sold a package of episodes of *The Young Doctors* to a regional station and, within a year, had hawked programmes such as *Prisoner: Cell Block H*, *The Restless Years* and *Sons and Daughters* in eleven of the fifteen regional commercial television markets (Moran 1998: 49). A real breakthrough occurred the following year, when the BBC licensed *Neighbours* for early afternoon broadcast. The Australian soap proved so popular that the BBC re-broadcast the programme in an early evening timeslot (Crofts 1995: 98–108; Cunningham & Jacka 1996:

122–29). By 1988, *Neighbours* had become the most popular programme on UK television, developing a cult following among British teenagers. The programme remained in the Top Ten for several more years. Subsequently, two other Grundy soaps, the Australian *Richmond Hill* and its New Zealand production *Shortland Street*, were sold to ITV.

It was time to take advantage of these developments by looking to format adaptation and programme production in the United Kingdom. In 1987, Grundy established a British subsidiary, Reg Grundy Productions (GB) Ltd. It opened an office in London, which was to serve as both a UK production centre and a European base. It also entered into several co-financing and co-production arrangements. In 1984, the company had obtained UK investment in the children's series *Secret Valley* and a miniseries co-production arrangement in 1987 with London's Central Television that would result in the miniseries *Tanamera: Lion of Singapore* (Cunningham & Jacka 1996: 130–31). British financial investment was also secured for the children's series *Professor Poopsnaggle's Steam Zeppelin* (Moran 1993: 369–70).

The most important activity of Reg Grundy Productions (GV) was its making of format-based quiz shows, panel games and light entertainment. *Neighbours* was the first programme to be stripped Monday to Friday on UK television, and Grundy was the master production provider for this kind of scheduling system. Following the success of *Neighbours*, the company sold its first quiz show to the BBC for weekday late-afternoon broadcast. This was *Going for Gold*, which began on air early in 1989 and would run until 1996. The format was an original one developed in Grundy's Los Angeles office with US network licensing in mind. That format, then entitled *Run for the Money*, initially had appealed to US ABC Network programmers. Three pilots had been produced in 1987, but the network had passed on a licensing deal (Grundy 2010: 297–98). Not so the BBC, which contracted to broadcast an adaptation of the format under the title *Going for Gold* (Evans 2001: 252). The following year, it was joined by three other Grundy entertainments, again using formats that the company either owned or on which it held options. These were *Sale of the Century* on satellite cable channel BSkyB, *Sky Star Search* on the Sky Channel and *Keynotes* on the commercial ITV network.

Reg Grundy Productions (GB) had made an auspicious beginning in a very important market. The British television system was second only to the United States in terms of wealth and was also an excellent launching pad for further expansion into Western Europe, a move that was increasingly on the radar of Grundy Worldwide. Before looking in that direction, however, it is worth taking stock of one other facet of company operations in the second half of the 1980s. This involves a brief examination of the fortunes of Reg Grundy Productions (US) in the wealthiest but most difficult of world television markets.

The United States

Compared with the company's breakthroughs in the sale of drama and the commissioning of quiz-show format adaptations in the UK market, there was little success to report from the company's operation in the United States in the second half of the decade. With the notable exception of *Prisoner: Cell Block H*, Grundy's drama programmes made for Australian audiences had limited sales appeal, even for syndication and cable buyers. Additionally, US daytime television had become even more fiercely competitive with the popularity of talk shows such as *Donoghue,* and especially the meteoric rise of *The Oprah Winfrey Show* from 1985 onwards (Murray 2004a: 750–52; Timberg 2004b: 2255–62; Marshall 2004: 2558–59). This development further squeezed the late-morning weekday slot in which game shows had been scheduled and redoubled the difficulty of game show packagers hoping to license to the networks.

Two Grundy quiz shows, *Sale of the Century* and *Scrabble*, were already in production, and continued broadcasting on NBC network daytime television – although the latter came to an end in 1989 (Hyatt 1997: 390). The only other quiz show to be licensed for broadcast in this period, Bruce Forsyth's *Hot Streak*, came and went in the first half of 1986 (Hyatt 1997: 73). Otherwise, Reg Grundy Productions (US) had little to show for its efforts. This was not for want of trying, however. Led by Reg Grundy himself, the Los Angeles production office was busy developing quiz-show formats that were variously being presented in rudimentary or more complete forms to the network programmers. In some instances, already noticed in Chapter 9, negotiations with the networks proceeded as far as the production of game show pilot episodes of would-be programmes. None of these was commissioned, however. After its earlier successes, Reg Grundy Productions had no further entries to mark on its US scorecard. It was time for a new (and what would prove to be a final) sales campaign. One of Reg Grundy's biggest business gambles will be examined in the next chapter.

Afterword

The 1980s had been a notable time for the Grundy group. Australian television programme production had proved to be very lucrative, even in the more difficult financial times between 1987 and 1989. The company had several programmes in both quiz show and drama serial form that had proved to be long-running and very successful, and these had put more money in its coffers to fund further transnational initiatives. They also provided it with programmes to take to other territories, either to distribute as finished canned programmes or to license as programme formats for adaptation as local programmes. The latter was a much more financially rewarding practice. Whether pursued as an independent operation in a new territory or undertaken in a joint venture arrangement with a domestic company, the remaking of a programme format – whether in the area of quiz and game shows or in drama serials – would generate valuable profits for Grundy by way of both production fees and format licensing fees. Grundy had an extensive library of programme formats that it had devised and owned outright, or had optioned from format owners elsewhere. Meanwhile, profound structural changes were continuing to occur in television systems around the world. How the company fared in this rapidly developing international market is the subject of the next chapter.

Chapter 11

Transnational Ambitions V: Worldwide, 1989-95

Introduction

Transnational expansion now exploded, with several elements contributing to this surge. The most important were the deregulation and privatization of public-service broadcasting, and the dramatic increase in the number of television channels on the air in different parts of the world, particularly Western Europe. This multiplication of television broadcasting services meant a general erosion of audiences for any particular channel. Broadcasters looked for some kind of insurance for the success of new programmes, and format-based adaptations promised to repeat triumphs already achieved in other markets. Grundy could also bring other advantages to the task of programme production in this new environment. These included a sizeable catalogue of programme formats, both owned and held under option. The company was remarkably expert in two key genres that form the backbone of broadcast schedules everywhere. Two other arms of Grundy also facilitated international co-production agreements, especially in new markets. The first was programme distribution. But early contact between Grundy and particular national broadcasters also occurred through various co-production arrangements on drama series and, most especially, children's series. The combined effect of these elements was to ensure the very rapid transnational development of Grundy in the period 1989–95. Production had never been so busy, and the revenue flow had never been so great. A change of name for the company was in order, given that its operations now circled the planet. Hence the discussion that follows covers a larger number of markets than has previously been the case. It also needs to spell out details on more productions and other initiatives than before.

Australia: quiz and game show output

By 1990, printed advertisements in international industry magazines could list some of the 77 quiz programmes, game shows and drama serial formats that Grundy Worldwide now had in its library. A significant number of these were held under regional option agreements with their owners, so that they might not be available for remaking in any particular territory. Other programme formats were owned outright or had been devised by the company so that these were available for remaking in any region. Even Australia was now no different from any other territory where the company had branches in terms of being a market for the remaking of formats deriving from company activities elsewhere. Format adaptation continued to be the name of the game so far as quiz and game shows were concerned, and the Australian television market underwent steady revival after the 1987–90 downturn in the economy and in the industry.

As usual, there was the standard run of shows that were short-lived and lacklustre in terms of audience numbers. Three of these were commissioned by the Ten Network and involved the recycling of well-known quiz and game show formats on which Grundy held options. The first was *Superquiz* in 1989, a remake of what itself had been a remake. The original was the most successful of early Australian television quiz shows, *Pick-a-Box*, broadcast on the Seven Network while its reversioning as the *Ford Superquiz* in 1981–82 had represented an attempt by Grundy and the Nine Network to repeat its popularity. Now it was the turn of the Ten Network to have another bash at a remake (Moran & Keating 2003: 120). Unfortunately, the new version also failed to capture the success of the original and was not licensed for a second season. *Let's Make a Deal* was a second unfortunate adaptation. Again, its format was familiar, with two previous outings on Australian television after its 1963 US network debut, where it had gone on to become one of the most popular game shows on the air (Schwartz, Ryan & Wosbrook 1987: 267–69). This 1991 version was Grundy's second revival, and it updated the pricing and trading game with a deliberate spirit of comic anarchy (Moran & Keating 2003: 89). However, the new version had no more success than *Superquiz* and was quietly forgotten. The same year witnessed the return of an even older format of romance and courtship in the shape of *Blind Date*. The format had first appeared on US television in 1949, and had given rise to at least two clones that appeared as *The Dating Game* and *Perfect Match* (Schwartz, Ryan & Wosbrook 1987: 118–21, 354–55). However, the 1991 update did not grab public attention and was soon off air (Moran & Keating 2003: 54).

Nor was this run of quiz and game show disappointments confined to only one network. For the Nine Network in 1992–93, Grundy produced *Supermarket Sweep* (Moran & Keating 2003: 119). As its title suggests, the programme involved contestants who, with limited time to gather grocery items, strive to achieve the largest value for their goods. The show was an update of a not very successful US network original from the mid-1960s, but proved not to have improved its appeal over time (Schwartz, Ryan & Wosbrook 1987: 432). A local Seven Network version of a recent Grundy acquisition from Germany, *Man O Man*, appeared in 1994 (Moran 1998: 83–88). This was an extended game show in which a bevy of beautiful women and judges put young contestants of the opposite sex through various contests in order to whittle down numbers to find one male champion. Unfortunately, the potential raunchiness of the format was ill-suited to the conservatism of Australian television in general and the Seven Network in particular, so that the series was not renewed for a second season.

Other quiz and game shows more than overcame these disappointments, with four long-term successes proving themselves revenue bonanzas. Both *Sale of the Century* and *Wheel of Fortune* continued their very successful twenty years-plus runs on Australian television. The former had several summer replacements designed to protect its timeslot. These included the 1992–93 substitute *Keynotes*, the Grundy US recasting of *Name That Tune*, while the 1994–95 proxy was the talent show *Pot of Gold*. Meanwhile, *Wheel of Fortune* briefly spawned a Perth-based superversion *Celebrity Wheel of Fortune*, which was broadcast in 1990–91. A third ratings triumph in this period was *Family Feud*, which was a second, very successful Australian outing of the Goodson-Todman format that had originally appeared in 1976 on the US ABC Network (Schwartz, Ryan & Wosbrook 1987: 164–67). The game show pitted members of two families against each other, with the teams attempting to pick the most popular response to questions as revealed by a programme survey. The new version of the format was broadcast by the Seven Network, and first ran in an early evening timeslot; however, its ratings improved considerably when it was moved to a late-afternoon time. *Family Feud* was broadcast from 1989 to 1996 and included a night-time 1990–91 spin-off in the shape of *Celebrity Family Feud* (Moran & Keating 2003: 56).

The last ratings triumph emerged from a less successful quiz and game show outing on the Ten Network. This was a 1993 version of *The Price is Right*, a brief prime-time revival (and network change) of the earlier highly successful *The New Price is Right* that had played on the Seven Network between 1981 and 1984 (Moran & Keating 2003: 108–10). The Grundy Organisation was undaunted by this latter casualty and, following a practice that it had used before and was to use again, it took the programme to the Nine Network a few years later. The result was yet another highly successful version of *The Price is Right* that was to run until 1998. (Even then, the series was only cancelled despite healthy ratings due to the popularity of *Catchphrase* in the timeslot during summer recess, and would reappear on the network in 2003.)

Australia: miniseries, children's and other fiction

Grundy's other slate of production in this period marked a distinct shift away from the domestically addressed high-volume fiction output that had been its staple for almost two decades. The only home-grown and Australian-oriented soap opera still in production was *Neighbours*, which continued its triumphant run on the Ten Network, although its BBC licensing was crucial to keeping it in production and on air. By the early 1990s, the Australian commercial networks had mostly lost their collective enthusiasm for drama serials, not only due to Nine's disastrous run with the form in the mid-1980s but also because of the downturn in the economy from 1987 to 1990. This shift was convenient enough for the Grundy Organisation, even if it missed out on the opportunity to put more revenue into its war chest. Grundy Worldwide was spreading its fiction wings elsewhere, and needed to dispatch experienced Australian writers and producers to other international markets where there were opportunities to initiate new Grundy soap operas.

In any case, even the Australian fictional output showed a marked turn towards internationalization. This was facilitated by a new division established for production in the areas of drama miniseries, telefilms and series output. Its first efforts were skewed deliberately towards co-production investment and international distribution. Highlighting this change, three programmes – *Embassy, Tanamera: Lion of Singapore* and *The Other Side of Paradise* – were all fictionally set in South-East Asia or the Pacific. *Embassy* was a co-production with the Australian Broadcasting Corporation (ABC), which, since 1986, had signalled its preparedness to enter into production partnerships with commercial companies. It was the first venture between it and Grundy. As the series' name suggests, the 51 hour-long episodes of *Embassy* were concerned with an Australian diplomatic outpost in a fictional South-East Asian country, with the situation and relationships of the embassy group dramatizing political comment, social awareness and diplomatic sensitivity (Moran 1993: 160–61). The Islamic country was given the name Ragaan, and the ambassador in the first series was Bryan Marshall. *Embassy* carried a financial involvement not only from the ABC but also from Television New Zealand, and was intended for sale in Asian markets. Malaysia took offence at the series, however, and suspended diplomatic relations with Australia. Its objection probably led to disappointing sales in Asia and the withdrawal of the New Zealand financial involvement for the second series. However, the controversy did trigger high viewer interest in Australia and elsewhere.

Meanwhile, Grundy had become involved in long-form fiction for the first time by producing two miniseries in association with the United Kingdom's Central Independent TV. The deal for the first miniseries was set up in 1987, with investment coming from Australia, New Zealand and the United Kingdom. *Tanamera: Lion of Singapore* was the first to go to air. It consisted of seven hour-long episodes and was broadcast in Australia in 1989 (Moran 1993: 445–46). *The Other Side of Paradise* featured four hour-long episodes and was put to air in early 1992 (Moran 1993: 333–34). The two miniseries followed similar fictional patterns of complex racial relations involving romance, rivalry, war and, in the case of *Tanamera*, communism. *Tanamera* was set in Malaya while *The Other Side of Paradise* was located on a Polynesian island under the protectorship of New Zealand. The Cook Islands provided the setting for *The Other Side of Paradise*, and possibly also helped with the program's taxation arrangements.

Another cab off the fiction rank was *Bony*. This was a 1992 action adventure crime series, set in outback Australia and produced by the Grundy Organisation in association with the German ZDF group (Moran 1993: 83–84). ZDF contributed two-thirds of the costs and Grundy picked up the rest. Although there had been a 1972 Australian series, *Boney*, produced on film and in colour, based on a group of earlier crime novels concerning an Aboriginal outback detective, Grundy ignored these sources. Instead, it licensed rights to only the detective's name, Napoleon Bonaparte, and proceeded to make the character a white man who had been raised by Aborigines, thereby developing an extraordinary and very useful (fictional) ecological consciousness. The rugged outback locations would have impressed the German backers, while each of the thirteen hour-long episodes had sufficient physical action in the form of chases, fights, killings and face-offs to please international distributors and broadcasters.

Australia's Most Wanted was a more anomalous contribution to Grundy's non-quiz-show output, although it had precedents of sorts in several public information programmes that the company produced in 1970. Highlighting the extent of format programme convergence that was now occurring between US television and television systems elsewhere, *Australia's Most Wanted* was based on a monthly German programme that had aired on the public-service ZDF channel, *Aktenzeichen XY: ungelost/File XY: Unsolved* (Bourdin 2011: 176). The format attracted no licensing interest until 1988, when it was picked up by the US Fox Network, which put it to air as *America's Most Wanted* (Seaton 2004: 102–04). As we saw in Chapter 10 with *Jeu Sans Frontieres/It's a Knockout*, European-derived programme formats needed to be picked up by US television broadcasters at this stage before they came to the attention of programme producers elsewhere in the world and were subsequently licensed. Grundy was quick to license an Australian adaptation of *America's Most Wanted*, which began on the Seven Network in 1989. The programme mixed dramatized re-enactment with actuality television, including live footage, victim and expert testimony, and commentary that frequently was self-promotional and congratulatory. Each episode retold and re-enacted one or more criminal cases, and this example of tabloid television soon captured a solid following. *Australia's Most Wanted* ran until 1994, then went off air only to return in half-hour form on the Nine Network, where it proceeded to run from 1996 to 1999.

Finally, there were also more telefilms. After more than a dozen years of inactivity in this kind of genre, the Grundy Organisation had an additional half-dozen television features to put alongside the Gemini Movie Package in its international distribution catalogue. One of these was a feature-length pilot for the *Bony* series, but the others were made by producer Roger Mirams for the international children's fiction market. As we saw in Chapter 7, Mirams had joined the Grundy Organisation in the early 1970s as an independent producer, pursuing international co-production deals on telemovies, films and children's series. This arrangement meant that there were inevitable ebbs and flows in terms of productions going to air. The period after 1989, however, saw a bevy of Grundy's outputs that had been coaxed into existence by Mirams. One group was a suite of five telemovies that were intended as pilots for possible children's series and also doubled as feature-length episodes for an anthology series, *South Pacific Adventures* (Moran 1993: 427). The adventures were, variously, about a wild horse, a masked Australian bushranger and a band of pirates on a deserted island. Miram's second production achievement was a series spin-off from one of these telemovies. *Mission Top Secret* depicted a secret organization of a select group of teenagers, who share the philosophy of one peaceful world with no boundaries (Moran 1993: 299). The programme was to run to two series, comprising 48 half-hour episodes. Arranged in the story form of an international chase, the series conveniently accommodated various national places that in turn encouraged overseas broadcasters to invest in the series. The two series of *Mission Top Secret* were broadcast in Australia in 1992 and 1995, respectively.

One other detail concerning the Australian operation should also be noted: the Grundy Organisation's attempt to buy the Seven Network in 1991 (Shoebridge 1991). Chapter 10 outlined the financial upheavals in the commercial network sector in the late 1980s and early 1990s. As a result, both the Seven and Ten Networks were up for sale at this time. The Australian head of the Grundy Organisation, Ian Holmes – who had been managing director of TEN10 until 1977 – was said to be interested in having the company purchase the broadcasting group (Weston 1995). However, no deal was struck involving Grundy and Seven and the matter lapsed.

New Zealand: quiz shows and *Shortland Street*

Despite the physical proximity of Australia to New Zealand and the common origin of the two as 'white settler societies', their television industries had little in common historically. However, like many of the television systems to be discussed later in this chapter, New Zealand television by 1989 involved a public-service system struggling to remain dominant following the unleashing of the forces of new technology, the occurrence of media deregulation, the advent of private commercial broadcasting and the multiplicity of television services (Lealand 1994: 214–27; Moran 1998: 53–54; Murdock 2004b: 1640–42).

Until the late 1980s, New Zealand's only involvement with Australian television producers had occurred through New Zealand's import of the latter's programmes. From the mid-1970s, Grundy had distributed many of its Australian-made drama programmes across the Tasman, including *Prisoner, The Young Doctors, Sons and Daughters* and *Neighbours*. It also distributed several US-produced game shows, which it represented internationally, and this distribution paved the way for its entry into the local production market. Formats were the bedrock of this development.

In 1989, the company sold its first New Zealand production, a local adaptation of its warhorse format, *Sale of the Century*, which ran from 1989 to 1993. Home-grown versions of other game show formats that Grundy had under licence from their US owners followed, including *Wheel of Fortune* (1990–93), *Perfect Match* (1990) and *Jeopardy!* (1992). *Neighbours* had already created a taste for stripped soaps in prime-time access, and in 1992 Grundy sold TV2 its own domestic daily soap set in an emergency medical centre, *Shortland Street* (Moran 1996a). This was an original drama format and was co-produced with South Pacific Pictures, a production arm of the channel. Grundy distributed the serial internationally, securing a good sale to ITV in the United Kingdom (Moran 1998: 53–54). Even more impressive was the fact that Grundy could achieve the economies of scale necessary to produce high-volume drama in a market of only 3.5 million people (Murphy 1995). *Shortland Street* proved to be far more durable than the quiz and game shows. It was still on air at time of writing.

The United States: quiz and drama stalemate

After a promising start in the early 1980s, the US television business had stalled in the second half of the decade for Reg Grundy Productions Inc. The early 1990s would mostly see this stalemate continue so far as programme licensing was concerned. The quiz-show format that was a champion elsewhere, *Sale of the Century,* had begun on NBC in 1983 but was cancelled in 1989 (Hyatt 1997: 390). In fact, *Scrabble* was the company's most successful quiz and game show to appear on US network television. It started on NBC in 1984 and ran until mid-1993 (Hyatt 1997: 380). Reg Grundy's memoirs detail several disappointments involving quiz-show presentations and pilots that never gained commissions (2010: 274–80). There were other setbacks, too. For instance, although the company had announced that it would produce a first-run syndication version of *Scrabble* in 1990, this failed to materialize. About the same time that *Scrabble* was coming to the end of a network run on NBC, another Grundy quiz show on the same network was also dying (Grundy 2010: 267–69). Late the previous year, NBC had commissioned another quiz show from Grundy based on a board game, *Scattergories.* The programme began early the following year (Hyatt 1997: 377); however, the network did not commission beyond its initial run, and *Scattergories* ended in mid-1994. It was to be the last of the Grundy programmes to be bought by one of the US networks, although there were to be two light entertainment programmes in 1997: a *Man O Man* special, produced for station UTN, and a season of *Small Talk* for The Family Channel. These were the last programmes produced in the United States by Reg Grundy Productions Inc. (US).

Grundy had two other surprises left in its cupboard as it struggled to remain active in US television production. Both initiatives involved drama serials, and both were inspired by the earlier broadcast success of *Prisoner: Cell Block H.* The first venture involved the fictional inhabitants of Ramsey Street. Besides its overwhelming success with audiences in Australia, *Neighbours* had done equally well in other English-language markets in the United Kingdom and New Zealand. This prompted Grundy to enter into licensing agreements that would see the serial aired on US television. Of course, network doors were closed to such a venture. The Big Three had long believed that only home-grown television fiction could attract the kind of audience numbers that they wanted. Syndication was another story, however. *Prisoner: Cell Block H* had been a breakthrough success in 1979, and had attracted an international minority cult audience (Curthoys & Docker 2004: 1825–26). Similarly, British drama, especially that produced by the BBC, had been scheduled successfully for many years by the US public broadcaster (Steemers 2004: 128–31). Grundy's hope was that *Neighbours* might achieve a similar triumph. The serial was launched in 1991 in New York and Los Angeles.

Reg Grundy, who had been masterminding the US operation for over ten years, also decided to push ahead with a US adaptation of *Prisoner: Cell Block H.* The new fiction, *Dangerous Women,* represented a kind of sequel serial to the original, in that it followed the circumstances of five women after they had been released from prison and had set up a guest lodge near a lake. The dramatic premise of the programme was that while they had left the prison, it would not stop affecting their lives (Moran 1993: 138–39; Grundy 2010: 247–51).

Dangerous Women was to prove one of the company's biggest gambles. In his memoir, Grundy confesses that he wanted to have complete artistic and financial control over the soap so that he ignored whatever opportunity there might have been to involve large television corporations such as Viacom or even CBS (2010: 247–49). The upshot was that Reg Grundy Productions Inc. (US) company poured a good deal of its own capital into producing 26 one-hour episodes of what it hoped would be the first of many seasons of *Dangerous Women* for US television syndication.

The company also needed to arrange coast-to-coast broadcasts of its serial. Working through a broker in New York, Reg Grundy Productions Inc. (US) roadshowed the serial, putting together a circuit of independent syndication stations in various urban markets. These included the Pineland Group's WPIX New York, KCOP Los Angeles, WPWP TV Chicago, the TVX Broadcast Group (which had several stations in Texas as well as one in Washington), Hubbard Broadcasting in Florida and the Chris Craft/United TV Station Group with stations on the Pacific seaboard as well as Minneapolis and Phoenix (Cunningham & Jacka 1996: 170–80; Moran 1998: 50–52). Altogether, this 'network' had the capacity to reach approximately 30 per cent of the US television viewing population.

Dangerous Women was screened twice weekly starting in the fall of 1991 and continuing into 1992. However, the adaptation fared no better than the imported *Neighbours* had a short time earlier (Crofts 1995: 108–15; Moran 1998: 48; Cunningham & Jacka 1996: 170–73; Grundy 2010: 249–51). Its lack of success must have left Reg Grundy wondering whether he could ever become a substantial production presence in the US television market (*Broadcasting* 1991: 247–51). By the mid-1990s, Reg Grundy Productions Inc. (US) found that it was mostly unable to sell either locally produced game shows or drama serials in the US television market. By then, the only English-language soap operas that it had to distribute were *Neighbours* and the New Zealand *Shortland Street*. The former had fared poorly in the United States in 1991 and the latter was unlikely to be more successful.

Instead, Reg Grundy Productions Inc. ended up as a de facto laboratory, developing new television programme formats for game shows and light entertainment. The primary intention was, of course, to license these to US television broadcasters. But this was a very difficult market, likely to generate a lot of unsuccessful formats that had not made it into production. In some instances, there were even pilot episodes of such casualties. Hence, Reg Grundy Productions Inc. (US) served as a very useful cog in the worldwide operation of the company by providing new programme formats for the transnational entity as a whole (Crystal 1995). Among the new Grundy quiz-show formats developed and piloted in the United States were *Going for Gold*, *Hot Streak* and *Keynotes*. Other arms of the company in other markets in Europe, Oceania and elsewhere would successfully adapt these formats (Cunningham & Jacka 1996: 82). Nevertheless, this was not what Reg Grundy himself had intended in studying US television programmes from 1959 onwards, undertaking format field trips to the United States beginning in 1966, spending more than ten years gaining US network acceptance as a quiz-show producer, and sinking a good deal of company revenue into various US-related enterprises particularly the production of *Dangerous Women*. There was some room for jubilation but a lot of grounds for disappointment in the fate of the US initiative. It is not surprising that, by 1993, Reg Grundy had decided to sell his international suite of companies.

The United Kingdom

Grundy's game shows for the UK public-service broadcaster followed in the wake of the highly successful *Neighbours*. There were casualties as well as champions (Cunningham & Jacka 1996: 121–26; Moran 1998: 44). The least successful was *The Main Event*. The programme had a distinct leaning towards novelties and stunts. Originated by an independent British devisor, it pitted two teams of families against each other. These were only seen on screen from their homes; however, they were represented by two teams of television celebrities in the studio. Rounds included a scavenger hunt and the miming of historical events. *The Main Event* went to air for thirteen weeks in 1993 but made little headway against stiff competition and was not renewed. It would, though, give rise to a French adaptation. *Eureka* was a revival of an earlier BBC hybrid that used re-enactment and humour to present moments of scientific invention. The new version also had a brief outing, running for one season in 1994.

Reg Grundy Productions (GB) had more luck with three other game shows. *Small Talk* began on BBC1 in 1994. A total of 51 episodes were produced and the programme ran until early 1996. Hosted by comedian Ronnie Corbett, this was a light-hearted quiz/game show for youngsters, based on children's views of the world (Evans 2001: 139). The *Small Talk* formula saw adult contestants attempt to guess how children contestants would respond to the quiz-show's questions (*Small Talk* website). The second of these more successful BBC shows was *How Do They Do That?* This was a game show format licensed from Time Warner and aired by the BBC between 1994 and 1998. It was less a quiz show and more a light-hearted audience-participation programme, where secrets of engineering, organization and scientific feats were explained to the viewer by a resident host and hostess, with the assistance of professionals and general experts. The programme was broadcast on Wednesday night and had a strong following, thanks to its many pranks. Each season opened with a stunt from one of the presenters, such as a car chase, a skydiver crashlanding into the studio or the entire studio being washed away.

The third show putting black ink on the books was *Going for Gold*, mentioned in Chapter 10. It was a remake of a US Grundy-original, *Run for the Money*, which had failed to get off the ground there. The UK remake revealed the format to be something of an old-fashioned quiz show with the emphasis falling on the knowledge and brains of contestants. *Going for Gold* confirmed the value of the *Run for the Money* format by airing for nine years until mid-1996. The quiz show had a strong European orientation, with each programme consisting of four rounds of questions involving seven contestants, each representing a different European country competing for the winner's prize. The heats were part of a series culminating in finals with a repackage twist unusual at the time whereby unsuccessful contestants from one day's show would return on the following day. *Going for Gold* was put to air each weekday on BBC1, immediately after the broadcast of *Neighbours*. It was also aired on the Super Channel (later the NBC Super Channel) in continental Europe, although the 1996 version only appeared on UK television because by then the programme only featured British contestants.

The game shows produced by Reg Grundy Productions (GB) for the ITV Network included several of the more classic US game show formats. Heading these was *Jeopardy!* (Hoerschelmann 2004a: 1222–24). This format had been immensely successful, appearing on US network television from 1964 to 1975, followed by a first remake in 1978–79, and a second from 1984 onwards (Schwartz, Ryan & Wosbrook 1987: 249–51). It was an ideal game show for UK television, with its commitment to public-service values. Hoerschelmann notes that, unlike most other game shows originating in the United States between the 1960s and mid-1990s, which concentrated on gambling, guessing and consumption, *Jeopardy!* offered the appearance of serious competition and educational concern. It varied the formula of the knowledge quiz by having contestants frame questions for supplied answers, with winnings accumulating in cash (Hoerschelmann 2004a: 1222–24; Hoerschelmann 2004b: 1871–74). Back in the 1970s, Grundy had been beaten to the format by a rival in the Australian television market, but now had been able to license it from Merv Griffin Productions for Western European markets, including the United Kingdom. *Jeopardy!* began on ITV in 1990 and ran until 1996. *Keynotes* was another success for Grundy, with the ITV Network screening the programme from 1988 to 1992. It was a music guessing game with cash prizes, trading in the nostalgia of classic recorded songs, including having contestants sing these tunes themselves. Reg Grundy had helped devise this format in the United States, although his company was to have far more success with this UK version than had been the case with the US Keynotes. The UK remake was initially produced for HTV West and then picked up by the ITV Network as a whole (Vahamagi 1996: 381; Evans 2001: 288). It ran for four years, with a total of 210 episodes split into five series.

Mention of four other light entertainment shows will round out this section. Reg Grundy Productions (GB) produced a version of *Celebrity Squares* for ITV between 1993 and 1996 (Vahamagi 1994: 414). The format had originated as *Hollywood Squares* on NBC daytime, airing between 1966 and 1981, whereupon it was re-versioned for syndication (Schwartz, Ryan & Wosbrook 1987: 214). The formula of the show, devised by Merrill Heatter and Bob Quigley, was simple: two contestants answered questions to complete a Tic Tac Toe sequence on a board game, where each square revealed a celebrity. As Chapter 8 noted, Reg Grundy Enterprises had produced a version of the show in Australia in 1975–76. *Pot of Gold* was another format-based show that appeared on ITV from 1993 to 1995. More a talent show than a game show, each episode had six acts attempting to please a panel of judges. Audiences at home played along and the pot of gold went to the home viewer who matched the judges' votes as well as the one whose combined score matched the studio points total. The third game show, *Press Your Luck*, was based on a 1983–86 US CBS Network original that featured three contestants hitting buzzers to answer quiz questions and get prize spins on a board (Schwartz, Ryan & Wosbrook 1987: 379–80). Grundy obtained a UK licensing from HTV West, in the hope that it might be picked up by the rest of the ITV network; this did not happen. Hence, *Press Your Luck* aired briefly in 1991–92, slipping first into a Saturday-afternoon broadcast slot and then into a Sunday lunchtime wasteland. One other programme came and went just as quickly. This was *Sky Star Search,* another earlier talent show for the new Sky satellite service that lasted only one season from 1989 to 1990.

By 1995, Reg Grundy Productions (GB) had registered significant achievements in the UK television market. *Neighbours* was very successful on BBC Television, and was effectively a British programme that just happened to be produced on Australian soil. The company had become part of the television production landscape so far as British broadcasters were concerned. It was selling to three networks: BBC, ITV and Sky. And while the parent company, Grundy Worldwide, was producing 45 hours a week of television programmes (*TV World*, 30 May 1993), Reg Grundy Productions (GB) had become the seventh largest independent producer in the United Kingdom, a position based on the company's volume of annual productions outlined here. By this stage, the company was also very active in Western Europe.

The Netherlands

Paralleling its experience in the US television market, Grundy had a very promising beginning in The Netherlands, which then mostly fizzled out. The circumstances and reasons were quite different, however. As we shall see in more detail in Chapter 13, Dutch television had already developed an independent production sector by 1989, making programmes for a hitherto limited public-service system swelled by the onset of a string of new commercial broadcasters (Cunningham & Jacka 1996: 151–56; Moran 1998: 55–57; Meers 2004: 1631–33). The commercially strongest of the latter were RTL4 and RTL5, stations that were linked to the CTL group in Luxembourg, which also owned new commercial stations in Germany (Chalaby 2009: 46–47). RTL4 wanted a strip drama as an anchor for its new evening programming, and asked the Dutch production group Joop van den Ende Productions (JE), which would rapidly become its major supplier of programmes, to devise a successful soap opera. JE investigated several drama serials being produced elsewhere, and asked Grundy to license one of its soap formats (Holmes 1992). The Australian transnational preferred a coventure arrangement, and in 1990 the two companies signed a co-production agreement to produce *Goede Tijden, Slechte Tijden/Good Times, Bad Times.* This was an adaptation of the format of the Australian soap opera *The Restless Years,* which had begun on air in 1977 (see Chapter 8), and had also given rise to a pilot for a US adaptation, *Starting Out,* in 1980 (see Chapter 9) (O'Donnell 1999: 65–69).

Goede Tijden, Slechte Tijden began on RTL 4 late in 1990 (Moran 1998: 123–34). The programme soon built and maintained a strong audience, making it the most popular daily drama serial in The Netherlands. The soap opera is still on air at the time of writing, more than twenty years later, making the offspring far more popular than its Australian predecessor. The Dutch success also helped Grundy sell a further adaptation, *Gute Zeiten, Schlechte Zeiten/Good Times, Bad Times* in Germany in 1992. Despite this very promising beginning, Grundy was unable to sell any more programmes to the Dutch broadcasters with the solitary exception of a short season of a *Man O Man* remake in 1996 (Moran 1998: 83–89). Three factors probably militated against the newcomer. The first was the linguistic barrier, although it has to be added that this may not have been insurmountable. The second was the fact that, by the early 1990s, two Dutch production companies, Joop van den Ende Productions and John de Mol Productions, already dominated independent television production in The Netherlands, probably leaving little space for a newcomer (Moran 1998: 557). Parochial attitudes also probably played a part, with no Dutch broadcaster offering Grundy any further programme commissions (Servaes 2004b: 820–26).

France

Of the European markets, France turned out to be only a little more successful than The Netherlands. After the consolidation of offices in the United States and the United Kingdom, Grundy decided to make a French base its next priority. In 1986, private television broadcasting had been introduced (Emmanuel 2004: 910–12). The sector soon achieved profitability and weakened the public-service sector. Grundy was not the only foreign production company to see the possibilities in the transformed French television market. In 1987, for instance, the US advertising agency Lintas was responsible for the importation and take-off of a French adaptations of classic US game show formats such as *Wheel of Fortune, Family Feud* and *The Dating Game* on one of the three public-service broadcasting channels (Cunningham & Jacka 1996: 151–54; Moran 1998: 64–69). In Grundy's case, there was already a short history of contact thanks to sales of such series as *Runaway Island, The Young Doctors* and *Neighbours*, although sales volumes were small and programmes badly scheduled (Macken 1989: 9; Cunningham & Jacka 1996: 154; Crofts 1995: 115–18).

Les Productiones Grundy only ever secured commissions for game shows, despite working on another adaptation of *The Restless Years* in 1992 for Tele (Baart 1995). Two game shows turned out to be enormously popular, however. The first commission was *Questions pour le Champion*, a further adaptation of the *Run for the Money/Going for Gold* format, which began in 1988 for the regional public broadcaster France 3. It is still on air at the time of writing, almost a quarter of a century later, making it the most successful Grundy game show format, alongside *Sale of the Century*. And, given its 'Ugly Duckling' beginnings as a US Grundy-devised format that none of the networks wanted, it is a format about which Reg Grundy might feel considerable pride.

A second game show, *Que le meilleur gagne*, was based on the format of *Everybody's Equal*. The formula of the show had been developed in the United Kingdom, where the format had its first outing on ITV between 1989 and 1990. The programme was an audience-participation game show, with the show's audience progressively eliminated as they voted for the most popular answers on keypads. Grundy took an option on the format and licensed it in 1991 to La Cinq, one of the new private networks. When the group went bankrupt the following year, there was yet another instance of a Grundy programme doing a station hop.

France 2 picked up *Que le meilleur gagne,* and it continued on air until 1996. There were 30-minute daytime and early evening versions as well as a 90-minute night-time, 'special event' offspring, *Que le meilleur gagne plus.* The two quiz shows *Questions pour le Champion* and *Que le meilleur gagne* maintained Grundy as the third most successful independent producer in the French market (Cooper-Chen 1994: 69–72).

Other game shows were more short-lived: *Le Jeu* (based on *The Main Event*) ran for two seasons, as did *Mais Comment Font Ils?* (based on the Time Warner format of *How Do They Do That?*) and *Cheri-Cheries* (based on Grundy's format of *Man O Man*), while *Keynotes* ran for one season in 1994. All these light entertainment adaptations, with the exception of the last, were produced for public-service networks. This congruence between the company and public-service broadcasters has already been mentioned in the case of the United Kingdom, and would be repeated with others, including Germany, Italy and New Zealand. In systems where the public-service monopoly had ended, Grundy Worldwide was winning as much if not more acceptance from public broadcasters as it was securing from new, private, commercial operators.

Germany

Germany was the largest and most lucrative television production market in Europe (Bleicher 2004: 981–85). It was fortuitous, then, that Grundy Worldwide would make a significant impact there, particularly in the very profitable area of drama serial output. Germany has been identified as sharing a common cultural orientation of European countries along the northwest rim of the continent that has been labelled 'Germanic' to distinguish it from a 'Latin' cultural rim in the south. This orientation gives Germany a loose common background not only with Britain but also with Australia (Cunningham & Jacka 1996: 151–56; Moran 1998: 69–72). Such commonality helps explain the long contact between Australian producers and German broadcasters that began as early as 1973 with *The Castaways,* a co-production between the ABC, Scottish Television and German broadcaster ZDF (Moran 1993: 1056). Grundy also benefited from these industry linkages, with the sale of programmes such as *Bellamy* and *Neighbours* to German broadcasters such as RTL and SAT1 (Macken 1989: 9). In 1991–92, the company was involved with the Kirch production group, owner of SAT1, in a co-production of the crime series *Bony,* with the latter providing two-thirds of the finance while Grundy paid the remainder (Holmes 1992).

Soon after 1987 and the establishment of a London office, Grundy set about building an infrastructure in Germany. Two companies were established: Grundy Television Produktions was set up to produce light entertainment and game shows; while Grundy UFA TV Productions was a coventure arrangement with UFA Film and TV Productions, itself a unit of the powerful Bertelsman media conglomerate, which was also a part owner of RTL Plus (Jones 2004: 247–48). Because UFA was a film production company, the association with Grundy proved to be a very stable and complementary relationship, and was one reason among many why Grundy Worldwide was so successful in Germany (Murphy 1995).

As in other territories, the company had its earliest successes with game shows, and these remained an important source of cash flow. The series *Ruck Zuck* was an adaptation of the format *Hot Streak,* which Reg Grundy Productions had first developed in the United States. As we saw in the previous chapter, *Hot Streak* had a brief 1986 appearance on US network television. The *Ruck Zuck* adaptation on German television proved to be a lot more appealing: it was broadcast first on Tele 5 and then on RTL2, running from 1989 to 1996 (Cunningham & Jacka 1996: 166; Moran 1998: 69). A children's version, *Kinder Ruck Zuck*, was spun off and aired between 1991 and 1992. Grundy's champion format, *Sale of the Century,* was also pressed into service under the title of *Top Oder Flop*. This adaptation ran from 1990 to 1993 (Moran 1998: 69). Additionally, in 1997 there were also several new Grundy game shows, including *Muuh! The Pet Show, Small Talk* and *Jeder gegen Jeden/Fifteen-to-One*.

If the success with game shows in Germany was encouraging, the record with soap operas was outstanding (Lewis 1994: 18). The partnership with UFA began slowly. Following the success in The Netherlands of the Dutch adaptation of *The Restless Years*, the German commercial broadcaster RTL commissioned a further adaptation, *Gute Zeiten, Schlechte Zeiten/Good Times Bad Times* in 1992. Following the example of the Dutch adaptation, this remake started by using the original Australian scripts and followed with new German ones after Episode 230. Unlike its Dutch counterpart, the German adaptation was slow to build an audience, and RTL showed a good deal of faith in retaining it on air. By late 1994, it was the second most popular soap in Germany (Cunningham & Jacka 1996: 168). Grundy received two further commissions for daily strip drama in 1994 (Moran 1998: 123–34). Broadcaster RTL wanted an early evening five-days-a-week drama serial that was strongly oriented towards youth. Later that same year, the new serial *Unter Uns/Among Ourselves* went to air. It was based on an original set of ideas, but would not last more than two seasons. Meanwhile, the company was also developing an adaptation of *Sons and Daughters, Verbotene Liebe/Forbidden Love* for the public-service broadcaster ARD. This began broadcasting early in 1995. Both serials were produced in separate studios in Cologne. Finally, late the following year came a further commission for a daily soap, this time from RTL2. *Alle Zusammen/All Together* began on air in late 1996, a little over a month after the serial went into production at studios in Berlin. Grundy had become a significant production presence in Germany in the space of just five years.

Italy

Television in Italy had been deregulated following a ruling in the Constitutional Court in 1973 and a new *Broadcasting Act* in 1975 (Noam 1992; Bechelloni and Buonanno 2004: 1191–95). When Grundy Worldwide sought to enter the Italian television market in 1993, it found that an extraordinary period of broadcasting libertarianism had left the service in the hands of the state broadcaster RAI on the one hand, and commercial owner Silvio Berlusconi on the other (Murdock 2004a: 243–45). As usual, the first market contact had been through the sale of Australian drama programmes, including *Bellamy* and *The Young Doctors* (Macken 1989: 9). It soon became clear that the public broadcaster, RAI, was very interested in obtaining Grundy's services for the production of game shows as well as a drama serial.

In 1994, in conjunction with the public broadcaster, Grundy produced a local adaptation of *Man O Man* entitled *Beatro Tra Le Donne/Happy Among Women* (Moran 1998: 88). The programme was a 'live' entertainment, which was broadcast by RAI1 in its summer season. The series did enormously well, generally capturing more than half the viewing audience, and led to repeat seasons until 1998. Meanwhile, the company was also engaged in discussions about a strip drama serial and, although these were protracted, in late 1996 Grundy's first soap opera in Italy went on the air on RAI3. *Un Poste Al Sol/A Place in the Sun* was an original format devised for RAI (Lewis 1994: 18; Moran 1998: 88; O'Donnell 1999: 214–16). As Buonanno (2009) points out, the soap was responsible for introducing Italian audiences to the genre of the continuing soap opera (2009: 255–69). *Un Poste Al Sol* is still on air at the time of writing. Another Australian Grundy drama format, *Sons and Daughters*, remade for RAI2 as *Cuori Rubati*, came and went in 2002–03. Meanwhile, in 1997 Grundy produced an Italian version of *Everybody's Equal* titled *Vinca il Migliore*. A new game show format was devised for RAI, appearing in the form of *Per Tutta La Vita/For Life* (Moran 1998: 88). Altogether, this body of programmes, produced in just four years, constituted an impressive beginning in the Italian market, one on which the company planned to build further.

Spain

Another European television market that attracted the attention of the Australian transnational producer was that of Spain. A public-service monopoly came to an end in 1990 with the introduction of commercial television and the outsourcing of some of the production needs of the sector as a whole (Maxwell 2004: 2152–57). Grundy again drew on the same catalogue of formats for adaptation that it was using elsewhere, and soon was receiving game show commissions. Its light entertainment productions for Spanish broadcasters have included *Txandka/Kids are Funny Too* for ETB in 1991, *Cuestionario Millionario/Going for Gold* for TV Madrid in 1991–92, *Aqui Jugomos Todas/Everybody's Equal* for TVE in 1997 and *Vore Qui Guanya/Let's See Who Wins* for TVVCanal 9, also in 1997. In 1994, a coventure agreement (CVA) was signed with Zepelin, and a first coventure was *Elles I Ells*, an adaptation of *Man O Man*, for TVVChannel 9, produced from 1993 to 1995; it was then sold to Telechino as *Uno Para Todas* for national broadcasting in 1996 and 1997 (Moran 1998: 87). Altogether, these licensings represented a reasonable beginning for Grundy in the Spanish television market.

Sweden

A further late coventure agreement in this period saw Grundy achieve a presence in Swedish television. Fulfilling some of the media needs of a social democracy, broadcasting had been a public-service monopoly until the late 1980s (Hulten 2004: 2238–41). Foreign satellite-delivered commercial television prompted the advent of Swedish commercial television as a means of protecting the advertising base of local newspaper groups, however. Once again, Grundy was already known to the broadcasters from the late 1980s, thanks to its 'calling card' of Australian-made drama such as *Neighbours* (Macken 1989: 8). In 1994, it developed a coventure arrangement with Wegelius TV, a Scandinavian production house, and commercial broadcaster TV3, to produce a pan-Scandinavian adaptation of *Man O Man* (Moran 1998: 87–88). The programme was distributed to Sweden, Norway and Denmark in their respective languages. To develop particular national identifications inside this pan-Scandinavian emphasis, individual episodes featured different national hosts and contestants, while the final was a Scandinavian affair. The programme ran for three seasons from 1994 to 1996. In 1996, Grundy entered into a second coventure arrangement with Swedish producer Jarowskij Productions to produce another game show, *Sommarpratarna*, an adaptation of the format of *Small Talk*, for TV 4. The show is still on air. Late in 1996, the company began producing its first drama serial in Sweden. *Skilda Varlder/Worlds Apart*, stripped in a 7.00 p.m. weekday timeslot, was yet another adaptation of the Australian *Sons and Daughters*, and ran from 1996 to 2002 (Daniel 1995; Moran 1998: 119–20). Once again, this incursion into another European television market represented a promising beginning.

Elsewhere

To complete this survey of Grundy Worldwide's activities up to 1995, a string of one-off productions in individual markets in Europe, South America and Asia should also be noted. Some of these occurred later than 1996 but are mentioned here to complete the account. First, let us examine Europe. A Grundy office was maintained in Monaco that handled legal and accounting matters, as well as programme distribution. It also serviced productions occurring in some nearby markets. Greece was one of these markets, with the Mega TV channel commissioning a series of *Ruck Zouk* in 1994 and its Star Channel broadcasting a Greek version of *Sale of the Century* that same year, while in 1998 a broadcaster licensed the format for *Sons and Daughters*, which aired briefly as *Apagorevmeni*. Nearby, United Channels of Israel also put an adaptation of *Hot Streak* to air, this time under the title of *Hamesh Hamesh*, and complemented it with a franchise of *Small Talk* entitled *Ma'ta Omer*, with both game shows broadcast in 1994.

Later still, there were two further spin-offs from the *Sons and Daughters* franchise. The first occurred in Croatia and was titled *Zabranjena ljubav*. It went to air on RTL Televizija between 2004 and 2008. Finally, there was one other revival of the format under the same name for Bulgaria's Nova TV that began on air in 2008 and is still being broadcast at the time of writing.

The second region is South America, where the company had reasonable success in smaller markets in the period under review (Pinne 1995). In 1992, the Australian wing obtained a sale to Chile's national channel for a game show, *Desafio Familiar/Family Feud*. This led to the establishment of a South American office in Chile. Two seasons of another Goodson format, *Blockbusters*, were also commissioned, one produced for Chile in 1994 and the other in Uruguay in 1997. The company also re-versioned two of its own formats: *Sale of the Century* was retitled *La Venta del Siglo*, and began in 1995 on Paraguay's SNT Canal 9 under a barter arrangement, running for five years (Moran 1998: 69–70). The fourth game show was a supranational version of *Man O Man* that appeared in 1997 (Moran 1998). Drawing inspiration from the Italian summer version, it was broadcast into Argentina (ARTER Channel 13), Uruguay (Channel 10) and Paraguay (SNT Channel 9). Lastly, the South American office licensed the Australian ABC's sitcom *Mother and Son* (Moran 1993: 301–02), and produced a Chilean version, *Madre e Hijo*, for the 1995 season. Subsequently, there would be further remakes of this sitcom in Denmark, Greece and Turkey, all of them produced by Grundy Worldwide.

The last world region into which the company embarked was Asia. As Chapter 9 noted, there had already been Grundy's productions in Hong Kong and Brunei in the early 1980s, but these had been spillovers from the Australian operation. However, Grundy was known to broadcasters in the region thanks both to the distribution of some of its Australian shows and to its financial and production partnerships on miniseries, drama series and children's series (Leong 1994: 26–29). It established an office in Singapore in 1994 as a base for renewed engagement with the region (Skinner 1995). Soon, four game shows were on the air in different markets (Moran 1998: 72). The first was *Famili Seratus*, another Grundy clone based on the Goodson-owned format *Family Feud*, broadcasting on Indonesia's Anteve channel from 1994 onwards. It soon was joined by a celebrity version of the format, *Bintang Bintang Famili Seratus*. Indonesia's Antennae commissioned a third game show, *Kata Fa Kecil*, an adaptation of *Child's Play*, which began broadcasting in 1997. Finally, there was also a sports-based light entertainment show, *Kricketl*, based on a format devised by the company. This was produced in 1995 in partnership with United Television of Bombay for broadcast on the Star Plus channel of Star TV.

A final profile

This chapter has reported in detail on the explosion of Grundy's production activities in the period 1989–96. It is useful in this penultimate section to offer some broader observations about Grundy Worldwide and its undertakings, both by way of summarizing achievements and also adding to the administrative and structural outlines offered in previous chapters. Unbeknown to most staff and sections of the media, a silent swan song was already in progress. By 1990–91, Grundy Worldwide was a pre-eminent transnational television organization, with production and distribution contributing about 70 per cent of its international revenue stream of A$140 million, up from A$9.5 million in 1979–80. Its programmes sold into more than 70 countries across the world, with about 40 per cent of revenue being derived from Australasia and 60 per cent generated elsewhere. In mid-1991, Grundy was employing some 600 staff, a figure that would have increased between then and 1995 (*Australian Financial Review* 1993: 15; *Variety* 1992: 6). These activities, as well as the company's global productions, had brought about this increase, with the company claiming to be the second largest light-entertainment producer on the planet and one of the world's largest independent production organizations (Cunningham & Jacka 1996: 84). By 1993, it was reported that the company was making about 50 hours of television programming each week (Gerrie 1992: 98–100).

Since 1980, Grundy had followed three different kinds of domestic involvement in pursuing market opportunities in Europe and elsewhere. The first had to do with the establishment of a distinct Grundy presence, and involved such operations as registering a distribution and production company in the national market. A string of these incorporated companies began setting up in different parts of Western Europe from 1985 onwards. Hence a 1991 newspaper review of Grundy Worldwide could report that the parent organization owned 30 such companies around the world, including companies incorporated in Australia, New Zealand, the United States, Britain, France, Germany, The Netherlands, Belgium and Hong Kong. Plans were also in train to incorporate in South America and Asia (*Business Review Weekly* 1991). Not all of these incorporations involved setting up a local Grundy office, however. This expense was only warranted if a show was about to go into production. Hence, even by 1995, the company had not established offices in less wealthy television markets such as those of Ireland, Denmark and Finland.

A second means of proceeding involved entering a joint-venture arrangement with an established domestic production company. This had the double advantage of piggybacking on the latter's industry knowledge and reputation, and saving on office establishment costs. Its drawback was having to share revenue with the local production partner. All the same, Grundy found it advantageous to follow this strategy in certain instances hence the establishment of Grundy/JE in The Netherlands and Grundy UFA in Germany for the purpose of remaking Grundy soap operas for local broadcasters. Often, there was considerable chopping and changing with coventure partners. In 1987, for example, Grundy settled on Tele Image as a coventure partner in France. It soon realized that Tele Image was a competitor not a collaborator (Baart 1995). In 1989, it tried again, having a brief arrangement with Ellipse, a division of Canal Plus, but this association did not last either. Hence, in 1994, Grundy Worldwide abandoned the idea of a joint venture agreement in France in favour of setting up its own wholly owned and operated company, Les Productiones Grundy. Finally, the third tactic in advancing the Grundy interest involved the licensing of its formats to local broadcasters or production companies in particular television markets. There were at least two determinations at work in such decisions:

the relative size of the national viewing population and the degree of affluence of that population. Grundy sub-licensings was the case with company-owned format productions in Greece, Israel and Indonesia.

Afterword

Grundy was most fortunate in the timing of its move into Europe, South America and elsewhere. The years 1989–95 saw an increasing number of commercial broadcasters coming on the air, as well as a significant expansion in broadcast time. Where new and existing television stations – especially those in Europe – were able to arrange their finances, they preferred to schedule domestic rather than imported programmes. These tended to give the broadcasters the largest audiences (Silj 1988: 27–31). Grundy Worldwide benefited enormously from this practice of producing domestic adaptations based on international programme formats. The explosion in output across many of the more affluent television markets around the world highlighted the fact that Grundy was at the pinnacle of its power and wealth. Yet, having become a global player, several weaknesses could be discerned in the transnational operation. Although remarkable, the US venture had not been able to achieve long-term success. Grundy had only a limited number of formats that it had devised and or that it owned. It was financially conservative, always having existed as a string of privately owned companies. While its accumulated revenues would support the establishment of new production offices in different markets, it would not stretch far enough to include mergers with and acquisition of other companies that would strengthen its market position in the face of aggressive competitors. The next chapter looks at the consequences of this situation.

Chapter 12

Buyout and Beyond: Since 1995

Introduction

In 1995, Reg Grundy sold his suite of companies and retired. A split occurred whereby an individual and the business empire that he had built over almost fifty years became separate entities. Grundy Worldwide was acquired by a British company, which itself underwent even more elaborate conglomerate changes over the next fifteen years. None of these alterations impacted on the capacity of the business to produce television programmes in markets across the world based on formats that it owned or licensed. Nevertheless, the Grundy name was to have less and less meaning as successive trade markings and brandings of the conglomerate took effect. Reg Grundy himself also changed roles. With no behind-the-scenes business commitments, he began to appear more often in the media spotlight. After almost half a century of business anonymity, the former TV format mogul began to recover a little of the public voice, face and presence that had been abandoned around the mid-1960s. This chapter deals with the sale of the Grundy business empire and its aftermath. It considers the detail of the buyout and examines the motives that are likely to have prompted the sale. The subsequent trajectories of Reg Grundy and Grundy Worldwide are also outlined. One became more public as the other ceased to exist. I also survey changes that have occurred in the practice of television programme adaptation and remaking over the period covered in this book.

The buyout

In 1993, Reg Grundy decided to sell his group of companies. A suitable price was fixed on and the search for a buyer commenced. Two regional television operators in Australia initially were interested, but they seemed to have been unwilling to meet Grundy's asking price and bowed out of negotiations (Potter 1994). None of the three major Australian commercial television networks was interested in purchasing the Grundy company because of the difficulties that would be encountered in selling programmes to its rivals (*Australian Financial Review* 1993). The only other possible buyers mentioned in press reports at the time were Kerry Packer's Consolidated Press Holdings and the US entertainment giants Warner Bros and the ABC Network (Tabagot 1995). Nothing eventuated, though, and the matter seemed to lapse. In fact, Grundy and his financial advisers pressed on with the task of selling the company over the next twelve months or longer. Reports had it that it was offered to a UK television company, but it was not interested in buying. Maybe the company in question was Pearson Television, which soon would return to the fray. Finally, because no private buyer had been found, plans were put in place to float the group by listing it on stock exchanges in New York and Sydney (*Sydney Morning Herald* 1994; *The Australian* 1995; Potter & Kidman 1994).

But then a more enthusiastic would-be buyer began negotiations in early 1995, and within three months a deal had been struck (Benchley 1995a, 1995b; Houseman 1995; Oliver 1995; Snoddy & Tait 1995). The buyer was the UK conglomerate Pearson Television, with the deal being negotiated by its new chairman and chief executive officer, Greg Dyke (Auicke 2004). Dyke previously had been chief executive at London Weekend Television, an ailing television giant whose fortunes he was credited with turning around. He had also acted as advisory consultant to Pearson and a consortium that had bid for the new UK commercial television franchise of Channel 5. He moved to Pearson Television in early 1995 when London Weekend Television was taken over by Granada. Reg Grundy and Greg Dyke settled on a sale price of US$279 million (A$380 million) for the Grundy suite of companies. The private owner himself would receive 85 per cent of this sum with the remainder going to two company executives (Tabagot 1995).

The selling price was within the range of the company's value nominated for the New York and Sydney stock exchange listings (*Sydney Morning Herald* 1994; *The Australian* 1995; Furness 1995). Financial commentators believed that Reg Grundy had gained the kind of price that he wanted. Opinion was more philosophical about the position of Dyke and Pearson. 'The price doesn't look outrageous,' one analyst said, 'provided they can keep the act going without him' (Furness 1995: 28). The act in question included a bevy of companies scattered across the world with catalogues of 4000 hours of drama, 1000 hours of quiz shows and a slew of formats in two very popular modes of television, facilitating distribution in 60 markets and production in 23 territories. Under the deal, Grundy executives would remain, and Grundy himself was also reported to be continuing as a consultant to the new owner (Moran 1997b).

Why did the Pearson board finally agree to the acquisition when it had previously rejected it? Grundy reports in his memoir that Dyke's recent appointment as chairman of Pearson Television may have helped persuade the board to agree to the deal (Grundy 2010: 312–16). Dyke's mandate had been to improve the market position of Pearson Television. He was enthusiastic about the acquisition of Grundy Worldwide, believing that it would strengthen and expand the capacity of Pearson Television. The board may have acquiesced to his decision, not wanting to negate such a recommendation so soon after his appointment (2010: 314–15). Press reports of the news of the buyout announced that Reg Grundy would remain as a consultant following his company's buyout. In fact, Dyke did not remain at the helm for long. He left to head up Channel 5 and soon moved again to become director-general of the BBC in 2000 (Auicke 2004: 769–70). Without Dyke, the former lack of regard for Grundy Worldwide may have resurfaced at Pearson Television.

In any case, various Grundy-appointed executives soon moved on to retirement or to work elsewhere. Reg Grundy seems not to have been actively sought out as a consultant on projects (Moran 1997b).

Deciding to sell

Why did Grundy sell his business empire? A series of interconnected answers can be suggested. First, there was his personal situation. The format mogul had no male heir to take over the business in the case of his death. His wife of almost 25 years was not directly involved in his companies, and his sole offspring, daughter Kim, had long been estranged. Selling his business interests in 1995 would give the group a larger value than it might have had had he died while still at the helm. After all, his father, Roy Grundy, had declined in health and died relatively suddenly and unexpectedly at the age of 54 and Grundy himself would turn 72 later in 1995. Mark Goodson had died in 1992, the same year that Grundy began thinking about selling the company. Nor was age on the side of some key executives that Reg Grundy was losing. Reg Watson, for instance, had retired around 1992 at the age of just 57, while Ian Holmes, by then in his early sixties, had indicated that he wanted to lighten his managerial duties in the company.

The general track record of television production groups in Australia and elsewhere is also worth bearing in mind. Business longevity was not common among television production companies. Working in Australian television for over 30 years, Reg Grundy had seen a string of programme packagers overtaken by financial collapse after being unable to follow up hit shows with other successful programmes. While the Grundy business was now mostly safe from such a calamity, nevertheless there was always the distant possibility of again encountering the problems associated with the simultaneous cancellation of programmes that Grundy himself had encountered twice in Australia in the 1960s. Such a fate was increasingly unlikely, although the recent bankruptcies of the Seven, Nine and Ten Networks in Australia may have sounded a warning bell of sorts.

Another factor – very possibly more important – may have been the disappointment of programme packaging for US television outlined in the last three chapters. From 1959 on, when he began to copy US television quiz shows, Reg Grundy probably harboured a dream of becoming a leading producer of television programmes for US television networks. The attempted implementation of that desire began in 1979, with the establishment of the Los Angeles production office for the Grundy Organisation. A string of quiz shows were sold for daytime programming by the networks in the 1980s, but this market had become even smaller and more difficult to penetrate with the rise of daytime talk shows, beginning with that of Phil Donoghue and followed by Oprah Winfrey's programme (*Broadcasting* 1991). Grundy's biggest disappointment in the US market undoubtedly lay with *Dangerous Women*, however. Much against his own practice of avoiding deficit financing on any production, Grundy was so determined to achieve a significant US production breakthrough that he underwrote much of the cost of the production and broadcast of *Dangerous Women* (Grundy 2010: 247–51). Unfortunately, this clone did not achieve the success of its predecessor, *Prisoner: Cell Block H* in the US market. Its demise left the company without either the vehicle, or perhaps even the funds, to commit to a second drama serial assault on the US network market. It is certainly the case that the decision to sell the company came hard on the heels of the *Dangerous Women* disappointment.

Grundy Worldwide's excellent fortunes in the years 1993–95 may also have been a contributing factor in the decision to sell. As I noted at the end of Chapter 11, over 50 per cent of income came from operations in the United Kingdom and Europe, and the prospects there and elsewhere looked excellent (with the obvious exception of the United States) (*Variety* 1992). Given a growing inclination towards selling the company, the period 1993–95 was an excellent time for it to be on the market. Recent business returns would help ensure that such an offering would only have attracted fire-sale offers. Company profit projections are made on the basis of recent trade, and such a valuation at the time would ensure that a satisfactory price might be achieved.

The mention of capital highlights another distinctive feature of Reg Grundy's business career and the company buyout. Grundy's companies, notably Reg Grundy Enterprises, the Grundy Organisation and Grundy Worldwide, had all been private companies, with most if not all of their stock owned by Reg Grundy himself. This situation had a clear upside, but it also had a downside. Personal ownership of the companies, and the fact that these were private entities, ensured that Reg Grundy was and remained safe from a possible business takeover. The drawback lay in the fact that any new initiatives or ventures on the part of the company had to be financed from existing capital.

Despite the value of his business, Grundy possibly realized that he did not have the financial resources to remain a significant player in the rapidly changing environment of the global television format business. Very large transnational players were on the scene, and acquisition and merger were the name of the game so far as rapid expansion was concerned. Conglomeratization required access to very large pools of finance. Reg Grundy had sufficient wealth accumulated over the years to pay for the establishment of an office in a new territory or the hiring of professionals identified as useful and important, but he did not have the funds required for a company takeover of the magnitude that was now becoming common.

Floating the company could have overcome this situation. Although he was prepared to go down this path in 1994, it was probably one that was not to his liking. As I suggest in the next chapter, this was not an attitude shared by other media moguls, whether hailing from Australia or elsewhere. Instead of remaining private and solely owned, the more common practice has been to list on the stock exchange while retaining majority shareholding. Indeed, two of Grundy's rivals in the television programme production business, Southern Star International in Australia (Cunningham & Jacka 1996: 105–16) and Endemol in The Netherlands (Moran 1998: 33–34), were also listed on stock exchanges, in Sydney and Amsterdam, respectively. Reg Grundy was probably in a good position to float his company in the public domain by, say, 1980 when his programme production had solid, mutually supportive foundations in quiz shows and drama serials. This did not happen, and the projected float in 1995 was readily abandoned once a willing buyer was found in the shape of Pearson Television. The business divorce brought about by the sale left both principal and company free to go their separate ways.

'Re-Grundification': Reg Grundy without Grundy Worldwide

The Pearson buyout of the Grundy group served to separate Reg Grundy from Grundy Worldwide. After almost half a century in broadcasting, Grundy no longer had a television business vehicle that demanded most of his time and effort, although he would remain busy in retirement. Reg Grundy had been involved in broadcasting for almost half a century when he parted with his company in 1995. While some moguls have planned to expire at the helm, others have passed over command whether to an offspring or to a business companion before health or other reasons trigger such a surrender. Subsequent regret is often common on the part of the previous owner. Sir Frank Packer, legendary hardman owner of the Australian media group Consolidated Press, for instance, later became disappointed that he had sold his *Sydney Daily Telegraph* to Rupert Murdoch in 1972 (Griffen-Foley 2000: 350), while US quiz-show devisor and packager Merv Griffen also came to rue his decision to sell his business interests (Timberg 2004a: 1034–35). In fact, at least one Grundy erstwhile partner and subsequent rival came back to television programme production after retiring. This was Dutch producer Joop van den Ende, who had joined with his Amsterdam competitor John de Mol to form Endemol in 1993, then retired from Endemol in 2000 only to be active again in the international television format production industry by 2010 (Edgecliffe-Johnson 2008: 16).

Like these and other figures, Grundy has voiced regret about selling his company from time to time (2010: 317–18). But he has found many ways to occupy his spare hours, and of course has had sufficient capital to support his preoccupations. The former mogul and his wife have pursued various interests, old and new, in keeping with their wealth. These pastimes have included art collecting, golf, scuba diving, photography and writing. Some of the fruits of these activities have gained public attention. Reg Grundy has had art exhibitions of his wildlife photography in galleries in Bermuda, Sydney and Brisbane and has published a coffee-table book collection of wildlife photography and a memoir. His wife, Joy Chambers, has published a series of novels combining history and romantic fiction. These interests are maintained and supported by a private staff that has collected around the principal and his partner, much like a family. Members of the retinue are identified in the memoir (2010: 317–30). Grundy's 'people' had its beginnings in the early 1970s and has grown to support the private, cosmopolitan activities of the couple. Highlighting the corporatization of the domestic and the domestication of the corporate that have been a feature of Grundy's life since he first entered television, there is even a small inner advisory board meeting held several times a year in whatever part of the world best suits different travel itineraries. The main task of this retinue – especially the inner brains trust in consultation with the Grundy couple – is to watch over the Grundy fortune, which began as US$279 million in 1995 and now approaches A$1 billion (*Australian Women's Weekly* 2005). Led by Reg Grundy, the group decides what to buy and sell, whether company shares, paintings and art objects, or larger assets such as yachts or houses.

Hence, although no longer a TV format mogul, Reg Grundy's trading activities, under the banner of his private company RG Capital, are reported from time to time in the financial pages. By the late 1990s, for instance, the company had bought as many as 39 FM radio stations in Australia, although it had unloaded these by 2004 (*Australian Women's Weekly* 2005). At another point, it had a minority shareholding in the Australian television production company Southern Star, while in 2008 it was reported as owning 29 per cent of Photon, an Australian-based advertising, marketing and ecommerce group (2010: 331). The last of a string of sailing boats, used for business and private functions, also came and went. Fittingly, what turned out to be the last yacht had been given a regal title, *Boadicea*, after the legendary Queen of the Anglo-Saxons who had commanded her army against the Romans, although the luxury yacht had actually been built in the Netherlands (Grundy 2010: 339–42).

Beyond these financial activities, Grundy's people organized large special events as well as more routine, less spectacular ones on an ongoing basis. The former have included the 2005 Sydney and Brisbane launches of the handsome glossy coffee-table book of wildlife photography, a lavish *This is Your Life* Sydney birthday party on Grundy's turning 85 in 2008, and the gala publication of his memoirs in Sydney in late 2010. There was also more regular travel, including field trips to such places as outback Australia to photograph endangered species, Canada to snap polar bears and the Kalahari Desert to photograph meerkats. These activities are launched from a series of Grundy residences, including a house in Bermuda, apartments in Los Angeles, London and Sydney, and a country house in southern NSW.

In between, there have been a string of honours, awards and homages, acknowledging Reg Grundy's contribution to the television industry in Australia, the United States and internationally, which consistently have thrust him into the public spotlight (Grundy 2010: 347). This acclaim began as early as 1983 with the award of the Order of the British Empire (OBE), Australia's highest award after the Australian government had abandoned its involvement in the British knighthood award system. Collectively, the continuing string of special events and tributes have played their part in forcing the television format pioneer into the public domain. Some of the secrecy associated with his business career has gone, and submitting to these public occasions has had the effect of gradually making the Grundy face and voice increasingly familiar to the Australian public in ways that parallel his social recognition by the broadcasting audience in the 1950s and early 1960s.

This kind of late public 'Grundification' or, rather, 're-Grundification' has been doubly ironic. After all, Grundy had consciously decided by the late 1960s to privatize his persona. This was not triggered by a mania for personal secrecy and anonymity as personified by US mogul Howard Hughes, although it was certainly in keeping with a general tendency, noticed by Tunstall, towards extreme privacy on the part of moguls in general, and media moguls in particular. With business imperatives mostly gone after 1995, Reg Grundy was consenting to a kind of re-publicizing of his imagined self. A parallel irony involved what was happening to Grundy Worldwide at the time of this 'Grundification' of the man. As the next section makes evident, the growing fame of the former was matched by the increasing business anonymity of the latter.

'De-Grundification': Grundy Worldwide without Reg Grundy

As Gomery (2004) suggests, company takeovers and buyouts have been the principal mechanism whereby television organizations have achieved substantial growth (2004: 1479–82). The vast majority of dominant enterprises have been assembled by merger and acquisition with other companies rather than by building from the ground up. In fact, as we saw in Chapter 7, Reg Grundy Enterprises demonstrated this in a minor way in the early 1970s in Australia, when it brought several writer/producers on board to give it immediate expertise in the area of drama. From 1995 onwards, the company was swallowed by a bigger corporate fish in the shape of Pearson Television.

Pearson Television had been established in 1993 as an arm of the UK Pearson group, whose origins lay mainly in publishing (Blumler 2004: 330–37). Major changes were afoot at the time in the UK media sector, and the move was part of a plan by Pearson PLC to establish itself as a transnational conglomerate in the areas of media and communications. Its immediate target in 1993 was the purchase of Thames Television, previously the provider of weekday commercial television programming for the London region (Bryant and Alvarado 2004: 322–27). Dyke had become chairman and chief executive officer of Pearson Television in early 1995, and immediately launched a flurry of aggressive mergers and acquisitions, beginning with the Grundy purchase and followed by further company buyouts in the United Kingdom, Italy, Germany and Finland in the area of television production and distribution (Auicke 2004: 769–70). Pearson Television also obtained an important stake in the consortium bidding for the new UK commercial television network Channel 5 (Blumler 2004: 330–37).

For Pearson Television, the purchase of Grundy Worldwide made a good deal of sense, as it already had a television division with broadcasting interests in companies such as BSkyB, UK Gold and UK Living in the United Kingdom, and European Satellite Television and TVB in Hong Kong, as well as owning another production company in the shape of Thames Television (Moran 1997b; Chalaby 2009: 55–57). The Channel 5 consortium in which it was represented further underlined the significance of the Grundy purchase by helping to develop a vertically integrated television operation in the United Kingdom as well as a rapidly developing production company in Europe, Latin America and Asia (Moran 1997b).

Over the next five years after the buyout, Grundy Worldwide underwent a change of identity, becoming a junior in the Pearson Television operation (Moran 1998: 69–70). Its headquarters was relocated to London, with the company becoming a UK group. Grundy

Distribution was integrated with Thames programme distribution, with Pearson Television overseeing all major expenditures. Frustrated at the new style at work in the larger company, several of the former Australian executives left.

Meanwhile, the conglomerate continued to grow in size. By 2011, it could point to twenty companies that it had swallowed up (Chalaby 2009: 55–60). The Grundy acquisition saw Pearson Television pick up a significant catalogue of programme formats, to which it added in 1997 when it acquired All-American International (AAI), whose format library included the series *Baywatch*. The UK company also picked up properties previously owned by Mark Goodson Productions and Fremantle International (Moran 1998: 69–70).

Because of its name, which soon would be adopted by the group, Fremantle International deserves a short note in passing. It had begun life in the 1950s, distributing B Western feature films starring Hopalong Cassidy, as well as Hal Roach silent Hollywood comedies. The company was founded by New York-based television distributor Paul Talbot, who first named the company Talbot/Fremantle (Grantham 1998). The latter referred to the Western Australian port city and signified the Antipodean origins of Talbot's wife. The earlier company's successor, Fremantle International, was active in many overseas television markets, including that of Australia. In 1969, it ventured into two local co-productions, one involving a comedy sitcom format remake using scripts of a US original that had starred Wally Cox (Moran 1993: 202–03). Ironically, in the 1980s and 1990s, Fremantle International distributed light entertainment formats and partnered with one of Grundy's Australian quiz-show rival producers (Moran 1993: 523–24).

As already mentioned, Dyke moved on to head up Channel 5 for the successful consortium and then became director-general of the BBC in 2000 (Auicke 2004: 769–70). In this capacity, he fell foul of the UK Labour government, which instigated a witchhunt of BBC reporting of events surrounding its decision to join the United States at war in Iraq (Dyke 2005). Dyke was heavily criticized in an inquiry headed by the conservative Lord Hutton, and resigned in early 2004. He soon rebounded. His account of these events was published the following year, and by 2010 he was in line to become editor of *The Independent* and *The Independent on Sunday* newspapers.

The dawn of the new millennium had also seen Pearson Television and CLTUFA merged as an even bigger conglomerate, the Luxembourg-based RTL (Radio Television Luxembourg) Group. A further name change was now necessary. The following year, the content production division of RTL (Pearson, UFA and Grundy UFA) was renamed as FremantleMedia. The past decade has seen the group continuing to acquire smaller companies, with the German Bertelsman Group picking up a 30 per cent majority share in the RTL Group (Moran & Malbon 2006: 94–96). FremantleMedia's worldwide headquarters is in London, and the organization is now a transnational conglomerate of considerable proportions (Chalaby 2009). It is second only in size and wealth to the Dutch company Endemol, whose growth is touched upon in the next chapter.

The name 'Grundy' soon began to disappear off company productions in different parts of the world, as the mergers and conglomeration continued after 1995. The label lingered in Australia for some time. In 1995, productions ceased to bear the imprint of the Grundy Organisation in favour of the name Grundy Television. In 2003, FremantleMedia acquired a second production company in Australia, Crackerjack Productions, and in 2006–07 it and Grundy Television were merged to become FremantleMedia Australia. Ironically, a number of companies have retained the founder's name in their title, including light entertainment companies in Germany, Spain and Italy as well as the joint venture drama producer Grundy UFA in Germany, with a subsidiary, Magyar Grundy UFA in Hungary and elsewhere (Grundy 2010: 261–62). Despite this process of 'de-Grundification', whereby the name of the originator has progressively been stripped away, an important business legacy remains in the FremantleMedia conglomerate, into which the Grundy group was merged. Regardless of changes in nomenclature, the particular business practice on which Grundy built his operation is now of major international cultural and economic significance, as the next section suggests.

World format trade explosion

This study has discussed two broad phases to Grundy's career in television format production. The first began around 1960 and lasted until 1980. In a study of US format adaptation on the part of European public-service broadcasters, Bourdin has usefully characterized this time as one when the practice of programme format adaptation and remaking was 'discrete, infrequent and often informal adaptation' (Bourdin 2011: 163–70). This was not the way that Grundy operated, however. Instead, as I suggested in Chapter 5, he set about systematizing the introduction of new US quiz-show formats to Australian commercial television by regular, planned and thorough survey trips to the United States. The only way in which Grundy's format borrowings coincided with those of the European public broadcasters discussed by Bourdin was because these adaptations were also informal. Few intellectual property arrangements were in place to hinder the free circulation of commercial and cultural ideas and know-how, and this certainly applied to television programme formats. A key event for both European and Grundy borrowings of US quiz-show formats occurred in 1979: the United States becoming a signatory to the latest revisions of the Berne Convention for the Protection of Literary and Artistic Works (Porter & Mun 2004: 591).

From this point on, US programme format owners and originators began to reap valuable, systematic rewards in markets in overseas territories such as Western Europe, the United Kingdom and Australia. Format catalogues became available, overseas producers signed territorial agreements with format owners to secure option rights on particular programmes, and companies began to pay format-licensing fees. This coincided with the onset of commercialization and channel multiplication in European public broadcasting, with the licensing of programme formats happening alongside the licensing of finished imported programming (Curtin 2004: 993–97). Bourdin has characterized this second phase as the 'open replication' era, which 'saw increased competition and new pressures forcing broadcasting systems to freely "adapt" successful American game show formulae' (2011: 70–74).

As we have seen, Grundy's activities between 1980, when his operation began to extend offshore, and 1995, when he sold his company, also conform to this second designation. As an important producer involved in the business of 'open replication', Grundy had accumulated expertise in adaptation and format origination, and even owned a number of formats in the areas of quiz shows and drama serials. The company became a transnational business, eyeing off opportunities for format development and remakes in the United States, Western Europe and elsewhere. One other qualification of Bourdin's characterization of this second era is in order, however. This relates to the fact that the flow of formats had become even less of a one-way flow from the United States to other places, including Australia and Western Europe. The traffic in television programme formats was increasingly multidirectional, even including the occasional format from elsewhere being adapted for US television screens.

Bourdin's third phase of international traffic in formats happened after Grundy's retirement from the business of adaptation and remaking. As we have seen, the Australian-born producer retired in 1995, when he sold his company to Pearson Television. On the other hand, the contemporary phase of the global format trade began in 1998–99. This era has seen a 'Euro-American convergence' that has involved 'the normalization of the format trade' and the transformation of 'once-public European entities (into) … active originators and participants in the contemporary format marketplace' (Bourdin 2011: 172).

The phase began dramatically with the launch of three game shows originating in the United Kingdom and The Netherlands, respectively. These were *Survivor* and *Big Brother*, and together with *Who Wants to Be a Millionaire?*, they ushered in a new era of international traffic in formats (Wilson 2004: 262–64; Murray 2004b: 1900–02; Blasini 2004: 2226–27; Hoerschelmann 2004d: 2536–37). These shows have been characterized by such superlatives as 'big', 'mega', 'beach-head', 'juggernaut' and 'bubble' formats designations that suggest the high visibility that many contemporary formats have attracted. *Big Brother*, for example, has been produced in more than 60 countries as well as in several regional versions, has often had repeat seasons stretching over a dozen years or more, and has had more written about it than any other television show in history (Wilson 2004: 262–64).

In the new international television landscape brought about by multichannelling, new technology and narrowcasting, other more expensive forms of content increasingly have been displaced in favour of less expensive forms whose economies were based in part on the 'parochial' remaking of what were seen to be international formats (to apply Reg Grundy's own formula of 'parochial internationalism'). Major new format distributing companies emerged, based in Western Europe rather than the United States. Format trade became a serious business at the international round of television markets (Moran 2009: 23–41). In 2000, a group of these companies came together and established an industry body, the Format Recognition and Protection Association (FRAPA). Lawyers also fought out several court battles, the collective outcome of which has been the beginning of legal recognition of television programme formats as valuable intellectual property (Moran &

Malbon 2006). Training courses have come into being and practitioner handbooks have also begun appearing, yet another sign of the coalescence and formalization of a worldwide format trade.

Programme remaking is now one of the pillars of the modern transnational system of television, and Reg Grundy has played an important role in its development. The industry is sufficiently consolidated for Grundy to have received two awards recognizing this contribution. The first was bestowed in 2003 at the Monte Carlo Television Festival, where he was honoured for the public understanding generated by his concept of 'parochial internationalism', while the second was presented in 2010 in the form of a 'lifetime achievement' award from FRAPA in Cannes (Grundy 2010: 346).

Afterword

This chapter has traced the different trajectories of the businessman and his business after the two were divorced from each other. It has been concerned with the details and significance of the buyout, Grundy's subsequent life and the fate of his company in a changing corporate set of arrangements. It has also marked the independent development of the global television format trade historically by looking at this practice when Grundy entered and exited the television business. There remains one outstanding matter for this career study to address: an overall assessment of Grundy's importance, both financially and culturally. How significant has Reg Grundy been, and what is the best way to measure his achievement? The last chapter addresses these questions.

Chapter 13

A TV Format Mogul Among TV Format Moguls

Introduction

Chapter 1 introduced the category of the media mogul and suggested the possibility of different types. I offered the 'TV format mogul' as a particular variant and have fleshed this out by examining Reg Grundy's business career in detail. But Grundy is far from being the only example of the TV format mogul. Accordingly, this chapter addresses two other instances of the figure as a means of extending awareness of the general type and helping to pinpoint Grundy's significance. The two case studies offered below concern figures who belong to different times, situations and national settings. They help contextualize the Australian mogul's business trajectory in television programme formats by offering differing career histories and examples and they help pinpoint the particular significance of Grundy's work in the television programme format trade. The two examples also assist us in understanding the television programme format business both before and after Grundy, thereby generating a more nuanced, historical insight into the twists and turns of the trade. Finally, the two case studies, together with the more extended example of Reg Grundy outlined in these pages, help us get a better grasp of the category of the TV format mogul itself.

Reg Grundy and Rupert Murdoch

First, some words about another Australian-born media mogul with whom Grundy is sometimes bracketed. On the face of it, there seems no point in comparing Reg Grundy and Rupert Murdoch although significant differences soon emerge. Murdoch is eight years younger than Grundy, being born in Melbourne in 1931 (Gunzerath 2004a, 2004b). He took control of two Adelaide newspapers inherited from his father in 1952 at the age of 21. Television stations followed, and these were soon joined by more newspapers in Australia and New Zealand. Soon, Murdoch moved to become a transnational media owner, buying two newspapers in the United Kingdom in 1968 and two others in the United States in 1973 and 1976. A further six newspapers were added over the next ten years. News International, Murdoch's media company, then proceeded to add television, book publishing and airline, oil and gas businesses to this slate of companies. In 1985, it was the turn of 20th Century Fox film studios and a string of Metromedia television stations to be gobbled up. Murdoch, now a US citizen, broke into network television broadcasting by establishing the Fox Television

Network. British Sky Broadcasting was under Murdoch's command by 1990 and Asia Star TV followed in 1993. He has continued to add to his assets, most especially in the area of new digital technologies over the past two decades.

These details mark important differences between the two Australian-born magnates. First and most obvious is the fact that Grundy began from scratch whereas Murdoch had a flying start by being bequeathed two newspapers. Murdoch is far wealthier and more powerful, not only in business matters but also in political ones. Grundy's empire was founded on a media content industry whereas Murdoch's rests not only on the output of content but, especially, upon the far more lucrative activity of carriage provision. The older man was never timid in his business dealings but the younger one soon showed even greater boldness and aggression in his newspaper and television tradings.

A ready supply of finance capital can help fuel corporate takeover although the owner puts some of his business control at the mercy of lending institutions and shareholders in such arrangements. Reg Grundy never endangered his company control by publicly floating his company, which remained a private concern until its 1995 sale. Rupert Murdoch, on the other hand, successfully gambled on retaining control of News Corporation even while using outside financial institutions as a war chest for further expansion. For Grundy, there was no heir to take over the business whereas Murdoch has several sons and daughters who have been variously groomed for such a task. Linked to the matter of succession is the matter of the mogul's departure. Grundy sold his business at the age of 72 whereas Murdoch, 80 years of age at the time of writing, continues to preside over his empire although the latter may be crumbling in the face of major corruption issues in his UK operations.

In short, a comparison of Grundy and Murdoch serves mostly to highlight the differences between the two. Most of these stem from the fact that the two twentieth-century, Australian-born moguls operated in different parts of media industries – Murdoch as the owner of a large number of media industry vehicles and Grundy as a television programme provider. Hence, to pinpoint Grundy's specific importance, it is more relevant to turn to two other figures who have been active in the area of television programme production, with format franchising forming a core part of their business. The two in question are American Mark Goodson and Dutchman John de Mol. The former predated Grundy, while the latter succeeded him in the television programme format trade. I outline these two careers so that general conclusions about Grundy's career as format mogul can be drawn.

Mark Goodson: background

Goodson belongs to an earlier generation of the programme format trade in broadcasting. He was born in 1915 to Russian immigrant parents in Sacramento, California (McDermott 2004: 1013–16). After a Depression-era boyhood and taking a degree from the University of California, gained through part-time work and scholarships, he landed a job at a local San Francisco radio station in 1937. Four years later, Goodson went to New York to break into network radio. He carried two recommendations with him: he had already devised a radio quiz show, *Pop The Question*, and had a letter of introduction from producer/host Ralph Edwards, an alumni of his university (Sterling 2004b: 539–40).

In New York radio, Goodson found work undertaking announcing and writing. At local station WABC, he worked on *Battle of the Boroughs* alongside Bill Todman and the two set up Goodson-Todman Productions in 1945. Goodson was to concentrate on the creative side of the business by devising new quiz and game shows while Todman was responsible for the practical end of things, including spotting weaknesses in quiz ideas, laying down programme rules, overseeing budgets and selling shows to broadcasters. The company licensed a string of new quiz and panel game shows to local radio stations. Goodson-Todman Productions also scored its first network sale with the licensing in 1946 of *Winner Take All* to CBS Radio. Following the end of the World War II, the US networks were also developing their television broadcasting so that *Winner Take All* was one of many radio shows simulcast on television running from 1948 to 1950.

Goodson as format devisor

By this stage, Mark Goodson was showing himself to be innovative and creative so far as pushing the boundaries of the quiz and game show genre was concerned (Mittell 1994: 1146–52). *Winner Take All* was the first show to use a lockout buzzer system; to pit two contestants against each other rather than against the quizmaster, one at a time; and to feature quiz champions returning until beaten by another contestant (McDermott 2004: 1011). As mentioned in Chapter 4, quiz and game shows had already developed a variety of types and Goodson-Todman focused on two particular styles of the genre in its offerings to the US television networks.

The first type was the celebrity panel game. Goodson-Todman's initial venture into the category was *What's My Line?*, which CBS bought in 1950 (Sherman 1965: 63–70). The concept for this cheerful, often funny show was rudimentary, with a contestant drawn from the public at large, answering questions about his or her occupation, put by a regular team of personality/celebrities, with the audience learning about the occupation before questioning got underway. *What's My Line?* proved to be immensely popular and ran in prime-time on CBS from 1950 to 1967. The year after its cancellation, it was remade for syndication broadcast and ran until 1975 (Schwartz, Ryan & Wosbrook 1987: 491–94). It was also one of the first of the Goodson-Todman game show ideas – it would be a long time before the term 'format' was used – to be adapted outside the United States, with the BBC paying the company a licensing fee, first for a radio version, then for a television version (Brunt 1985: 23).

Goodson-Todman also concentrated on quiz and game shows that highlighted ordinary people as contestants. *Beat the Clock* chose these from a studio audience and set various stunts to be performed, usually within 60 seconds, frequently featuring custard pies, whipped cream, breakable dishes and exploding balloons. The show proved to be very popular and durable. It ran from 1950 to 1958 on CBS prime-time and spun off a CBS daytime version 1957 to 1958. The company persuaded the ABC Network to take a daytime version from 1958 to 1961 after CBS had cancelled the show. *Winner Take All* then bounced back in a syndicated version between 1969 and 1974 and even briefly revived for CBS daytime between 1979 and 1980 (Schwartz, Ryan & Wosbrook 1987: 34–37).

Goodson-Todman's changing fortunes

On the other hand, Goodson-Todman had mostly steered clear of the large prize-winning quiz shows that became the rage with networks and audiences from 1954 to 1958. This meant that none of their shows was cancelled in the aftermath of the quiz-show scandal when it became clear that contestants had been told answers beforehand and coached about their appearances (Hoerschelmann 2004b: 1871–74). Indeed, the company was largely unaffected because of its excellent reputation inside the trade. On the other hand, Goodson-Todman, like other quiz and game show packagers, was affected by the decision of networks, in the aftermath of the scandals, to mostly restrict the genre to daytime broadcast, a decision that affected licensing prices.

The 1950s had seen Goodson-Todman at the height of its powers as the largest and most successful quiz-show producer in the US television industry. Among its winners were *What's My Line?*, *I've Got a Secret*, *Tell the Truth*, *Concentration* and *The Match Game*. After this golden era, its fortunes slowly declined. According to McDermott, the company was largely coasting on past successes in the quiz and game show genre by the 1960s. That decade had also seen a final end to its ambitions to be a producer of the more lucrative genre of television drama when the old-style anthology fiction series *The Richard Boone Show* had been cancelled in 1964. Worse was to come. CBS decided to programme for a more youthful demographic and in 1967 cancelled several of Goodson-Todman's more long-running game shows. This shift was contagious so that by 1970 all three networks had dropped almost all game shows from their daytime programming (McDermott 2004: 1013–16).

New licensings of Goodson formats

As we saw in Chapter 5, many Goodson-Todman shows were being adapted and remade elsewhere from the 1950s onwards (Bourdin 2011; Schmitt, Bisson & Fey 2005). Some of these remakes occurred under licence but most were unauthorized. The company was probably unaware of the extent of such borrowing and was, in any case, powerless to oversee it because the United States was not a signatory to the Berne Agreement on copyright (Porter & Mun 2004: 593–97). In any case, Goodson-Todman itself joined this trend of recycling its old programme ideas when the 1971 implementation of the Prime Time Access rule opened up a new set of buyers for its wares in the shape of the US television syndication market. It had over twenty years of popular game shows in its catalogue and proceeded to remake most of these for the new syndication marketplace.

At the same time, the networks relented in their attitude towards game shows when faced with syndication competition (Hoerschelmann 2004b: 1871–74). Many new glossy game show extravaganzas came and went, some from Goodson-Todman. However, the company had not really lost its touch and, once again, had success with a new version of *The Price is Right*, and especially with two new programme formats, *Family Feud* and *Card Sharks*.

In 1979, Todman died and the private company became Mark Goodson Productions. By then, the company was mostly trading on its many past successes. In the United States, the rise of talk shows had squeezed the market for game shows (Timberg 2004: 2255–62). However, the Berne Agreement had been signed so that a more formalized international system for remaking programme formats was coming into being. This ensured a steady licensing income accruing to the company. Additionally, television channels in many other parts of the world, beginning with Western Europe, were multiplying in number, thanks to new technology, commercialization and privatization (Servaes 2004a: 820–24). The licensing prospects for the Goodson quiz-show catalogue were expanding considerably. Mark Goodson was, by then, probably more interested in other activities, including a chain of small community newspapers that he owned as well as his commitments to the performing arts that he had always esteemed above the devising of quiz shows. He died in 1992 worth about $400 million and the Goodson quiz-show format catalogue was sold to All-American International (AAI), soon ending up in the format library of FremantleMedia. As noted in the previous chapter, the latter is a giant transnational television programme format producer, second only to another European format conglomerate, Endemol. The co-founder of the latter is the subject of the next TV-programme format mogul profile.

John de Mol: background

The other mogul relevant to a fuller understanding of Grundy's media career is John de Mol. De Mol is a significantly younger man who was born in The Netherlands in 1955. Like Goodson and Grundy, he also started from scratch (Bickerton 2004: 27). All the same, he benefited from a show-business family background that provided useful industry contacts and opportunities. His father, who bore the same name, was a popular singer-entertainer, a kind of Dutch Frank Sinatra. John de Mol's childhood ambition was to be a professional footballer but he got his media start as an assistant on Radio Noordzee, the Dutch pirate radio station. The stint included some DJ work. Still a teenager, de Mol then landed a job at the Dutch state-television's NOS channel's highly popular Sunday-night sports program where his task was to edit 90-minute videotapes of Dutch football games into three-minute grabs of highlights.

At 21, the neophyte married into another show-business family, which helped him get a start as a television director at public broadcaster TROS. But de Mol was very ambitious and impatient, so he soon set up his own television production company, John de Mol Productions. The year was 1979 and he was 24 years old. As might be expected, the television company's first work was in music programming, which included producing specials for Dutch broadcasters. In 1984, John de Mol Productions sold its first weekly programme, *Pop Formulae*, a pop music magazine programme that was to run until 1991. The same year saw a second major boost when Sky Channel in the United Kingdom signed a three-year contract for a daily music programme, *Euro Chart Top 30*. A year later, Sky contracted to broadcast *DJ Catshow*. The latter was presented by de Mol's highly attractive sister, Linda de Mol, who was 21 at the time. She became very popular with Dutch viewers and was, in effect, John de Mol Productions' first star, a situation reminiscent of Joy Chambers' relationship with Reg Grundy Enterprises.

de Mol's rival

de Mol's most significant Dutch competitor was JE Productions, owned by Joop van den Ende. As we saw in Chapter 11, JE partnered with Grundy World Wide in setting up The Netherlands' and Europe's first daily soap opera in the form of *Goede Tijden, Slechte Tijden/ Good Times, Bad Times* for RTL 4 in 1990. van den Ende had started his organization in 1969 as a special events and theatre production company. Soon, it was involved in the televising of these live events by the public broadcasters and then moved into producing television programmes in its own right. Many were based on imported formats for quiz, drama and sitcoms. However, JE Productions was also adept at developing its own 90-minute variety hybrids that would include *The Honeymoon Quiz*, *The Soundmix Show* and *The Playback Show* (Moran 1998: 33–39). By 1988, JE was the largest television producer in The Netherlands. However, an aborted attempt to become a broadcaster in its own right provoked a boycott by the public broadcasters and created the opportunity for the spectacular growth of John de Mol Productions.

By then, the latter company was no longer confined to making music programmes; instead, it had expanded into game shows, drama and comedy. It acquired the Dutch licence for several of the most successful US game show formats and produced local versions of programmes such as *Wheel of Fortune, The Price is Right* and *The Dating Game*. John de Mol Productions also saw the need to create new shows that it might license into other territories. One of the earliest and most successful of these was the game show *Love Letters*, hosted by Linda de Mol, which pitted three engaged couples against each other, vying for the grand prize of a lavish on-air wedding ceremony. The 90-minute programme was sold to Germany and to several other broadcasters in Western Europe.

Major changes in television ecology were afoot in The Netherlands, nearby Germany and elsewhere in Europe at this time. Especially significant was the rise of the RTL group (Chalaby 2009: 47–49). The latter was a pioneering international broadcaster originating in 1931 when the Compagnie Luxembourgeoise de Radiodiffusion (CLR) came on the air as an advertising-supported broadcaster. It was granted a television licence in 1954, changing its acronym to CLT, and broadcasting into Luxemburg, France and Wallonia. In 1984, CLT partnered with Bertelsmann to launch Germany's highly successful RTL Plus while in 1989 it launched what became RTL 4 in The Netherlands. The entity was eager to guarantee content for these new broadcasting ventures.

Both John de Mol Productions and JE Productions benefited significantly. In 1992, John de Mol's company finalized a three-year output deal with RTL 4, covering all areas of programming and worth US$65 million (Moran 1998: 33). That same year, encouraged by CTL, it opened an office in Germany to provide programmes for RTL Plus. The need to supply new programmes to the Dutch and German markets led to the expansion of the company's format library. Additional formats that it devised included *The 100,000 Guilder Show* and *Will They or Won't They?* in the variety/game show genre, the drama serial *Foreign Affairs* and particularly the creation of 'sob' game show entertainments such as *Forgive Me* and *All You Need is Love*.

The advent of RTL 4 helped break the financial drought for John de Mol Production's rival, JE Productions. In 1989, it signed a three-year contract with RTL4 worth more than US$75 million and extended it in 1992 for an additional three years for a package worth more than US$100 million. In turn, the relationship with CTL led to the setting up of a German subsidiary, JE Entertainment Productions, established in Cologne in 1991, which entered into a three-year, US$160 million output deal with Germany's RTL Television. By then, JE was also back-selling programmes to some of the Dutch public-service broadcasting networks. But then, the two production companies decided on a daring initiative.

Endemol

In 1994, a merger was brokered between JE Productions and John de Mol Productions that resulted in Europe's largest independent programming company, Endemol. Although various elements suggested that they might draw closer, nevertheless the union represented a bold business move by van den Ende and de Mol. There was an immediate jump in growth for each company over what it could have achieved by itself. The new conglomerate would produce 2,500 hours of television a year spread across The Netherlands, Belgium, Germany, Spain, Scandinavia, the United Kingdom and Greece. Van den Ende and de Mol already moved in the same Dutch show-business circles and had complementary business styles with the younger man being more aggressive in deal-making but also throwing himself enthusiastically into programme format development. The merger also made sense in view of protectionist policy adopted by the European Commission that stipulated that at least half of all television programmes put to air in Europe should be of European origin (Servaes 2004b: 824–26). RTL probably also encouraged the marriage, preferring to do output deals with a large European group rather than dealing in any extended way with companies originating outside Europe.

Nor did Endemol rest on its laurels but immediately launched further initiatives. In 1995, it set about forming a vertically integrated group that would have resulted in oligopolistic control of Dutch television broadcasting but left the group because of European Community anti-trust stipulations (Servaes 2004b: 825). The following year, the company was floated on the Amsterdam Stock Exchange (Moran 1998: 33–34). This gave it the finance necessary to continue to buy television production houses in different national television markets, which, in turn, increased the profits being derived from the production of format programmes elsewhere in the world. By this time, it was increasingly clear that John de Mol was the driving force behind Endemol. There was often tension between him and the older man who, in any case, had medical problems.

Endemol was already a large company but now a new programme format was to transform it into a mega international conglomerate. In 1997, de Mol and Endemol's creative team came up with a radically innovative game show format that was named *Big Brother* (Thal Larsen 2000; Wilson 2004: 262–64; Murray 2004b: 1990–92). Only one Dutch broadcaster was willing to air the programme, provided Endemol paid half of its production costs. De Mol agreed because a first broadcast was vital to help license the format into other territories. The gamble paid off and *Big Brother* went on to become the most watched television programme ever, being adapted in over 50 markets worldwide and still running in some of these after more than a dozen years. The dot-com bubble was at its height worldwide and there was talk within media industries of synergy and convergence. Soon, Endemol had a marriage proposal.

de Mol: in and out of Telefonica

Early in 2000, it was announced that van den Ende and de Mol had sold Endemol to Telefonica, a Spanish telecommunications giant, for $5.5 billion (Levine 2003: 88–96). The intention was to provide content for broadcasting companies as well as for the Internet, third-generation mobile telephone and other distribution platforms. As the brains behind *Big Brother*, de Mol agreed to remain for a further five years as both chief executive and principal creative officer. Van den Ende took the opportunity to retire on the grounds of ill-health and bought back his theatrical business. Endemol's distribution arm was also sold. The plan was to concentrate on the production of content for television and interactive networks. Chalaby has provided a recent profile of Endemol as follows:

> By 2007, it became a global production house, launching 15 start-ups and acquiring full or part-ownership of 25 new media and TV production companies. Endemol is currently present in over 20 territories around the world, but its main markets are those of the UK, the United States, Spain, the Netherlands, Italy and Germany, in that order. Endemol UK alone incorporates seven companies, such as Brighter Pictures (*Big Brother UK* [2000–present] and derived shows), Cheetah Television (*Gok's Fashion Fix* [2008]; *Deal or No Deal* [2005–present]; *Ready,*

Steady, Cook [1994–present]), Initial (*The One and Only … Golden Balls* [2007–present]), and Zeppotron (*Would I Lie to You?* [2007–present]). Globally, Endemol's most profitable formats are *Big Brother, Deal or No Deal, 1 versus 100* and *Star Academy*.

(Chalaby 2009: 57)

Meanwhile, the relationship with Telefonica was unravelling. Buying at the height of the media market, the telco had paid too much for Endemol. Mostly, the expected synergies had not eventuated while there was little geographic overlap between the telco's market in Spain and South America and the content provider's footprint in the West. Meanwhile, de Mol became increasingly unhappy with the Telefonica union even while he kept his financial hand in, buying shares in dozens of bluechips including EMI, Fox Kids Europe and Manchester United using his cash-rich private company, Talpa Capital. He resigned from Endemol in mid-2004. By then, Telefonica had grown less interested in a future with the Dutch content group. Needing capital to finance other deals, including a 2005 purchase for £17.7 billion of O2, a mobile telecom company, it sold 25 per cent of shares in Endemol. Thus, in 2007, de Mol, in a consortium with Italian mogul Silvio Berlusconi and an investment fund owned by Goldman Sachs, was able to buy back 75 per cent of Endemol from Telefonica for $3.5 billion (Pfanner 2007: 8).

The last four years furnishes little further significant detail (Edgecliffe-Johnson 2008: 16). Endemol continues to be the largest and most successful transnational television production company on the planet and de Mol is one of the richest men in The Netherlands with a fortune valued at $3 billion in 2007 (van Tiggelen 2007: 16). He remains very active as a creator of new programme formats for television. To bypass the difficulties encountered in the past where a new format had to find a broadcaster prepared to take a chance on its success, de Mol established his own television channel, Talpa TV, in 2005 where he can get new formats to air when he decides that they are ready. The broadcaster had the poorest audience share in The Netherlands although this may be turning around with the enormous success of the singing talent show *The Voice* (Netherlands) in 2010 (Wikipedia: John De Mol). de Mol's major career goal now is to create a television programme format that will repeat if not surpass the success that he achieved with *Big Brother* (van Tiggelen 2007: 16).

The TV format mogul reconsidered: Goodson, Grundy and de Mol

A string of interconnected resemblances and differences emerge if we link Reg Grundy's career in television programme format production with those of the other two figures. Some of these are accidental, others stem from temperament and personality, while the most crucial have been structural. Let us trace these patterns, using points raised by Tunstall's account of the media mogul outlined in Chapter 1.

First, the beginnings of their broadcasting career: de Mol was quickest off the mark, setting up his own production company at the age of 24, while both Mark Goodson and

Reg Grundy were well into their 30s before they were able to establish their own companies. The latter two served time as staffers in radio broadcasting, apprenticeships of sorts, before going out on their own as independent programme producers. de Mol did not quite enjoy the advantage of Rupert Murdoch, who inherited the kernel of a media organization. Nevertheless, his father provided invaluable show-business contacts, which obviated the need for a long apprenticeship for the television production business.

Glancing ahead to the end of their business lives is also revealing. All three ended up very wealthy with Goodson and Grundy amassing around $400 million each. Coincidentally, Mark Goodson Productions and Grundy World Wide were acquired by the same conglomerate, now known as FremantleMedia. De Mol, the youngest of the three, is still in the throes of his career and owns a large chunk of Endemol and is worth several billion dollars, confirming that the format trade is even more lucrative now than it was earlier.

Personal style and abilities also interact in all three cases. Goodson, Grundy and de Mol were prepared to take risks at particular points in their careers, although John de Mol has been the most adventurous and Mark Goodson probably the least so, with Reg Grundy lying somewhere in between. On the other hand, Grundy was the least innovative so far as the development of new programme formats was concerned while Goodson and de Mol have more substantial track records with originating formats. In addition, both Goodson and de Mol have been seminal figures in the generic development of the quiz show by introducing key changes that crucially altered elements of the genre in their wake.

Reg Grundy's spotty record in devising game shows was partly a matter of circumstance. In Australia, from 1959 onwards, it made more business sense for the producer to adapt existing US game shows than to attempt to devise them from scratch. On the other hand, he and his company did originate a handful of quiz-show formats in the 1980s and early 1990s for US and other markets. Coupled with that is the Grundy Organisation's extraordinary triumph in originating successful drama serial formats from 1974 onwards. Neither Goodson nor de Mol can match this achievement.

Goodson, Grundy and de Mol operated private companies or, in the case of the latter, a company under his control with other key investors. Allied to this have been high degrees of media shyness or secrecy. Mark Goodson was, in part, ashamed of his work in game show development and preferred to see himself portrayed as a patron of the arts. Reg Grundy avoided publicity, interviews and photographs as his television production career got underway. de Mol – whose name, coincidentally, refers to a creature that likes to remain hidden – also avoids publicity and interviews except where it is to his general business advantage.

As part of their overall business operation, all three format moguls diversified to a greater or a lesser extent into other activities and trading that was in part aimed at building their fortune. But there was also diversification designed to directly support and protect their core activity in television format programme production. On balance, the least successful of these initiatives was that of Goodson and his partner Todman, and their attempt to become a permanent presence in the production of drama series for US network television between 1950 and 1964, even though five series went to air. On the other hand,

Jon de Mol has been the most successful of the trio. The latter not only gained television production output in other genres besides quiz and game shows but also secured his own television station, Talpa TV, from which to launch new programme formats. Grundy belongs somewhere between the two thanks to very successful output in drama serials and series, telemovies and children's series.

More general conclusions about the pattern of Grundy's format career as opposed to those of the other two can also be drawn. Both Goodson and de Mol achieved stunning success in the business of devising quiz-show formats early in the lifetime of the television production companies that they founded. Goodson secured this triumph in the 1950s and, while there were later individual quiz-show format triumphs, nevertheless he was largely coasting on this early success in later years. de Mol's situation was similar with the stunning achievement of *Big Brother* around the turn of the millennium when he was in early middle age. This has left him with the continuing ambition to devise another show that will match or even cap the radical breakthrough and success that was *Big Brother*. As he has put it: he is 'not even half way yet' (Bickerton 2004: 27).

Reg Grundy, by contrast, had a more even, upward career progression between 1959 and 1995 and, while there were disappointments along the way, there were also a string of incidental triumphs. The result was that Grundy World Wide went from strength to strength and was at the height of its financial and industry power when it was sold.

A last afterword

An even broader conclusion can be offered about Reg Grundy in the company of these other TV format moguls as a means of rounding out this chapter and this book. This has to do with the more general, historical circumstances of television, both national and international, in the twentieth and early twenty-first centuries. For there is no doubt that different institutional possibilities presented themselves to each of the three format moguls. Common to all was the situation of a continuing expansion in television markets, whose ever-growing demand for programmes has made the adaptation and remaking of existing programmes more imperative, even spawning a name for such an activity. Goodson had a taste of this expansion with the institutional shift from radio broadcasting to television. He witnessed it again with the development of the US television syndication market. Grundy experienced the same phenomenon with a steady increase in the overall television market inside Australia and more international market growth after 1980, thanks to the advent of new technologies, commercialization and privatization. de Mol has seen the later, fuller results of this continuing growth in Western Europe and elsewhere with the development of international television networks.

Finally, the general phenomenon of television programme market development allows the further delineation of various overlapping stages in which Reg Grundy and the other two format moguls can be located. The periodization also helps in pinpointing the nature of the television format trade at specific times over the past 60 years. The first era buttresses those that follow. It can be earmarked as the Foundation Stage and occurred from 1950 to 1960. Movement in programme ideas was confined to the most advanced and wealthiest television systems, notably those of the United States and, to a lesser extent, that of the United Kingdom. No specific name had been coined to designate the idea of practical programme knowledge that would help another producer make a facsimile programme. Mark Goodson was active in this period with the idea of existing content being remade for new outlets as circumstances dictated. A string of radio quiz and other shows were copied for the new television service but there were also instances where programmes were revived and remade on different stations or at different times.

A second period of the development of the transnational format trade got underway in the late 1950s as many television services came on the air elsewhere in the world. The era lasted until 1980. It can be identified as the Primitive Stage to highlight its main features. The adaptation of formats was spontaneous and mostly happened on a one-off basis; it was neither organized or codified, formats were frequently copied without licence or even without the knowledge of their devisor or owner; and the dispersal of formats in other television markets outside such centres as the United States and the United Kingdom was slow and erratic. Television was mostly either a regional or a national rather than an international affair so that there was little sense of obligation to license or pay fees even if some broadcaster did obtain authorization for the remaking of programmes.

Reg Grundy was one of the many overseas television producers who derived programme ideas from the United States, including from Goodson-Todman Productions, during this phase. Meanwhile, Goodson may or may not have been aware that some of his and partner Bill Todman's programme formats were being copied elsewhere in the world. In any case, the advent of the television syndication market in the United States after 1970 would finally have crystallized his awareness that programme formats were valuable commodities in their own right, even outside the programmes that gave rise to them.

The beginning of the third period of the format business coincided with the United States' ratification of the Berne Convention on Copyright. It lasted until 2000 and can be labelled the Formalization Stage. Much of the ad hoc element disappeared from the trade and was replaced by organization and codification. There were plenty of exceptions but licensings and fee payment were normalized. Formats became a trade that was increasingly international, with events such as trade fairs helping to put format owners and potential licensees in touch with one another. Catalogues and libraries were collected together so that large-scale territorial agreements were entered into. By then, Mark Goodson was in semi-retirement but a catalogue of his past formats, some almost 30 years old, continued to be a valuable asset, still returning profit from international licensings. Reg Grundy remained very active in this period while John de Mol entered the trade in The Netherlands, adapting the formats of others and devising new ones.

The format trade entered a fourth era from 2000 onwards. This period is the contemporary one that is still with us. It can be tagged the Global Stage of the television programme format industry. As has been suggested elsewhere, this period has seen the rapid integration of television production into a transnational, worldwide system. The game changers were *Who Wants to Be a Millionaire?*, *Big Brother* and *Survivor*. *Big Brother* was devised by de Mol and its dispersal was rapid, aiming at high saturation on a global scale. Endemol was confirmed as one of a handful of transnational television production giants with an astonishing capacity to ensure production in 50 television territories across the planet, whether through national Endemol branches, JVAs or format licensing agreements.

Reg Grundy retired in 1995 and has played no part in the modern or Global era of the format trade. Nevertheless, he has four enduring claims to fame as a TV format mogul. First, he was among the first Australian independent programme 'packagers' and the only Australian television producer to take his business offshore, becoming an important transnational media presence in the process. Second, he amassed a sizeable fortune in the course of his production career, now said to be worth about A$1 billion. Third, he brought daily soap opera to Western Europe for the first time so that some of his programmes, originals and remakes, are still on air after more than twenty years. And, finally, he helped develop a mighty programme format industry that has changed the face of television across the world.

Appendix

Grundy's Television and Film Output

Where a programme title has not been sourced, the format on which it was based is indicated in brackets. Where a broadcaster has not been identified, this is indicated by a question mark.

1. Australia

ABBA: Down Under 1976, television documentary
ABBA: The Movie 1977, feature film
All at Sea 1977, TEN10, telemovie
Alternative, The 1976, telemovie
Ampol Big Game 1966, GTV9, quiz/game show
Ampol Stamp Quiz 1964–65, TCN9, children's quiz show
Anything Can Happen 1972–73, ADS7, quiz/game show
Australian Idol 2003–10, TEN10, talent show
Australia's Most Wanted 1989–94, 1996–99, ATN7, TCN9, public-interest/reality show
Bandstand 1976–77, TCN9, variety show
Barry McKenzie Holds His Own 1974, feature film
Beat the Odds 1970–72, BTQ7, quiz/game show
Bellamy 1981, TEN10, drama series
Bert's Family Feud 2006–07, GTV9, quiz/game show
Better Sex, The 1977–78, STW9, quiz/game show
Big Challenge 1969–71, QTQ, children's quiz show
Big Challenge 1971, BTQ7 (?), quiz/game show
Billion Dollar Baby (?) 1976, telemovie
Blankety Blanks 1985, GTV9, quiz/game show
Blankety Blanks 1996–97, GTV9, quiz/game show
Blind Date 1967–70, TEN10, quiz/game show
Blind Date 1974, ATV0, quiz/game show
Blind Date 1991, ATV10, quiz/game show
Bony 1990, telemovie pilot
Bony 1992, drama series
Case for the Defence 1976, TCN9, drama series/telemovie
Cash Bonanza 2001, QTQ9, quiz/game show
Casino 10 1975–77, TVQ0, quiz/game show

Celebrity Family Feud 1990–91, ATN7, quiz/game show
Celebrity Game, The 1969, QTQ9, quiz/game show
Celebrity Game, The 1976–77, TEN10, quiz/game show
Celebrity Game Challenge 1976, TEN10, quiz/game show
Celebrity It's a Knockout 1987, ATV10, quiz/game show
Celebrity Squares 1975–78, TCN9, quiz/game show
Celebrity Tattletales 1979–80, BTQ7, quiz/game show
Celebrity Wheel of Fortune 1990–91, SAS7, quiz/game show
Celebrity Wheel of Fortune 1998 (?), quiz/game show
Celebrity Who Wants to Be a Millionaire?, 2000, GTV9, quiz/game show
Chopper Squad 1976, telemovie pilot
Chopper Squad 1978, TEN10, drama series
Class of '74/75 1974–75, TCN9, drama serial
Concentration 1959–64, TCN9, quiz/game show
Concentration 1965–67, QTQ9, quiz/game show
Concentration 1973–74, ADS7, quiz/game show
Confessions of Ronald Biggs 1977, documentary feature
Crossfire 1987–88, GTV9, quiz/game show
Darryl and Ozzie Show, The 1978, ATV0, variety show
Death Train, The 1978, telemovie
Demolition 1978, telemovie
Embassy 1990–92, ATCTV, drama series
Emergency Line 1973–74, ADS7, advice show
Escape of the Artful Dodger 2001, children's drama series
ESP and All That 1971, factual/entertainment
Everybody's Talking 1968–69, quiz/game show
Family Feud 1977–84, TVW7/GTV9, quiz/game show
Family Feud 1989–96, Seven Network, quiz/game show
Family Game, The 1967, TEN10, quiz/game show
First Impressions 1966, QTQ9, quiz/game show
Ford Superquiz 1982, GTV9, quiz/game show
Funny You Should Ask 1972–74, QTQ9, quiz/game show
Gambit 1973–74, TCN9, quiz/game show
Generation Gap 1969, TEN10, quiz/game show
Get the Message 1966–72, TVQ0, quiz/game show
Glenview High 1977–78, ATN7, drama series
Gone to Ground 1976, telemovie
Graham Kennedy's Blankety Blanks 1977–78, TEN10, quiz/game show
Great Temptation, The 1971–74, ATN7, quiz/game show
Greed 2001, TEN10, quiz/game show
Guessing Game, The 1966–67, GTV9, quiz/game show
Have a Go Show, The 1980–81, TVQ0, variety/talent show
Heartline 1970–71, BTQ7, advice show

High Adventure 1984 (?), documentary series
High Rollers 1975, ATN7, quiz/game show
Hotline 1970, BTQ7, advice show
Hot Streak 1998 (?), quiz/game show
Hypnotism and All That 1971 (?), factual entertainment
Ideal Fun Day 1970 (?), quiz/game show
Image of Death 1977, telemovie
Inside Australian Idol 2003–05, TEN10, information/reality show
In Town Tonight 1967–69, TEN10, variety show
Is Anybody There? 1975, telemovie
Island Trader 1982, children's telemovie
It Could Be You 1984, TEN10, quiz/game show
It's a Knockout 1985–87, TEN10, quiz/game show
I've Got a Secret 1966–69/1970–74, SAS7, quiz/game show
I've Got a Secret 1966–74, QTQ9, quiz/game show.
Jackson High 1977 (?), telemovie pilot
Junior Moneymakers 1972–73, ATV0/TVQ0/SAS10, quiz/game show
Keynotes 1992–93, TCN9, quiz/game show
Let's Make a Deal 1977, TCN9, quiz/game show
Let's Make a Deal 1991, TEN10, quiz/game show
Lion's Share, The 1977, telemovie
Kevin Arnett's World of the Supernatural 1977 (?), factual/entertainment
Killers of the Great Barrier Reef 1979, documentary feature
King's Men 1976, TCN9, drama series
Lucky Seven 1970, ATN7, quiz/game show
Mama's Gone a-Hunting 1976, telemovie
Man O Man 1994, HSV7, quiz/game show
Marriage Game, The 1966–67, TEN10, quiz/game show
Martins & McCoys, The 1974, telemovie pilot
Martin St James 1971, TVQ0, factual/entertainment
Match Game, The 1969, ATV0, quiz/game show
Matchmates 1981–83, TCN9, quiz/game show
Missing Link 1969, BTQ7, quiz/game show
Mission Top Secret 1991, children's drama telemovie
Mission Top Secret 1992–97, children's drama series
Moneymakers 1971–73, TVQ0, quiz/game show
Name That Tune 1971, BTQ7, quiz/game show
Name That Tune 1975, ATN7, quiz/game show
National Star Quest 1978–79, variety/talent show
Neighbours 1985, ATN7/TEN10, drama serial
Nerds F.C. 2006–07, SBS, game show
Newlywed Game, The 1968, TEN10, quiz/game show
Newlywed Game, The 1986–87, TEN10, quiz/game show

Newman Shame, The 1978, telemovie
New Price is Right, The 1981–84, HSV7, quiz/game show
Nightnurse, The 1977, telemovie
Numbers Game, The 1967, ADS7, quiz/game show
$100 000 Moneymakers 1981–82, TVQ0, quiz/game show
One in a Million 1975, TVQ0, quiz/game show
One Way Ticket 1997, telemovie
Other Side of Paradise, The 1991, drama, miniseries
Password 1972–73 (?), quiz/game show
Pay Cards 1969, ATN 7, quiz/game show
Penthouse Club 1972–75, ADS7, quiz/game show
Perfect Match 1978, TVQ0, quiz/game show
Perfect Match 2002, ATN7, quiz/game show
Price is Right, The 2003–06, GTV9, quiz/game show
Personality Squares 1967–69, TEN10, quiz/game show
Personality Squares 1981, TEN10, quiz/game show
Phantom Horseman, The 1991, children's telemovie
Pirate's Island 1991, children's telemovie
Play Your Cards Right 1984–85, BTQ7, quiz/game shows
Plunge into Darkness 1977, telemovie
Poor Fella Me 1973, documentary feature
Possession 1984–85, TCN9, drama serial
Pot Luck 1987, SAS10, variety/talent show
Pot of Gold 1975–78, ATV0, variety/talent show
Pot of Gold 1994–95, TCN9, variety/talent show
Press Your Luck 1987–88, HSV7, quiz/game show
Pretty Petrol 1983, telemovie pilot
Price is Right, The 1973–74, ATV0, quiz/game show
Price is Right, The 1989, ATV10, quiz/game show
Price is Right, The 1993–98, GTV9, quiz/game show
Prisoner (aka *Prisoner: Cell Block H*) 1979–84, drama serial
Professor Poopsnaggle's Steam Zeppelin 1985–86, children's drama series
Punishment 1981, TEN10, drama serial
Pyramid Challenge 1978, TVQ0, quiz/game show
Queensland's Celebrity Game 1970, QTQ9, quiz/game show
Restless Years, The 1977–81, TEN10, drama serial
Richmond Hill 1987–88, TEN10, drama serial
Return to the Good Old Days 1977 (?), talent show
Rogue Stallion 1991, children's telemovie
Ron Cadee Show 1970, QTQ9, variety show
Roses Bloom Twice 1978, telemovie
Runaway Island 1981, children's series
Sale of the Century 1980–2001, TCN9, quiz/game show

Appendix

Say When 1962–64, TCN9, quiz/game show
Scalp Merchant, The 1978, telemovie
Search for Treasure Island, The 1998–99, children's drama series
Second Chance 1977–78, TVQ0, quiz/game show
Second Guess 1987, Seven Net, quiz/game show
Secret Valley 1980, telemovie, pilot
Secret Valley 1981, children's series
Seven Million Dollar Fugitive 1982, documentary feature
$7000 Question 1971 (?), quiz/game show
Shafted 2002, GTV9, quiz/game show
Showdown 1968, TVQ0, quiz/game show
Silent World of Buster Fiddess, The 1964 (?), pilot
Sons and Daughters 1982–85, ATN7, drama serial.
South Pacific Adventures 1991, children's drama miniseries/telemovie
Special Place, A 1980, telemovie pilot
Spending Spree 1971–74, TCN9, quiz/game show
Split Personality 1967, TEN10, quiz/game show
Split Second 1972–73 TCN9, quiz/game show
Starting Out 1983, TCN9, drama serial
Supermarket Sweep 1992–93, GTV9, quiz/game show
Superquiz 1989, TEN10, quiz/game show
Surprise Package 1961, TCN9, quiz/game show
Surprise Package 1970s (??), TEN10, quiz/game show
Super Seven 1976, BTQ7, quiz/game show
Tanamera: Lion of Singapore 1989, drama miniseries
Taurus Rising 1982, TCN9, drama serial
Tell the Truth 1971 (?), HSV7, quiz/game show
Tell the Truth 1971, TEN10, quiz/game show
Tell the Truth 1971, ADS7, quiz/game show
Tell the Truth 1971, STW9, quiz/game show
Temptation 1970–74, ATN7, quiz/game show
Temptation 2005–08, GTV9, quiz/game show
Three on a Match 1972–75, ADS7/SAS10, quiz/game show
Tic Tac Dough 1960–64, TCN9, quiz/game show
Travellin' Out West 1972–79, NBN3, variety show
$200 00 Question 1987 (?), quiz/game show
Two-Way Mirror 1974 telemovie pilot.
Until Tomorrow 1975, BTQ7, drama serial
Waterloo Station 1983, TCN9, drama serial
What Do You Know? 1970, BTQ7, quiz/game show
Wheel of Fortune 1959–62, TCN9, quiz/game show
Wheel of Fortune 1970, BTQ7, quiz/game show
Wheel of Fortune 1981–2006, SAS10/7; ATN7, quiz/game show

Who Wants to Be a Millionaire? 1999–2006, GTV9, quiz/game show
Win Roy's and H.G.'s Money 2000, ATN7, quiz/game show
Women's World 1969 BTQ7, magazine program
Wreck of the Batavia 1973, documentary feature
Young Doctors, The 1976–86, TCN9, drama serial
You've Got to Be Joking 1971–72, BTQ7, audience-participation show
X Factor, The 2005, Network Ten, talent show
Xtra Factor, The 2005, TEN10, documentary feature
Your Life on the Lawn 2003, ATN7, quiz/game show
You've Got to Be Joking 1987, TEN10, audience-participation show

2. Elsewhere

Argentina/Uruguay/Paraguay

(*Man O Man*) 1997, Channel 13 Argentina/Channel 10 Uruguay/SNT Channel 9 Paraguay, quiz/game show.

Belgium

Rap Klap/Hot Streak 1990–91 (?), quiz/game show

Brunei

Matchmates 1982–86, Brunei TV, children's quiz show

Bulgaria

Zabranjena ljubav/Sons and Daughters/Forbidden Love 2008, Nova TV, drama serial

Chile

Blockbusters 1994 (?), quiz/game show
Desafio Familiar/Family Feud 1992 (?), quiz/game show
Madre y Hijo/Mother and Son 1995, comedy series

Appendix

Croatia

Zabranjena ljubav/Sons and Daughters/Forbidden Love 2004–08, RTL Televizija, drama serial

Denmark

(*Mother and Son*) post-1995, comedy series

France

Cheri-Cheries/Man O Man 1996, France 2, quiz/game show
Jeu, Le/The Main Event 1992–93 (?), quiz/game show
Keynotes 1994 (?), quiz/game show
Mais Comment Font Ils?/How Do They Do That? 1995, France 3, quiz/game show
Que le Meilleur Gagne/Everybody's Equal 1991–96, La Cinq/France 2, quiz/game show
Que le Meilleur Gagne Plus/Celebrity Everybody's Equal 1992–96, France 2, quiz/game show
Questions pour un Champion/Going for Gold 1988, France 3, quiz/game show

Germany

Alle Zusammen/All Together 1996, RTL2, drama serial
Gute Zeiten, Schlechte Zeiten/Good Times, Bad Times 1992, RTL2, drama serial
Hopp oder Top/Sale of the Century 1990–93, Tele 5/DSP, quiz/game show
Jeder gegen Jeden/Fifteen-to-One 1997, RTL2, quiz/game show
Kinder Ruck Zuck/Junior Hot Streak 1991–92, Tele 5, quiz/game show
Muuh! The Pet Show 1997, ARD, quiz/game show
Small Talk 1997, RTL2, quiz/game show
Ruck Zuck/Hot Streak 1989–96, Tele 5/RTL 2, quiz/game show
Verbotene Liebe/Forbidden Love 1995, ARD, drama serial
Unter Uns/Among Us 1994, RTL2, drama serial

Greece

Apagorevmeni/Sons and Daughters/Forbidden Love 1998–99, drama serial
(*Mother and Son*) post-1995 (?), comedy series
Ruck Zouk/Hot Streak 1994, Mega TV Greece, quiz/game show
(*Sale of the Century*) 1994, Star Channel Greece, quiz/game show

Hong Kong

Dai Pai/Card Sharks 1982, RTV, quiz/game show
Dai Sou But/Sale of the Century 1982, RTV, quiz/game show

Indonesia

Belahan Hati/Two Hearts/Sons and Daughters/Forbidden Love 2001–02 (?), drama serial
Bintang Bintang Famili Seratus/Celebrity Family Feud 1994, Antennae, quiz/game show
Famili Seratus/Family Feud 1994–98, Anteve, quiz/game show
Kata Fa Kecil/Child's Play 1997, Antennae, quiz/game show

India

Kricket! 1995, Star Plus, quiz/game show

Israel

Hamesh Hamesh/Hot Streak 1994, United Channels Israel, quiz/game show
Ma'ta Omer/Small Talk 1994, United Channels Israel, quiz/game show

Italy

Beato Tra Le Donne/Man O Man 1994–08, RAI1, quiz/game show
Cuori Rubati/Sons and Daughters/Forbidden Love 2002–03, RAI2, drama serial
Per Tutta La Vita/For Life 1997, RAI, quiz/game show
Un Posto al Sole/A Place in the Sun 1996, RAI 3, drama serial
Vinca il Migliore/Everybody's Equal 1997, RAI3, quiz/game show

The Netherlands

Goede Tijden, Slechte Tijden/Good Times, Bad Times 1990, RTL4, drama serial
(*Man O Man*) 1994 (?), quiz/game show

New Zealand

Jeopardy 1992, TVNZ, quiz/game show
Perfect Match 1990, TVNZ, quiz/game show

Appendix

Sale of the Century 1989–93, 1995 (?), quiz/game show
Shortland Street 1992, TVNZ, drama serial
Wheel of Fortune 1990–93 (?), quiz/game show

Paraguay

Venta del Siglo, La/Sale of the Century 1997–2001 (?), quiz/game show

Spain

Aqui Jugomos Todas/Everybody's Equal 1997, TVE, quiz/game show
Elles I Ells/Man O Man 1993–95, TVChannel 9, quiz/game show
Questionario Millionario/Going for Gold 1991–92, TV Madrid Quiz/game show
Txandaka/Kids are Funny Too 1991 ETB, quiz/game show
Uno Para Todas/Man O Man 1996–97, Telechino, quiz/game show
Vore Qui Guanya/Let's See Who Wins 1997, TVVCanal 9, quiz/game show

Sweden

Man O Man 1994–96, TV3 Sweden/Pan Scandinavia, game show
Sommarpratarna/Small Talk 1996, TV4, quiz/game show
Skilda Varlder/Worlds Apart/Forbidden Love 1996–2002, drama serial

Turkey

(*Mother and Son*) post-1995 (?), comedy series

United Kingdom

Celebrity Squares 1993–96, ITV, quiz/game show
Eureka 1994, BBC, factual entertainment show
Going for Gold 1989–96, BBC, quiz/game show
How Do They Do That? 1994–98, BBC, factual entertainment show
Jeopardy! 1990–96, ITV, quiz/game show
Keynotes 1988–92, ITV, quiz/game show
Main Event, The 1993, BBC, quiz/game show
Pot of Gold 1993–95, ITV, talent/game show

Press Your Luck 1991–92, HTV West, quiz/game show
Sale of the Century 1990–91, 1997, BSkyB, quiz/game show
Sky Star Search 1990, Sky, talent show
Small Talk 1994–96, BBC, quiz/game show

Uruguay

Blockbusters 1997 (?), quiz/game show

United States

Bruce Forsyth's Hot Streak 1986, ABC, quiz/game show
Dangerous Women 1991–92, Syndication 'network', drama serial
Man O Man 1997, UTN, quiz/game show special
Sale of the Century 1983–89, NBC, quiz/game show
Scrabble 1984–93, NBC, quiz/game show
Scattergories 1994, NBC, quiz/game show
Small Talk 1997, Family Channel, children's game show
Time Machine 1984, NBC, quiz/game show

References

Anderson, C. (2004), 'American Broadcasting', in H. Newcomb (ed.), *Museum of Broadcast Communication Encyclopedia of Television*, New York: Fitzroy Dearborn, pp. 87–91.

Anon. (1946), *The Big Store: 80th Anniversary Bulletin 1866–1946*, Adelaide: Advertiser Newspaper.

Attallah, P. (1991), 'Of Homes and Machines: TV, Technology and Fun in America, 1944–84', *Continuum: An Australian Journal of the Media*, 4: 2, pp. 58–98.

Auicke, A. (2004), 'Dyke, Greg', in H. Newcomb (ed.), *The Museum of Broadcast Communication Encyclopedia of Television*, Chicago: Fitzroy Dearborn, pp. 769–70.

The Australian (1995), 'Expansion Spurs Grundy to $144m in Float', 30 March, p. 25.

Australian Financial Review (1993), 'Millions Roll In and the Soaps Roll On', 22 October, p. 15.

Australian Women's Weekly (2005), 'Wildlife Passions: Reg Grundy's side', 10 August, http://www.ninemsn.com.au/aww. Accessed 20 March 2011.

Baart, L. (1995), Interview with A. Moran, Paris.

Baker, G. (1979), 'Abba the World: Australia', Billboard, 'Abba Five Years' Special Insert, 8 September, pp. 8, 24.

Bard, K. J. (1983), 'The History of Vaudeville in Australia from 1900 to 1930', Bachelor of Letters Dissertation, Armidale, NSW: University of New England.

Battema, D. (2004), 'Sports on Radio', in C. H. Sterling (ed.), *Encyclopedia of Radio*, Chicago: Fitzroy Dearborn, pp. 1320–23.

Battye, D. (1980), Interview with A. Moran, Sydney.

Bechelloni G. and Buonanno, M. (2004), 'Italy', in H. Newcomb (ed.), *The Museum of Broadcast Communication Encyclopedia of Television*, Chicago: Fitzroy Dearborn, pp. 1191–5.

Beck, C. (1984), *On Air: 25 Years of Television in Queensland*, Brisbane: One Tree Hill.

Becker, C. (2004a), 'Talent Raids', in C. H. Sterling (ed.), *Encyclopedia of Radio*, Chicago: Fitzroy Dearborn, pp. 1364–66.

——— (2004b), 'Wheel of Fortune', in H. Newcomb (ed.), *The Museum of Broadcast Communication Encyclopedia of Television*, Chicago: Fitzroy Dearborn, pp. 2527–28.

Beilby, P. (1981), *Australian Television: The First 25 Years*, Melbourne: Nelson.

Benchley, F. (1995a), 'Grundy Pulls Plug on Float and Sells to Pearson', *Australian Financial Review*, 30 March, pp. 1, 28.

——— (1995b), 'Spinning a Fortune from a Chocolate Wheel', *Australian Financial Review*, 31 March, p. 28.

Berger, A. A. (2004), 'The Prisoner', in H. Newcomb (ed.), *The Museum of Broadcast Communication Encyclopedia of Television*, Chicago: Fitzroy Dearborn, pp. 1829–30.

Bickerton, I. (2004), 'The Reality is, de Mol Isn't Even Half Way Yet', *Financial Times*, 20 December, p. 27.

Blasini, G. M. (2004), 'Survivor', in H. Newcomb (ed.), *The Museum of Broadcast Communication Encyclopedia of Television*, Chicago: Fitzroy Dearborn, pp. 2226–27.

Bleicher, J. (2004), 'Germany', in H. Newcomb (ed.), *The Museum of Broadcast Communication Encyclopedia of Television*, Chicago: Fitzroy Dearborn, pp. 981–85.

Blumler, J. G. (2004), 'British Television', in H. Newcomb (ed.), *The Museum of Broadcast Communication Encyclopedia of Television*, Chicago: Fitzroy Dearborn, pp. 330–37.

Bordowitz, H. (2004), *Turning Points in Rock and Roll*, New York: Citadel Press.

Bourdin, J. (2011), 'From Discrete Adaptation to Hard Copies: The Rise of Formats in European Television', in T. Oren and S. Shahaf (eds), *Global Television Formats: Understanding Television Across Borders*, Los Angeles: Routledge, pp. 163–89.

Braithwaite, J. (2005), *Markets in Vice, Markets in Virtue*, Sydney: Federation Press, pp. 36–40.

Brasher, N. (1985), *The Model Store 1885–1995: 100 Years Serving Sydney*, Sydney: Kevin Weldon.

Breen, M. (2004), 'Australian Programming', in H. Newcomb (ed.), *The Museum of Broadcast Communication Encyclopedia of Television*, Chicago: Fitzroy Dearborn, pp. 188–94.

Broadcasting (1991), 'Grundy in U.S. State of Mind', 29 April, p. 11.

Broadcasting Abroad (1989), 'Global Grundy', 1 October, pp. 10–13.

Brower, S. (2004), '*Dallas*', in H. Newcomb (ed.), *The Museum of Broadcast Communication Encyclopedia of Television*, Chicago: Fitzroy Dearborn, pp. 649–52.

Brownhill, R. (1978), *Unemployed Workers: A History of the Great Depression in Adelaide*, Brisbane: University of Queensland Press.

Brunt, R. (1985), 'What's My Line?', in L. Masterman (ed.), *Television Mythologies*, London: Comedia, p. 218.

Bryant, S. and Alvarado, M. (2004), 'British Programming', in H. Newcomb (ed.), *The Museum of Broadcast Communication Encyclopedia of Television*, Chicago: Fitzroy Dearborn, pp. 322–27.

Buonanno, M. (2009), 'A Place in the Sun: Global Seriality and the Revival of Domestic Drama in Italy', in A. Moran (ed.), *TV Formats Worldwide: Localizing Global Programs*, Bristol: Intellect, pp. 255–69.

Business Review Weekly (1991), 'Ian Holmes Interview', 26 January, p. 37.

Buxton, F. and Owen, W. H. (1972), *The Big Broadcast, 1920–1950*, New York: Viking.

Carrick, D. (2006), 'Austin Ashe, Retired Family Court Judge', *The Law Report*, ABC Radio National, 19 September, http://taxjustice.blogspot.com/2009/10/footreport.html. Accessed 11 May 2005.

Casey, R. (1995), Interview with A. Moran, Sydney.

Chalaby, J. K. (2009), 'Broadcasting in a Post National Environment: The Rise of Transnational TV Groups', *Critical Studies in Television*, 4: 1, pp. 39–64.

Coleman, A. (2009), *One Door Shuts*, Bloomington, IN: Trafford.

Colwell, M. and Naylor, A. (1977), *Adelaide: An Illustrated History*, Adelaide: Lansdowne Press.

Cooper-Chen, A. (1994), *Games in the Global Village: A 50-Nation Study of Entertainment Television*, Bowling Green, IN: Bowing Green State University Popular Press.

References

Craven, I. (1989), 'Distant Neighbours: Notes on Some Australian Soap Operas', *Australian Studies*, 3, pp. 1–35.

Crofts, S. (1995), 'Global Neighbours', in R.C. Allen (ed.), *To Be Continued ...: Soap Operas Around the World*, London: Routledge, pp. 98–121.

Cromie, A. (1989), 'Treasure Hunt', *Business Review Weekly*, 9 June, pp. 62–70.

Crystal, B. (1995), Telephone Interview with A. Moran, Los Angeles.

Culliton, J. (2009), Interview with A. Moran, Huonville, Tasmania.

Culliton, T. (1995), Interview with A. Moran, Sydney.

Cunningham, S. (1993), 'Television', in G. Turner and S. Cunningham (eds), *The Media in Australia*, Sydney: Allen & Unwin, pp. 19–41.

——— (2004a), 'Australian Production Companies', in H. Newcomb (ed.), *The Museum of Broadcast Communication Encyclopedia of Television*, Chicago: Fitzroy Dearborn, pp. 181–88.

——— (2004b), 'International Television Program Markets', in H. Newcomb (ed.), *The Museum of Broadcast Communication Encyclopedia of Television*, Chicago: Fitzroy Dearborn, pp. 118–34.

——— (2004c), 'Neighbours', in H. Newcomb (ed.), *The Museum of Broadcast Communication Encyclopedia of Television*, Chicago: Fitzroy Dearborn, pp. 1623–25.

Cunningham, S. and Jacka, E. (1996), *Australian Television and International Mediascapes*, Melbourne: Cambridge University Press.

Curtin, M. (2004), 'Globalization', in H. Newcomb (ed.), *The Museum of Broadcast Communication Encyclopedia of Television*, Chicago: Fitzroy Dearborn, pp. 993–97.

Curthoys, A. and Docker, J. (2004), 'Prisoner', in H. Newcomb (ed.), *The Museum of Broadcast Communication Encyclopedia of Television*, Chicago: Fitzroy Dearborn, pp. 1825–26.

Daniel, J. (1995), Interview with A. Moran, Cologne.

Davies, E. and Moran, A. (2012), 'TV City: Brisbane 1959–65', *Studies in Australasian Cinema*, 5: 3, pp. 239–50.

Davison, G. (1998), 'Postwar Reconstruction', in G. Davison, J. Hurst and S. Macintyre (eds), *The Oxford Companion to Australian History*, Melbourne: Oxford University Press, pp. 520–22.

Davison, G., Hurst, J. and Macintyre, S. (eds) (1998), *The Oxford Companion to Australian History*, Melbourne: Oxford University Press.

Day, C. (1980), 'How Rich Reg Grundy Plans to Get Richer', *National Times*, 17 May, p. 58.

Deleuze, G. and Guattari, F. (1983), 'What is a Minor Literature?', trans. R. Brinkley, *Mississippi Review*, 11: 3, pp. 13–33.

Docker, J. (2004), 'Kennedy, Graham', in H. Newcomb (ed.), *The Museum of Broadcast Communication Encyclopedia of Television*, Chicago: Fitzroy Dearborn, pp. 1247–48.

Donnelly, D. S. (2004), 'Color Television', in H. Newcomb (ed.), *The Museum of Broadcast Communication Encyclopedia of Television*, Chicago: Fitzroy Dearborn, pp. 554–55.

Drummond, M. (1995), Interview with A. Moran, Sydney.

Dyke, G. (2005), *Inside Story*, New York: Harper Collins.

Edgecliffe-Johnson, A. (2008), 'The Return of *Big Brother*'s Daddy: The Television Tearaway has Bought Back His Reality TV Baby and is Plotting his Next Notorious Endeavour', *Financial Times*, 14 July, p. 16.

Eilam, E. (2005), *Reversing Secrets of Reverse Engineering*, New York: Wiley.

Emmanuel, S. (2004), 'France', in H. Newcomb (ed.), *The Museum of Broadcast Communication Encyclopedia of Television*, Chicago: Fitzroy Dearborn, pp. 910–12.

Evans, J. (ed.) (2001), *The Penguin TV Companion*, New York: Penguin.

Fabe, M. (1979), *TV Game Shows*, New York: Doubleday.

Fang, I. (2004), 'Videotape', in H. Newcomb (ed.), *The Museum of Broadcast Communication Encyclopedia of Television*, Chicago: Fitzroy Dearborn, pp. 2438–40.

Felsenthal, N. (2004), 'Simulcasting', in H. Newcomb (ed.), *The Museum of Broadcast Communication Encyclopedia of Television*, Chicago: Fitzroy Dearborn, pp. 2094–95.

Finney, R. (2004), 'Radio Corporation of America', in C. H. Sterling (ed.), *Encyclopedia of Radio*, Chicago: Fitzroy Dearborn, pp. 1163–65.

Fletcher, J. E. (2004), 'Syndication', in H. Newcomb (ed.), *The Museum of Broadcast Communication Encyclopedia of Television*, Chicago: Fitzroy Dearborn, pp. 2247–48.

Franco, J. (2008), Interview with A. Moran, Sydney.

Fung, A. (1989), 'Corporate Shelter from the Storm', *Chartered Accountant*, 13: 1, pp. 45–50.

Furness, M. (1995), 'No Sale of the Century but the Price Isn't Half Bad', *Financial Review*, 30 March, p. 15.

Gerrie, A. (1992), 'Teaching the US to Suck Soap', *The Bulletin*, 6 June, pp. 98–100.

Gillespie-Jones (formerly Grundy), L. (1995), Interview with Margaret Pullar, Canberra.

Goldberg, D. T. (1998), 'Call and Response', *Journal of Sport and Social Issues*, 22: 2, pp. 98–119.

Gomery, D. (2004), 'Mergers and Acquisitions', in H. Newcomb (ed.), *The Museum of Broadcast Communication Encyclopedia of Television*, Chicago: Fitzroy Dearborn, pp. 1479–81.

―――― (2007), 'Talent Raids and Package Deals: NBC Loses Its Leadership in the 1950s', in M. Hilmes (ed.), *NBC: America's Network*, Berkeley: University of California Press, pp. 153–68.

Gonzerath, D. (2004a), 'Murdoch, Rupert K', in H. Newcomb (ed.), *The Museum of Broadcast Communication Encyclopedia of Television*, Chicago: Fitzroy Dearborn, pp. 1558–60.

―――― (2004b), 'News Corporation Ltd', in H. Newcomb (ed.), *The Museum of Broadcast Communication Encyclopedia of Television*, Chicago: Fitzroy Dearborn, pp. 1646–48.

Gordon, N. (1975), *My Life at Crossroads*, London: W.H. Allen and Company.

Gorman, J., Kirk, C. and Rozin, S. (1994), *The Name of the Game: The Business of Sports*, New York: Wiley.

Graham, J. (1988), *Come on Down! The TV Game Show Book*, New York: Abbeville Press.

Grant, A. (2004), 'Digital Television', in H. Newcomb (ed.), *The Museum of Broadcast Communication Encyclopedia of Television*, Chicago: Fitzroy Dearborn, pp. 705–06.

Grantham, B. (1998), Interview with A. Moran, Brisbane.

Griffen-Foley, B. (1999), *The House of Packer: The Making of a Media Empire*, Sydney: Allen & Unwin.

―――― (2000), *Sir Frank Packer: The Young Master*, Sydney: HarperCollins.

―――― (2009), *Changing Stations: The Story of Australian Commercial Radio*, Sydney: UNSW Press.

Griffin, J. (2004), *John Wren: A Life Reconsidered*, Melbourne: Scribe.

Grimes, W. (2010), 'Art Linkletter, TV Host Who Got Kids to Say the Darndest Things, Dies at 97', *New York Times*, 27 May, pp. 33–34.

Grundy, R. (2010), *Reg Grundy*, London: Pier One Books.

References

Gwinn Wilkins, K. (2004), 'Hong Kong', in H. Newcomb (ed.), *The Museum of Broadcast Communication Encyclopedia of Television*, Chicago: Fitzroy Dearborn, pp. 1129–32.

Hall, S. (1976), *Supertoy: 20 Years of Australian Television*, Melbourne: Sun Books.

Hampson, R. (1995), Interview with A. Moran, Melbourne.

Henderson, B. (1995), Telephone interview with A. Moran, Sydney.

Hilmes, M. (1990), *Hollywood and Broadcasting: From Radio to Cable*, Urbana, IL: University of Illinois Press.

―――― (2004a), 'Hollywood and Radio', in C. H. Sterling (ed.), *The Museum of Broadcast Communication Encyclopedia of Radio*, Chicago: Fitzroy Dearborn, pp. 718–20.

―――― (2004b), 'Hollywood and Television', in H. Newcomb (ed.), *The Museum of Broadcast Communication Encyclopedia of Television*, Chicago: Fitzroy Dearborn, pp. 1109–11.

Hobson, D. (1982), *Crossroads: The Drama of a Soap Opera*, London: Methuen

Hoerschelmann, O. (2004a), 'Jeopardy', in H. Newcomb (ed.), *The Museum of Broadcast Communication Encyclopedia of Television*, Chicago: Fitzroy Dearborn, pp. 1222–24.

―――― (2004b), 'Quiz and Game Shows', in H. Newcomb (ed.), *The Museum of Broadcast Communication Encyclopedia of Television*, Chicago: Fitzroy Dearborn, pp. 1871–74.

―――― (2004c), '$64,000 Question, The/The $64,000 Challenge', in H. Newcomb (ed.), *The Museum of Broadcast Communication Encyclopedia of Television*, Chicago: Fitzroy Dearborn, pp. 2105–6.

―――― (2004d), '*Who Wants to Be a Millionaire?*' in H. Newcomb (ed.), *The Museum of Broadcast Communication Encyclopedia of Television*, Chicago: Fitzroy Dearborn, pp. 2536–37.

Hogan, B. (1994), 'A Reflection on Deregulation', *Economic Papers*, 13: 1, pp. 45–50.

Holmes, I. (1980), Interview with A. Moran, Sydney.

―――― (1992), Interview with Stuart Cunningham and Marie Delofsky, Sydney.

Hooke, G. (1992), 'The Exchange Rate, Economic Activity and the Current Account Balance' *Economic Papers*, 11: 1, pp. 1–14.

Houseman, M. (1995), '€175m nets Pearson Australian TV Firm', *The Independent*, 30 March, p. 11.

Hulten, O. (2004), 'Sweden', in H. Newcomb (ed.), *The Museum of Broadcast Communication Encyclopedia of Television*, Chicago: Fitzroy Dearborn, pp. 2238–41.

Hyatt, W. (1997), *The Encyclopedia of Daytime Television*, New York: Billboard.

Inglis, K. (1983), *This is the ABC*, Melbourne: Melbourne University Press.

Jacka, E. (1993), 'Film', in S. Cunningham and G. Turner (eds), *The Media in Australia*, Sydney: Allen & Unwin, pp. 72–85.

―――― (2004), 'Gyngell, Bruce', in H. Newcomb (ed.), *The Museum of Broadcast Communication Encyclopedia of Television*, Chicago: Fitzroy Dearborn, pp. 1045–48.

Jones, C. (1995), *Something in the Air: A History of Radio in Australia*, Sydney: Kangaroo Press.

Jones, C. and Bednall, D. (1980), *Australian Television History Through the Ratings*, Sydney: Australian Broadcasting Tribunal.

Jones, J. P. (2004), 'Bertelsmann, A. G.', in H. Newcomb (ed.), *The Museum of Broadcast Communication Encyclopedia of Television*, Chicago: Fitzroy Dearborn, pp. 247–48.

Kasson, J. (1978), *Amusing the Millions: Coney Island at the Turn of the Century*, New York: Hill & Wang.

Kingsley, H. (1989), *Soap Box: The Australian Guide to Television Soap Opera*, Melbourne: Sun Books.

Lane, R. (1994), *The Golden Years of Australian Radio Drama: 1923-60*, Melbourne: Melbourne University Press.

Leach, W. (1993), *Land of Desire: Merchants, Power, and the Rise of a New American Culture*, New York: Vintage.

Lealand, G. (1994), 'New Zealand', in S. Cunningham and E. Jacka (eds), *Australian Television and International Mediascapes*, Melbourne: Cambridge University Press, pp. 214-27.

Leong, S. C. (1994), 'Programming: What Constitutes a Good Program?' *Online*, September, pp. 2-69.

Levine, J. (2003), 'Sex, Money & Videotape', *Forbes*, 171: 6, 17 March, pp. 88-96.

Lewis, D. (1994), 'Europeans Troppo Over Grundy Soap', *Sydney Morning Herald*, 13 August, p. 13.

'Long Boom' (1998), in G. Davison, J. Hurst and S. Macintyre (eds), *The Oxford Companion to Australian History*, Melbourne: Oxford University Press, p. 399.

Lucas, C. (2004), 'Broadcasting', in H. Newcomb (ed.), *The Museum of Broadcast Communication Encyclopedia of Television*, Chicago: Fitzroy Dearborn, pp. 343-46.

McCabe, L. (1980), Interview with A. Moran, Sydney.

McDermott, M. (2004), 'Goodson, Mark and Todman, Bill', in H. Newcomb (ed.), *The Museum of Broadcast Communication Encyclopedia of Television*, Chicago: Fitzroy Dearborn, pp. 1013-16.

Mackay, I. (1956), *Broadcasting in Australia*, Melbourne: Melbourne University Press.

—— (1959), *Macquarie: The Story of a Network*, Sydney: Macquarie Network.

Macken, D. (1989), 'Invasion of the Aussie Soaps', *Sydney Morning Herald Good Weekend*, 8 April, p. 9.

Mant, G. (1972), *The Big Show: 150th Anniversary Royal Agricultural Society of NSW*, Sydney: Horwitz.

Marshall, P. D. (2004), 'Winfrey, Oprah', in H. Newcomb (ed.), *The Museum of Broadcast Communication Encyclopedia of Television*, Chicago: Fitzroy Dearborn, pp. 255-89.

Mason, B. (1980), Interview with A. Moran, Sydney.

—— (2010), Interview with Albert Moran, Sydney.

Matthews, J. J. (2004), *Dance Hall and Picture Palace: Sydney's Romance with Modernity*, Sydney: Currency Press.

Mauger, L. (2006), Interview with A. Moran, Sydney.

Maxwell, R. (2004), 'Spain', in H. Newcomb (ed.), *The Museum of Broadcast Communication Encyclopedia of Television*, Chicago: Fitzroy Dearborn, pp. 2152-57.

May, A. (2010), 'Dancin' with My Darlin'', in A. Moran and M. Keane (eds), *Cultural Adaptation*, London: Routledge, pp. 19-29.

Mazzarella, S. R. (2004), '*Dynasty*', in H. Newcomb (ed.), *The Museum of Broadcast Communication Encyclopedia of Television*, Chicago: Fitzroy Dearborn, pp. 771-73.

Meers, P. (2004), 'Netherlands, The', in H. Newcomb (ed.), *The Museum of Broadcast Communication Encyclopedia of Television*, Chicago: Fitzroy Dearborn, pp. 1631-33.

Miller, T. with George Yudice (2004), *Cultural Policy*, Thousand Oaks, CA: Sage.

Mittell, J. (2002), 'Before the Scandals: The Radio Precedents of the Quiz Show Genre', in M. Hilmes and J. Loviglio (eds), *Radio Reader: Essays in the Cultural History of Radio*, London: Routledge, pp. 319–42.

—— (2004), 'Quiz and Audience Participation Programs', in C. H. Sterling (ed.), *Encyclopedia of Radio*, Chicago: Fitzroy Dearborn, pp. 1146–52.

Moran, A. (forthcoming), 'Television Program Formats: Their Making and Meaning', in M. Buonanno, H. Gray and T. Miller (eds), *Handbook of Television Studies*, Thousand Oaks, CA: Sage.

—— (1985), *Image and Industry: Australian Television Drama production*, Sydney: Currency Press, p. 232.

—— (1991), *Projecting Australia: Government Film Since 1945*, Sydney: Currency Press.

—— (1993), *Moran's Guide to Australian TV Series*, Sydney: Australian Film, Radio and Television School.

—— (1996a), 'National Broadcasting and Cultural Identity: New Zealand Television and *Shortland Street*', *Continuum: An Australian Journal of Media and Culture*, 10: 1, pp. 168–86.

—— (ed.) (1996b), *Film Policy: International, National and Regional Perspectives*, London: Routledge.

—— (1996c), 'National Identity and the Television Comedy Game Show: The Case of *Man O Man*', *Continuum: An Australian Journal of Media and Culture*, 10: 2, pp. 78–96.

—— (1997a), 'TRY and TRY Again: *The Restless Years* and Nationalizing Television Drama', *Australasian Drama Studies*, 30, pp. 57–68.

—— (1997b), 'Foreign Exchange: Reflections on the Grundy Buy Out', *Media International Australia*, 83, pp. 123–34.

—— (1998), *Copycat TV: Globalisation, Program Formats and Cultural Identity*, Luton: University of Luton Press.

—— (2004a), 'Australia', in H. Newcomb (ed.), *The Museum of Broadcast Communication Encyclopedia of Television*, Chicago: Fitzroy Dearborn, pp. 173–80.

—— (2004b), 'Crawford, Hector', in H. Newcomb (ed.), *The Museum of Broadcast Communication Encyclopedia of Television*, Chicago: Fitzroy Dearborn, pp. 627–28.

—— (2004c), 'Grundy, Reg', in H. Newcomb (ed.), *The Museum of Broadcast Communication Encyclopedia of Television*, Chicago: Fitzroy Dearborn, pp. 1041–42.

—— (2004d), '*I've Got a Secret*', in H. Newcomb (ed.), *The Museum of Broadcast Communication Encyclopedia of Television*, Chicago: Fitzroy Dearborn, pp. 1199–2000.

—— (2005), 'Configurations of the New Television Landscape', in J. Wasko (ed.), *A Companion to Television*, Malden, MA: Blackwell, pp. 291–307.

—— (2009). *New Flows in Global TV*, Bristol: Intellect.

—— (2010), 'TV Nation or TV City?', *Continuum: Journal of Media and Cultural Studies*, 24: 3, pp. 343–56.

Moran, A. and Keating C. (2003), *Wheel of Fortune: Australian TV Game Shows*, Canberra: Screen-Sound Australia.

—— (2007), *Historical Dictionary of Australian Radio and Television*, Lanham, MD: Scarecrow Press.

Moran, A. and Malbon, J. (2006), *Understanding the Global TV Format*, Bristol: Intellect.

Moran, A. and Vieth, E. (2005), *Historical Dictionary of Cinema in Australia and New Zealand*, Lanham, MD: Scarecrow Press.

Morotoff, G. (1995), Interview with A. Moran, Sydney.

Morrisby, T. (1988), *Unpackaged Tours: World Travels Off the Beaten Track*, New York: Taplinger.

Murdock, G. (2004a), 'Berlusconi, Silvio', in H. Newcomb (ed.), *The Museum of Broadcast Communication Encyclopedia of Television*, Chicago: Fitzroy Dearborn, pp. 243–45.

—— (2004b), 'New Zealand', in H. Newcomb (ed.), *The Museum of Broadcast Communication Encyclopedia of Television*, Chicago: Fitzroy Dearborn, pp. 1640–42.

Murphy, J. (1981), 'Light Entertainment', in P. Beilby (ed.), *Australian Television: The First 25 Years*, Melbourne: Nelson, pp. 60–89.

Murphy, M. (1995), Personal interview with Albert Moran, London.

Murray, S. (1996), *Australia on the Small Screen, 1970-1995*, Melbourne: Oxford University Press.

—— (2004a), 'Donahue, Phil', in H. Newcomb (ed.), *The Museum of Broadcast Communication Encyclopedia of Television*, Chicago: Fitzroy Dearborn, pp. 750–52.

—— (2004b), 'Reality Television', in H. Newcomb (ed.), *The Museum of Broadcast Communication Encyclopedia of Television*, Chicago: Fitzroy Dearborn, pp. 1900–02.

Nicholson, P. (1994), 'Neighbours to the World', *Television Business International*, September, pp. 44–46.

—— (1994), '1994 is the Year of Restructuring at Grundy', *European Media Business and Finance*, 24 October, p. 17.

Noam, E. (1992), *Television in Europe*, New York: Oxford University Press.

O'Callaghan, G. (1995), Telephone interview with A. Moran, Sydney.

Odell, C. (2004), 'Kinescope', in H. Newcomb (ed.), *The Museum of Broadcast Communication Encyclopedia of Television*, Chicago: Fitzroy Dearborn, pp. 1263–64.

O'Donnell, H. (1999), *Good Times, Bad Times: Soap Opera and Society in Western Europe*, Leicester: University of Leicester Press.

O'Farrell, P. (1987), *The Irish in Australia*, Sydney: UNSW Press.

O'Grady, J. (1980), Interview with A. Moran, Sydney.

—— (1995), Interview with A. Moran, Sydney.

Oliver, R. (1995), 'Union Jack Flies Over Ramsay Street', *Sydney Morning Herald*, 1 April, p. 33.

O'Regan, T. (1992), *Australian Television Culture*, Sydney: Allen & Unwin.

Palm, C. M. (2002), *Bright Lights Dark Shadows: The Real Story of Abba*, London: Omnibus Press.

Patterson, G. (1956), *Life Has Been Wonderful: Fifty Years of Adventures in Advertising at Home and Abroad*, Sydney: Ure Smith.

Peake-Jones, K. (1978), *St Peter's College*, Adelaide: Lutheran Publishing.

Peiss, K. (1986), *Cheap Amusements: Working Women and Leisure in Turn-of-the-Century America*, Philadelphia, PA: Temple University Press.

Penberthy, J. (1980), 'The Irresistible Rise of Reg Grundy', *National Times, Business Review*, 28 September, pp. 1314–15.

Perry, J. H. (1991), *Screen Gems: A History of Columbia Pictures Television from Cohn to Coke, 1948-1983*, Metuchen, NJ: Scarecrow Press.

Pfanner, E. (2007), 'Endemol Founders to Return as Owners', *International Herald Tribune*, 15 May, p. 8.

Pickering, D. (2004a), 'Grade, Lew', in H. Newcomb (ed.), *The Museum of Broadcast Communication Encyclopedia of Television*, Chicago: Fitzroy Dearborn, pp. 1017–19.

—— (2004b), 'Whicker, Alan', in H. Newcomb (ed.), *The Museum of Broadcast Communication Encyclopedia of Television*, Chicago: Fitzroy Dearborn, pp. 2530–31.

Pike, A. and Cooper, R. (1981), *Australian Film 1900–1977: A Guide to Feature Film Production*, Melbourne: Oxford University Press.

Pinne, P. (1995), Telephone interview with A. Moran, Santiago, Chile.

Pitts, C. (2004), 'Simulcasting', in C. H. Sterling (ed.), *Encyclopedia of Radio*, Chicago: Fitzroy Dearborn, pp. 1271–72.

Porter, V. and Mun, S. H. (2004), 'Copyright Law and Television', in H. Newcomb (ed.), *The Museum of Broadcast Communication Encyclopedia of Television*, Chicago: Fitzroy Dearborn, pp. 593–98.

Potter, B. (1994), 'Prime, Sunshine Out of Race for $278 Grundy', *Sydney Morning Herald*, 11 February, p. 2.

Potter, B. and Kidman, M. (1994), 'Grundy Revives Plans to Float Worldwide Production Interests', *Sydney Morning Herald*, 9 November, p. 17.

Potts, J. (1988), *Radio in Australia*, Sydney: UNSW Press.

Prest, W. (1998), 'Adelaide', in G. Davison, J. Hurst and S. Macintyre (eds), *The Oxford Companion to Australian History*, Melbourne: Oxford University Press, pp. 161–67.

Price, A. G. (1947), *The Collegiate School of St Peter 1847–1947*, Adelaide: Advertiser Printing Office.

Pusey, M. (1992), *Economic Rationalism in Canberra: A Nation-Building State Changes its Mind*, London: Cambridge University Press.

Rutherford, P. (2004), 'Advertising', in H. Newcomb (ed.), *The Museum of Broadcast Communication Encyclopedia of Television*, Chicago: Fitzroy Dearborn, pp. 28–32.

Schatz, T. (2004), 'Development', in H. Newcomb (ed.), *The Museum of Broadcast Communication Encyclopedia of Television*, Chicago: Fitzroy Dearborn, pp. 696–98.

Schmitt, D., Bisson, G. and Fey, C. (2005), *The Global Trade in Television Formats*, London: Screen Digest.

Schwartz, D., Ryan, S. and Wosbrook, F. (1987), *The Encyclopedia of TV Game Shows*, New York: Zoetrope.

Scurfield, J. (1998), 'Manufacturing', in G. Davison, J. Hurst and S. Macintyre (eds), *The Oxford Companion to Australian History*, Melbourne: Oxford University Press, pp. 410–11.

Seaton, E. (2004), 'America's Most Wanted', in H. Newcomb (ed.), *The Museum of Broadcast Communication Encyclopedia of Television*, Chicago: Fitzroy Dearborn, pp. 102–04.

Selleck, R. J. W. (1998), 'Economy', in G. Davison, J. Hurst and S. Macintyre (eds), *The Oxford Companion to Australian History*, Melbourne: Oxford University Press, pp. 203–06.

Sen, K. (2004), 'Southeast Asia', in H. Newcomb (ed.), *The Museum of Broadcast Communication Encyclopedia of Television*, Chicago: Fitzroy Dearborn, pp. 2145–49.

Servaes, J. (2004a), 'European Union Television', in H. Newcomb (ed.), *The Museum of Broadcast Communication Encyclopedia of Television*, Chicago: Fitzroy Dearborn, pp. 822–24.

—— (2004b), 'European Union Television Policy', in H. Newcomb (ed.), *The Museum of Broadcast Communication Encyclopedia of Television*, Chicago: Fitzroy Dearborn, pp. 824–26.
Shaw, P. (1987), 'Generic Refinement on the Fringe: The Game Show', *Southern Speech Communication Journal*, 52: 4, pp. 403–10.
Shawcross, William (1992), *Rupert Murdoch: Ringmaster of the Information Circus*. New York: Pan.
Sherman, A. (1965), *A Gift of Laughter*, New York: Atheneum.
Shoebridge, N. (1991), 'Why Grundy is Set on TV Ownership', *Business Review Weekly*, 25 January, pp. 29–30.
Silj, A. (ed.) (1988), *East of Dallas: The European Challenge to American Television*, London: British Film Institute.
Simmons, T. (1995), Interview with A. Moran, Sydney.
Skinner, T. (1995), Telephone interview with A. Moran, Singapore.
Smith, J. (1984), *Australian Country Music*, Sydney: Berghouse Floyd Tuckey.
Snoddy, R. and Tait, N. (1995), 'Pearson to Tune into Neighbours with Grundy Deal', *The Financial Times*, 31 March, p. 21.
Solomon, L. (1989), 'The Oz Invasion', *The Age Green Guide*, 24 March, p. 1.
Spearritt, P. (1978), *Sydney Since the 1920s*, Sydney: Hale and Ironmonger.
Steemers, J. (2004), *Selling Television: British Exports in a Global Marketplace*, London: British Film Institute.
Sterling, C. H. (2004a), 'Deregulation', in H. Newcomb (ed.), *The Museum of Broadcast Communication Encyclopedia of Television*, Chicago: Fitzroy Dearborn, pp. 688–89.
—— (2004b), 'Edwards, Ralph 1913', in C. H. Sterling (ed.), *Encyclopedia of Radio*, Chicago: Fitzroy Dearborn, pp. 539–40.
Stern, L. (1982), 'The Australian Cereal: Home Grown Television', in S. Dermody, J. Docker and D. Modeskja (eds), *Ginger Meggs, Nellie Melba and Friends: Essays in Australian Cultural History*, Melbourne: Kibble Books, pp. 1032–33.
Strover, S. (2004), 'Cable', in H. Newcomb (ed.), *The Museum of Broadcast Communication Encyclopedia of Television*, Chicago: Fitzroy Dearborn, pp. 389–97.
Sydney Morning Herald (1994), 'Grundy Prepares to Pass on the Torch', *Sydney Morning Herald*, 22 January, p. 44.
Tabagot, N. (1995), 'Grundy Spins a Fortune from the Chocolate Wheel', *Australian Financial Review*, 30 March, p. 28.
Taub-Pervizpour, L. (2004), 'Independent Production Companies', in H. Newcomb (ed.), *The Museum of Broadcast Communication Encyclopedia of Television*, Chicago: Fitzroy Dearborn, pp. 1168–71.
Thompson, R. (1980), 'David Jones in War and Peace', BA(Hons) thesis, Macquarie University.
Timberg, B. M. (2004a), 'Griffen, Merv', in H. Newcomb (ed.), *The Museum of Broadcast Communication Encyclopedia of Television*, Chicago: Fitzroy Dearborn, pp. 1034–35.
—— (2004b), 'Talk Shows in the United States', in H. Newcomb (ed.), *The Museum of Broadcast Communication Encyclopedia of Television*, Chicago: Fitzroy Dearborn, pp. 2255–63.
The Times (1995), 'Greg's New Neighbour', 30 March, p. 14.

References

Toohey, B. (1973), 'TV Packagers to Gain Most from Points System', *Australian Financial Review*, 2 July, pp. 2–3.

Tunstall, J. (ed.) (1970), *Media Sociology: A Reader*, London: Constable.

—— (ed.) (2001), *Media Occupations and Professions: A Reader*, New York: Oxford University Press.

—— (2008), *The Media Were American: US Mass Media in Decline*, New York: Oxford University Press.

Tunstall, J. and Palmer, M. (1991), *Media Moguls*, New York: Routledge.

—— (2001), 'Media Moguls in Europe', in J. Tunstall (ed.), *Media Occupations and Professions: A Reader*, New York: Oxford University Press.

TV Week (1959), 'We Don't Rig Our Shows', 14–20 November, p. 5.

—— (1962), 'The Other Face of Mr. Grundy', 25 August, p. 11.

—— (1971), 'The Man Who Gives Money Away', 9 October, p. 7.

—— (1973), 'TV King Joins the Drama Race', 4 September, p. 14.

—— (1977), 'Reg Grundy's Multi Million Dollar Gamble', 3 December, p. 13.

Vahamagi, T. (1996), *British Television: An Illustrated Guide*, Oxford: Oxford University Press.

van Manen, J. R. (1994), *Televiseformats: eniden naar Netherlands Recht*, Amsterdam: Otto Cramwinckle Uitgever.

van Tiggelen, J. (2007), 'Who Wants to Be a Billionaire?', *Sydney Morning Herald*, 14 April, p. 16.

Variety (1992), 'Grundy's the Format Wizard of Oz', *Variety*, 21 January, p. 19.

Watson, R. (1980), Interview with A. Moran, Sydney.

Walker, R. R. (1973), *The Magic Spark: The Story of the First Fifty Years of Radio in Australia*, Melbourne: Hawthorn Press.

Weiten, J., Murdock, G. and Dahlgren, P. (eds), (2000), *Television Across Europe: A Comparative Introduction*, London: Sage.

Weston, B. (1995), Interview with A. Moran, Brisbane.

Whitelock, D. (1977), *Adelaide 1836–1976: A History of Difference*, Brisbane: University of Queensland Press.

Whitfield, W. (2005), Interview with A. Moran, Magnetic Island, Townsville.

Wilson, P. (2004), '*Big Brother*', in H. Newcomb (ed.), *The Museum of Broadcast Communication Encyclopedia of Television*, Chicago: Fitzroy Dearborn, pp. 262–64.

Wolfers, H. (1980), 'The Big Stores Between the Wars', in J. Roe (ed.), *Twentieth Century Sydney: Studies in Urban & Social History*, Sydney: Hale & Iremonger.

Websites

BHP Billiton: http://ww.bhpbilliton.com/home/aboutus/ourcompany/Pages/ourHistory.aspx, viewed 20 September 2011.

Ernest Hillier: http://www.ernesthillier.com.au/history.html, viewed 20 September 2011.

History of Country Music: http://www.historyofcountrymusic.com.au, viewed 20 August 2011.

Julian Ashton Art School: http://julianashtonartschool.com.au/about/history, viewed 3 November 2011.

Qantas history: http://www.qantas.com.au/travel/airlines/history/global/en, viewed 18 April 2011.
Reg Grundy Wildlife: http://www.rgwildlife.com, viewed 20 June 2011).
Small Talk: http://www.ukgameshows.com/ukgs/Small_Talk, viewed 9 August 2011.
Wikipedia: John de Mol: http://en.wikipedia.org/wiki/John_de_Mol,viewed 8 February 2011.
Wikipedia: Reverse engineering: http://en.wikipedia.org/wiki/Reverse_engineering, viewed 30 September 2010.

Index

$10,000 Moneymakers, 144; see also Moneymakers
$25,000 Great Temptation, 114
$64,000 Question, The, 59, 66, 73
   in Germany 59
   see also Coles £3000/$7000 Question
0–10 Network, see Ten Network

A

ABBA: Down Under, 130
ABBA: The Movie, 129–30
Adventures of Barry McKenzie, The, 111, 116–17, 121
Adventures of Long John Silver, The, 171
Adventures of the Sea Spray, 108, 135
advertising
   agencies in radio, 28
   spot ads, 103
All at Sea, 127
All Star Anything Goes, 164
All Together
   in Germany, 190
All-American International (AAI), 217
Almost Anything Goes, 164–65
Alternative, The, 127
Amalgamated Wireless Australasia (AWA), 31, 46
America's Most Wanted, 181
American Bandstand, 123
American Broadcasting Company (ABC), 151, 199
Americanization, 102
Ampol Big Game, 88, 163
Ampol Stamp Quiz, 67–68, 88
Anything Can Happen, 117
Ashe, Austin, 73

Ask the Army, 42
Auction Quiz, 44
Australia's Most Wanted, 181
Australian Broadcasting Commission
   establishment, 28
   restructuring of ABC TV, 80–81
Australian Broadcasting Control Board (ABCB) 82–83, 115
   abolition, 122
   see also Frequency Assignment Plan
Australian Broadcasting Tribunal (ABT), 222
Australian programmes
   increased popularity of, 80
Azcarraga, Emilia, 5

B

Balance Your Budget, 62
Bandstand, 59, 123, 130
BAPH stations 83–84, 90
   local autonomy, 84, 88
Barovick, Richard, 152
Battye, Don, 109
Beat the Clock, 215
Beat the Odds, 112
Beck, Ron, 43
Bellamy, 145–46
   in Germany, 189
   in Italy, 191
Beresford, Bruce, 110–11, 116–17
Berlusconi, Silvio, 5
Berne Convention for the Protection of Literary and Artistic Works, 69, 163, 207, 224
Bertelsmann family, 5
Bertelsmann Group, 7, 206, 219
Better Sex, The, 131

Big Brother, 125, 208, 220–21, 225
Big Challenge, 112
Big Chief Littlewolf, 35
Big Sister, 58
Billion Dollar Baby, 128
Blankety Blanks, 124, 168
Blind Date, 81, 87, 104, 112, 144, 168, 178
Blockbusters
  in Chile 193
  in Uruguay, 193
Blondie, 43, 59
Bob Stewart Productions, 112–13
Bond, Alan, 167
Boney, 180
Bony, 180, 181
Bourdin, Jerome, 4, 207–08, 216
Bruce Forsyth's Hot Streak, 124, 154, 184
Brunei
  Grundy game shows in, 156, 193
Bruning, Robert 107, 108, 125, 145

C

C (Children's) classification, 122
Cadee, Ron, 96, 112, 117
Calling the Stars, 29, 31
Can You Take It?, 43, 44
Candid Camera, 168
Card Sharks, 217
Carrick, Damien, 73
Carruthers, Jimmy, 34
Case for the Defence, 127, 129, 171
Casino 10, 124
Castaways, The
  in Germany, 189
Celebrity Game, The, 87, 124, 127
Celebrity It's a Knockout, 165
Celebrity Squares, 124, 186
Celebrity Tattletales, 124, 143
Celebrity Wheel of Fortune, 179
Chalaby, Jean, 220–21
Chambers, Joy, 96, 112, 156–57, 201, 203–04, 218

Child's Play
  in Singapore, 193
children's programmes, 6, 68, 88, 108, 112, 114, 117, 122, 128, 144, 145–46, 156, 158, 164, 169–70, 172, 177, 179–82
Chile
  Grundy shows in, 193
Chopper Squad, 128, 129, 171
Chuck Barris Productions 87
Clarke, Dick, 123
Class of '74/'75, 108, 115, 125, 129
CLTUFA, 206
Cold War, 41
Colda Music Quiz, 44
Coleman, Alan, 110, 115
Coles £3000/$70 000 Question, 73, 81, 111
Colgate-Palmolive Radio Unit, 28–29
Colgate-Palmolive Affair, 60, 63, 81
Colin Eggleston Productions, 128
Columbia Broadcasting System (CBS) (US), 28, 151
Concentration, 66, 67, 74, 80, 84–85, 87, 93, 112, 113, 216
Confessions of Ronald Biggs, 130
Cop Shop, 147, 148
Cop the Lot, 44
co-production arrangements, 177
Coronation Street, 110
Cox, Wally, 206
Crackerjack Productions, 207
Crawford Productions, 75, 80, 135, 137, 146–47
  proposed amalgamation with Grundy, 92, 106–07
Crawford, Dorothy, 75, 137
Crawford, Hector, 75, 92, 106, 137
Criminal Justice, 166
Crossroads, 110
Crystal, Bob, 105, 150, 151
Culliton, John, 91, 109

D

Dai Pai (Hong Kong), 155
Dangerous Women, 125, 183–84, 201–02

Dating Game, The, 144, 168, 178, 218
   in France, 188
Davey, Jack, 31, 44, 49
de Mol, Jon, 188, 203, 217–23, 224
de Mol, Linda, 218
Deals on Wheels, 49
Death Train, 127
Department of Communication, 102
Department of the Media, 102
Depression, *see* Great Depression
deregulation, 142
Division Four, 171
documentaries, 116–17, 121
Donovan, Jason, 169
drama production, 109, 128–29
   pilots, 116
   see also soap opera
Dulux Show, The, 44, 45
Dutch, Max, 104
Dyer, Bob, 31, 43, 44, 60, 143
Dyer, Dolly, 143
Dyke, Greg, 200, 205, 206
DYT, 70

E
E Street, 170
Edwards, John, 108, 115
Embassy, 180
Emergency Line, 117
Endemol, 92, 202, 219–20
   sale to Telefonica, 220–21
ESP and All That, 117, 130
Euro Chart Top 30, 218
Everage, Dame Edna, *see* Humphries, Barry
Everybody's Equal
   in France, 188–89
   in Spain, 191

F
Family Feud, 131, 179, 217
   in Chile, 193
   in France, 188
   in Indonesia, 193
   in Singapore, 193
   in Uruguay, 193
Family Game, The, 87
fiction programming, 101, 114–15, 145–46, 179–82
   see also soap opera
film production
government support for, 102
First Impressions, 86, 169
First Light Frazer, 29
Flying Doctors, The, 170
Fogarty, John, 73
For Life (Italy), 191
Ford Superquiz, 143, 178
format
   definition, 3–4
format adaptation, *see* programme format adaptation
Format Recognition and Protection Association (FRAPA), 208, 209
formats, *see* programme formats
Four Corners, 59
France
   Grundy shows in, 188–89
Fremantle International, 206
FremantleMedia, 206, 207, 217, 222
   FremantleMedia Australia, 207
Frequency Assignment Plan 82–83
Funny You Should Ask, 112

G
Gambit, 113
game shows, 81
   see also quiz shows
Generation Gap, 81, 85, 88
George Patterson Advertising Agency, 28, 60
Germany
   Grundy programs in, 189–90
Get the Message, 87, 88
Gillespie-Jones, Simon, 74
Give It a Go, 44, 45
Glenview High, 125, 128, 129, 171
Godfathers, The, 107

Going for Gold, 172, 184, 185
  in France, 188
  in Spain, 191
Gone to Ground, 127
Good Times, Bad Times, 218
  in Germany, 190
  in Netherlands, 187–88
  see also *The Restless Years*
Goodson, Jonathan, 93
Goodson, Mark, 93, 107, 201, 214–17, 221–23
  as format devisor, 215–16
Goodson-Todman Productions, 66, 69, 87–88, 93, 112, 113, 124, 144, 152, 215, 216, 224
Gordon, Bruce, 135
Gordon, Noele, 110
Grade, Sir Lew, 109–10
Graham Kennedy's Blankety Blanks, 124, 168
Great Depression, 28
  impact on Grundy, 11, 13
Great Temptation, The, 86, 106, 114, 115, 145, 154
  see also *Temptation*
Griffen, Merv, 203
  see also Merv Griffen Productions
Grundy companies, 6, 132, 92, 131–33, 161–63
  European offices, 162
  move to Bermuda, 156–57, 162
  move to Monaco, 132–33
  possible stock exchange float, 202–03
  sale of companies, 199–203
  see also Grundy Organisation; Grundy Television Produktions; Grundy Worldwide; Les Productiones Grundy; Reg Grundy Enterprises; Reg Grundy Services; Reg Grundy Productions (GB) Ltd; Reg Grundy Productions (US); transnationalization
Grundy House, 105, 130–31
Grundy Leisure, 134

Grundy's Surfers Paradise Centre, 134
Grundy Organisation, 6, 69, 70, 94, 121, 128. 132–34, 136, 138, 141–7, 150, 151, 154, 162, 165–66, 167–70, 178, 180, 202, 207, 222
  attempted purchase of Seven Network, 181–82
  establishment of US offices, 152, 201
  in Hong Kong, 155
  move into South-East Asia, 155
  move to Bermuda, 156
  in United Kingdom, 171
Grundy Television Produktions, 189
Grundy Travel, 133–34
Grundy UFA TV Productions, 189, 194, 207
Grundy Worldwide, 6–7, 92, 162–3, 189, 202, 222
  de-Grundification, 206–07
  format catalogue, 163–64
  Grundy International Distribution, 166
  post-sale to Pearson Television, 205–07
  sale to Pearson Television, 199–203
  strategies for programme formatting, 163–64
Grundy, Clive (uncle), 12
Grundy, Hazel (aunt), 12
Grundy, Irene (Dot) (aunt), 12
Grundy, Jean (aunt), 12
Grundy, John (grandfather), 12
Grundy, John (Jack) (uncle), 12
Grundy, Kim Robin
  birth, 53–54
  custody, 73–74, 95–96
  estrangement from father 118, 201
Grundy, Lillian Josephine (mother), 11, 53, 95–96, 118, 158; death, 118
Grundy, Lola
  courtship, 37–38
  divorce, 72–74
  marriage, 53
  motherhood, 53–54
  TV appearances, 65, 73

Grundy, Reg
  anonymity, 91, 137
  Army Reserve 16–18
  art school, 17–18
  awards, 204
  birth, 6
  books, 203–04
  childhood in Sydney, 11–13
  confidentiality, 92–93
  control of business, 92–93
  custody of daughter, 73–74
  divorce from Lola, 72–74
  early quiz shows, 48–50
  early years in TV, 57–76
  first job at David Jones, 16–17
  growing up in Adelaide, 13–15
  Grundification, 203–05
  as host of *Wheel of Fortune*, 67
  lateral thinking, 71–2
  livestock reporting at Royal Easter Show, 21–22
  marriage to Joy Chambers, 96
  marriage to Lola, 53
  memoir, 203–04
  move to Pittwater, 118
  parents' marriage, 11
  Pay Corps during World War II, 18–19
  personal style, 7, 91, 136–37
  photography, 203–04
  post-retirement, 203–05
  at radio station 2CH, 16, 17 53
  at radio station 2SM, 23, 27–37
  relocation to Bermuda, 156–57
  sale of companies, 199–203
  as salesman extraordinaire, 132
  schooldays, 14–15
  staff, 203–04
  This is Your Life, 204
  trading activities, 204
  travel, 204
  underwriting of shows, 125, 138, 202
  voiceovers, 36
  yacht, 204

  see also Grundy companies; Joy Chambers; Kim Grundy; Lillian Grundy; Lola Grundy; RG Capital
Grundy, Roy Harold (father), 11
  at David Jones Sydney, 15–17
  death, 53, 200
  at Ernest Hillier, 12–13
  at John Martin Restaurant Adelaide, 14, 15
Grundy/JE (Netherlands), 194
Guessing Game, The, 96
Gyngell, Bruce, 62, 64, 69, 70, 74, 109–10, 114

H
Hall, Ken, 62, 74
Hall, Sandra, 123
Hallstrom, Lasse, 130
Hamesh Hamesh (Israel), 192
Hancock, in Finland, 59
Hannam, Ken, 110
Hannan, Jimmy, 72, 113
Harper, John, 22–23, 32
Hatos-Hall, 124
Hearst, William Randolph, 3, 5
Heartline, 117
Heatter, Merrill, 186
Heatter-Quigley Productions, 87, 113, 124
Hersant, Robert, 5
High Rollers, 123–24
Holmes, Ian, 132, 136, 152, 182, 201
Home and Away, 169
Homicide, 80, 108, 174
Hong Kong
  Grundy game shows in, 155–56, 193
  RTV, 155
Hotline, 117
How Do They Do That?
  in France, 189
  in United Kingdom, 185
Hughes, Howard, 91, 204–05
Humphries, Barry, 116
Hyde, Frank, 37
Hypnotism and All That, 117

I

I've Got a Secret, 85, 86, 87, 96, 112, 113, 131, 169, 216
Ideal Fun Day, 117
Image of Death, 127
In the Groove with Grundy, 48
In Town Tonight, 85, 87, 111
Information Please, 49
Intervilles, 164
Is There Anybody There?, 127
It Could Be You, 143
It Pays to be Funny, 44, 45
It's a Knockout, 164–65, 168, 181
Italy
    Grundy shows in, 190–91

J

J. Walter Thompson Advertising Agency, 28
Jack Davey's Auction Quiz, 49
Jackson High, 128
Janus, 166
Jeder gegen Jenden (Fifteen-to-One), 190
Jeopardy!, 182, 186
Jeu Sans Frontieres, 164, 181
    see also *It's a Knockout*
Jon de Mol Productions, 188, 217–23
Jones-Howard Productions, 114
Joop van den Ende Productions (JE Productions), 187, 188, 218–19
Julian Ashton Art School, 17–18
Junior Almost Anything Goes, 164
Junior Moneymakers, 114

K

Kennedy, Graham, 124
Kevin Arnett's World of the Supernatural, 129
Keynotes, 154–55, 172, 179, 184
    in France, 189
Kids are Funny Too (Spain), 191
Killers of the Great Barrier Reef, 130
Kinder Ruck Zuck (Germany), 190
King's Men, 128–29, 145

Kinging, Glen, 71
Kricket! (India), 193

L

Lees, Lillian, *see* Grundy, Lillian Josephine
Leonetti, Tommy, 105
Les Productiones Grundy, 188–89, 194
Let's Make a Deal, 124, 178
licensing agreements, 135
licensing fees, 135
Life with Dexter, 43
light entertainment programming, 87, 123–24
Linkletter, Art, 43
Lintas advertising agency, 188
Lion's Share, The, 128
Long Arm, The, 107
long boom, 101, 141
Love Game, The, 144
Love Letters, 218
Lowy, Frank, 167
Lunchbox, 110
Lux Radio Theatre, The, 31, 58

M

Macquarie Network, 28
Magyar Grundy UFA, 207
Main Event, The, 185
    in France, 189
Major Network, 28
Mama's Gone a-Hunting, 127
Man O Man, 178
    in France, 189
    in Italy, 191
    in South America, 150
    in Spain, 191
    in Sweden, 192
    international options on, 164
Mark Goodson Productions, 155, 163–64, 166, 206, 222
Marriage Game, The, 81, 85, 86, 88, 143
Martin St James, 117
Martins & the McCoys, The, 116

Mason, Bill, 103, 136
Match Game, The, 87, 88, 124, 216
Matchmates, 144
  in Brunei, 156
McCabe, Lyle, 136
McGoohan, Patrick, 126
McLean, Ron, 107, 108, 109, 129, 145–46
McManus, Tom, 152
Meany, Monsigneur James, 31, 36, 38, 74
media organizations
  occupational hierarchy, 4–5
Meet the Press, 59
Merrill Heatter Productions, 186
Merv Griffen Productions, 124, 144–45, 168, 186
Michelson, Charles, 69, 151
miniseries, 179–82
Minogue, Kylie, 169
Mirams, Roger, 107–08, 109, 128, 146, 170, 181
Missing Link, 86, 87
Mission Top Secret, 181
Mitchell, Cameron, 128
mogul
  definition, 3, 5
  types 5
Moneymakers, 101, 104, 113–14, 144
Morotoff, George, 46
Morrisby, Ted, 110, 111
Mother and Son
  in Chile, 193
Murdoch, Rupert, 3, 5, 122, 142, 151, 203, 213–14
Muuh!, 190

N
Name That Tune, 59, 62, 66, 112, 124, 154, 179
  in Belgium, 59
National Broadcasting Company (NBC) (US), 28, 45, 151
National Star Quest, 123
Neighbours, 6, 96, 112, 135, 165–66, 169, 171–72, 179, 182, 183

  cross-subsidization of production costs, 165–66
  in Germany, 189
  in Sweden, 192
  success in United Kingdom, 165–66, 185, 187
Netherlands, The
  Grundy shows in, 187–88
New Price is Right, The, 144, 158, 168, 179
New Zealand
  Grundy shows in, 172, 182
  see also Shortland Street
Newlywed Game, The, 167
Newman Shame, The, 127
News Corporation, 214
News Limited, 122, 151
  control of 0–10 Network 142
Newton, Bert, 143
Newton, Patti, 143
Nicholson Muir Productions, 89
Night Nurse, The, 127
Nine Network
  as market for Grundy quiz shows, 88–9
  reversion to Kerry Packer, 167
  sale to Alan Bond, 167
NLT, 70
Noah, Bob, 152, 153
Number 96, 103, 108, 114–15, 132, 171
Numbers Game, 87
Numbers Please (?), 87, 88

O
O'Callaghan, Garry, 17
O'Grady, John, 48, 51
One in a Million, 124
Other Side of Paradise, The, 180
outsourcing of production, *see* production packaging

P
Packer, Frank, 32, 60, 75, 203
Packer, Kerry, 3, 199
Pails, Didi, 46

Panorama, 59
Pantomime Show, The, 45, 50
Paraguay
   Grundy shows in, 38, 193
Paramount Pictures, 135
parochial
   internationalism 148–50, 152, 208
   intranationalism, 149–50
   supranationalism, 150
Parramatta Hour, 47
Password, 112, 113
Pay Cards, 89
Pearson Television, 7, 166
   purchase of Grundy Worldwide, 199–203, 205–07
Penthouse Club, 117
People are Funny, 43
People Next Door, The, 107
Perfect Match, 144, 158, 167, 178, 182
Personality Squares, 85, 86, 87, 143–44
Pet Show, The, 190
Photon, 204
Pick-a-Box
   move to TV, 60, 81
   on TV, 111, 143, 178
   on radio, 43, 44, 45, 50, 60
Place in the Sun, A (Italy), 191
Play Your Cards Right, 144
Play Your Hunch, 87, 96
Plunge into Darkness, 127
Points System, 102–03, 122
Polar Music International, 130
Poor Fella Me, 116
Pop Formulae, 218
Pop the Question, 215
Portia Faces Life, 58
Possession, 148, 170
post-Fordist world view, 141
Postmaster General's Department, 33
Pot Luck, 168
Pot of Gold, 123, 179, 186
Powell, Lola, *see* Grundy, Lola
Press Your Luck, 168, 186

Pressure Pack Show, The, 44, 45, 50
Price is Right, The, 179, 217, 218
Prime Time Access rule, 216–17
Prisoner, 6, 125, 126, 158, 182
Prisoner: Cell Block H (US), 126, 152–53, 155, 171, 173, 183, 202
   see also Prisoner
Professor Poopsnaggle's Steam Zeppelin, 170, 172
Professor Quiz, 42, 49
programme distribution
   transnational, 134–35
   see also programme adaptation; transnationalization
programme format adaptation, 178, 194
   elements of, 148–50
   Euro-American convergence phase, 208
   Formalization Stage, 224
   Foundation Stage, 224
   Global Stage, 224–25
   informal phase, 207
   open replication era, 207–08
   parochial internationalism, 148–50
   phases of, 207–09
   Primitive Stage, 224
   travelling producer, 149
   see also programme formats; transnationalization
programme formats
   in early years of TV, 59
   formalization of format remaking, 69–70
   format spotting, 68–71, 89–90
   international explosion in, 207–09
   international strategies, 163
   knowledge adaptation, 70
   mega-formats 208
   phases of quiz show format adaptation, 68–69
   remaking for radio 58
   reverse engineering, 70–71
   see also programme format adaptation
programme packaging, 63–64
   increased acceptance of, 103

see also programme format adaptation; programme formats
public service broadcasting
  deregulation of, 177
  Grundy's role in, 166–67
Punishment, 147
Pyramid Challenge, 131

Q

Queensland's Celebrity Game, 96
Quigley, Bob, 186
Quigley-Hall Productions, 152
Quiz Kids, The, 29, 42, 45
quiz shows
  changed structure, 81
  distribution, 90–91
  during 1969–74, 111–14
  during 1979–85, 143–45
  during 1985–89, 168
  during 1989–95, 177–79
  Grundy's introduction to, 48–50
  increased output 1965–70, 86–89
  interstate production, 81
  prizes, 90
  programme economies, 90
  on radio, 43–44
  on TCN9, 64–68
  in United States, 153–55
  United States as source, 88
  US scandals, 60, 63, 81
  see also game shows

R

Radio
  adaptation of American shows, 42–43
  appeal to Grundy, 29–30
  Australianization of, 29
  quiz shows, 43–4
  US imports, 42
Radio Corporation of America (RCA), 45
Radio Noordzee, 217
Radio station 2CH, 31, 41, 45–53
  resignation, 53

Radio station 2SM, 230–32
  boxing broadcasts, 32–33, 34
  employment with, 23, 27, 30–32
  resignation, 36–37
  Rugby League broadcasts, 33–34
  as sports director, 31, 32–33
Radio stations
  2GB Sydney, 30, 42
  2GZ Orange, 21–22
  2KY Sydney, 22–23
  2KY Sydney, 30–31
  2UE Sydney, 30, 32
  2UW Sydney, 30
  see also Radio station 2CH; Radio station 2SM
Radio Television Luxembourg (RTL), 206
Ralph Edwards Productions, 124, 143
Reagan, Ronald, 151
Reg Grundy Enterprises, 132, 202
  cancellation of shows, 6, 74–75, 79
  confidentiality, 92–93
  consolidation of Australian market, 79–97
  diversification, 70–1
  division of labour, 93–94
  drama serial division, 6
  incorporation, 6, 63–64, 131
  international offices, 105
  interstate locations, 94–95
  licensing to other networks, 104
  light entertainment programmes, 123–24
  marketing of programmes, 104
  OB van, 106
  relocation of office, 104–05
  selling shows, 93–94
Reg Grundy Productions (GB) Ltd, 172, 185–87
Reg Grundy Productions (US), 131, 172–73, 183–84
Reg Grundy Services, 63, 67, 68, 79, 80, 82, 84, 85–96, 103, 111, 114, 115, 123, 126, 128, 132
  potential merger with Crawford Productions, 106–07

programme distribution, 104
relocation of offices, 104–05
Reg Grundy Television, 132
Reg Grundy's Wheel of Fortune, 124
  see also Wheel of Fortune
Restless Years, The, 6, 125, 129, 146, 147, 153, 171
  in France, 188
RG Capital, 204
RG Records, 72, 117
Richard Boone Show, The, 216
Richmond Hill, 170, 172
Rise and Shine, 29, 42
Rod Cadee Show, The, 117
Roses Bloom Twice, 127
Rovers, The, 108
Roy, John, 51
Royal Commission on Television, 44
Royal Easter Show, 19–20, 21–22
Ruck Zouk (Greece), 192
Ruck Zuck (Germany), 190
Run for the Money, 172, 185
  in France, 188
Runaway Island, 146, 158
runaway productions, 81, 84
Russell Becker Productions, 70

S

sale of companies, 199–203
  decision to sell, 199
  sale price, 200
Sale of the Century, 6, 137, 145, 150, 158, 164, 168, 173, 178–79, 182
  Dai Sou But (Hong Kong), 155–56
  in France, 188
  in Germany, 190
  in Greece, 192
  original US version 69, 70, 85, 114, 136, 153–54
  in Paraguay, 138, 193
  US network version, 154, 155, 172, 183
Sands, Davde, 35
Say When, 67, 69, 71, 74, 93, 113

Scalp Merchant, The, 128
Scattergories, 183
Scoop the Pool, 49, 50
Scrabble, 154, 155, 173, 183
Second Chance, 131
Secret Valley, 128, 146, 174
Seven Network
  Grundy's attempt to buy, 181–82
  as market for Grundy shows, 89
  sale to Christopher Skase, 167
Sherwood, John, 33;
    see also Tuohill, Patrick
Shortland Street, 172, 182
Showdown, 87
Silent Number, 108
Silent World of Buster Fidess, The, 71
Simmons, Ted, 37
Singapore: Grundy shows in, 193
Skase, Christopher, 167
Skippy, 135
Sky Star Search, 172, 187
Small Talk, 183, 185
  in Germany, 190
  in Israel, 192
  in Sweden, 192
soap opera, 114–15, 146–48
Sons and Daughters, 6, 147, 148, 158, 169, 170, 171, 182
  in Bulgaria, 192–93
  in Croatia, 192
  in Germany, 190
  in Greece, 192
  in Italy, 191
  in Sweden, 192
Sorbent Show, The, 50
South America
  Grundy shows in, 138, 150, 193
South Pacific Adventures, 181
South-East Asia
  Grundy shows in, 155–56, 170
Southern Star International, 202, 204
Spain
  Grundy shows in, 191

Special Broadcasting Service (SBS), 122
  SBS TV, 122, 142
Spending Spree, 113, 114
spillover productions, 81
Split Personality, 81, 86, 87
Split Second, 113
Spoiler, The, 107
Sporting Scrapbook, 48, 49
sports broadcasting on radio
  boxing, 32–3, 34, 35
  Rugby league, 33–34
  wrestling, 34–35
Sportsmen in the Spotlight, 48
Spy Force, 108
Starting Out, 148
Starting Over, 153
Stern, Lesley, 96
Stop the Music, 49
strip programming, 103
Stump the Sportsman, 48–49
Sullivans, The, 125, 147
Super Seven, 124, 131
Supermarket Sweep, 178
Superquiz, 168, 178
  see also Ford Superquiz
Surprise Package, 67
Survivor, 208, 225
Sweden
  Grundy shows in, 192
Sydney Entertainment Centre
  Grundy's involvement in, 134

T
Tanamera: Lion of Singapore, 172, 180
Taurus Rising, 147–48, 170
tax incentives for film, 142
TCN9
  quiz shows on, 61–65, 66–68
  cancellation of Grundy shows, 74–75, 79
  see also Nine Network
Telefonica, 220–21
telemovies, 126–28
television

  in Adelaide, 58, 61, 82, 83
  in Brisbane, 58, 61, 82, 83
  from 1964–70, 79–81
  growth in number of stations, 60–61, 80
  impact of colour, 121, 122–23, 135
  introduction of, 44–45, 58
  in Perth, 82, 83
  in Sydney, 60–61
  minor capital TV stations, 83–84
  in United States, 150–52
  see also Nine Network; Points System;
       programme formats; Seven Network;
       Ten Network: Special Broadcasting
       Service; Australian Broadcasting
       Commission
television stations, see TCN9
Tell the Truth, 59, 62, 112, 113, 216
Temptation, 69, 85, 114, 115, 137, 145, 154
  see also The Great Temptation;
       $25,000 Great Temptation
Ten Network
  introduction of, 80, 82–83
  as new market, 82–83
  sale to Frank Lowy, 167
That Was the Week That Was
  in the Netherlands, 59
Thatcher, Margaret, 171
This Day Tonight, 59
Three on a Match, 112–13
Tic Tac Dough, 66–67, 74
  board game, 71
Time Machine, 154
Today Tonight, 59
Todman, Bill, 215, 222
Tonight show, 124
Toweel, Vic, 34
transnationalization, 142, 155, 161, 166, 194–95
  joint-venture arrangements, 194
  licensing to local companies, 194–95
  local offices, 194
Travellin' Out West, 117, 133
Truth or Consequence, 49
Tunstall, Jeremy, 4–5, 7, 67, 73, 91, 95, 149, 205

Tuohill, Patrick, 33, 35
Turner, Ted, 151
Twenty One, 66
Two-Way Mirror, 116

U
UE Calling, 44
United Kingdom
   Grundy shows in, 170–72, 185–87
   see also Neighbours; Reg Grundy
      Productions (GB) Ltd
United States
establishment of US offices, 152, 201
   Grundy productions in, 6, 150–52, 164, 172–73, 182–84, 195
   quiz shows, 153–55
   television industry, 150–51, 182–84, 201
   see also licensing of game shows, 163–64; Reg Grundy Productions (US)
Until Tomorrow, 126
Uruguay
   Grundy shows in, 193

V
van den Ende, Joop, 187, 203, 218–19
Vanity Fair, 28
Voice, The, 221

W
Warner Bros, 130, 199
Wasserman, Lew, 63
Waterloo Station, 148, 158, 170
Watson, Reg, 110, 115, 125, 146, 147, 169, 171
Weston, Barry, 125
What Do You Know?, 112
What's My Line?, 59, 66, 96, 113, 215, 216
   in Germany, 59
Wheel of Fortune, 6, 88, 124, 131, 144–45, 158, 163, 168, 178–79, 182, 218
   in France, 188
   on radio, 50–52, 54, 112
   move to television, 58, 59, 60, 61, 62–65, 71
   Reg Grundy as host, 67
Whicker's World, 110
Who Wants to Be a Millionaire?, 208, 225
Willow B: Women in Prison, 153
Winner Take All, 215, 216
Women's World, 81, 87, 111
World War II
   impact on Grundy, 11
Worlds Apart (Sweden), 192
   see also Sons and Daughters
Wreck of the Batavia, The, 116

Y
You've Got to Be Joking, 168
Young Doctors, The, 6, 96, 125, 129, 138, 146, 165, 171, 182
   in Italy, 191
Youth Show, The, 29

www.ingramcontent.com/pod-product-compliance
Ingram Content Group UK Ltd.
Pitfield, Milton Keynes, MK11 3LW, UK
UKHW050522150426
5217IPUK00026B/1757